D1515371

THE
ITALIAN KITCHEN

THE
ITALIAN KITCHEN

Consulting Editor
Gabriella Mariotti

HERMES
HOUSE

First published in 1999 by Hermes House

© Anness Publishing Limited 1999

HERMES HOUSE books are available for bulk purchase for sales promotion and for
premium use.
For details, write or call the sales director, Hermes House, 27 West 20th Street
New York, NY 10011; (800) 3549-657

Hermes House is an imprint of Anness Publishing Inc.

All rights reserved. No part of this publication may be reproduced, stored in a retrieval
system, or transmitted in any way or by any means, electronic, mechanical, photocopying,
recording or otherwise, without the prior written permission of the copyright holder.

ISBN 1-84038 518 9

A CIP catalogue record for this book is available from the British Library

Publisher: Joanna Lorenz
Project Editor: Cathy Marriott
Designers: Peter Butler, Siân Keogh, Peter Laws, Alan Marshall,
Adrian Morris, Brian Weldon
Recipes: Carla Capalbo, Jacqueline Clarke, Maxime Clarke, Frances Cleary,
Carol Clements, Roz Denny, Matthew Drennan, Joanna Farrow, Christine France,
Sarah Gates, Shirley Gill, Carole Handslip, Christine Ingram, Patricia Lousada,
Norma MacMillan, Sue Maggs, Elizabeth Martin, Sarah Maxwell, Janice Murfitt,
Annie Nichols, Angela Nilsen, Louise Pickford, Hilaire Walden, Laura Washburn,
Steven Wheeler, Kate Whitman, Judy Williams, Elizabeth Wolf-Cohen, Jenni Wright
Photographers: Karl Admson, Edward Allwright, David Amstrong, Steve Baxter,
James Duncan, Michelle Garrett, Amanda Heywood, Tim Hill, Don Last,
Patrick McLeavey, Michael Michaels, Peter Reilly
Stylists: Madeleine Brehaut, Hilary Guy, Jo Harris, Maria Kelly, Fiona Tillett

Previously published in three separate volumes:
Pasta Pizza Presto, Italian Classics and Low Fat Pasta

Printed and bound in Italy

1 3 5 7 9 10 8 6 4 2

For all recipes, quantities are given in both metric and imperial
measures, and where appropriate, measures are also given in standard
cups and spoons. Follow one set, but not a mixture, because they are
not interchangeable.

CONTENTS

INTRODUCTION

Italian cooking is strongly regional—the dishes of Florence, Venice, Genoa, Piedmont, Rome and Naples all have their own character. This is largely because Italy was not unified until 1861, and although the regions are now more able (and willing) to share their natural produce, they still rely heavily on what they can grow themselves. Sun-ripened tomatoes, eggplants and peppers feature strongly in the cuisine of the south, fish is the staple food on the coast, Parmesan cheese is at its best in Parma, dairy products are used in much of the cuisine of the north (with, for example, butter replacing olive oil in many of the dishes) and the best beef is reared in Tuscany. Each area has its "classic" dish—Milan has its creamy risotto, Bologna its tagliatelle with meat sauce, Naples its pizza and Rome its lamb cooked with anchovies and herbs.

Despite the diversity of Italian cooking, the one unifying factor is the freshness of the ingredients. Produce is bought daily, sometimes even twice daily, at the local market. Dishes are often very simple—meats and fish are grilled or roasted, sauces often take no longer than the pasta to cook and delicious pizzas can be created in minutes—allowing the quality of the ingredients to do the work.

Olive oil plays a vital role in Italian cooking, and is used in nearly every recipe, from a simple salad tossed with extra virgin olive oil vinaigrette to a classic tomato sauce for pasta or the warm and crusty bread served with every meal. It is rich in monounsaturated fat and, like the low-fat carbohydrates provided by the pasta, rice and vegetables that are the base of so many dishes, contributes to the healthy diet prevalent in Italy.

Italians love their food and they love sharing it with friends and family. They take time in its preparation and time in its eating. All the delicious and authentic recipes in this book will help to capture the Italian enthusiasm for food, whether you choose to serve a simple salad or an elaborate meal.

The Italian Meal

One of the many attractions of the Italian meal is the relaxed way in which it is eaten and enjoyed. Most meals in Italy start with a plate of antipasti, particularly if pasta is not being served as a course. It could simply contain a selection of delicious olives, but will more usually include a variety of cold roasted or marinated vegetables, cold meats such as prosciutto or Parma ham, and delicious breads such as ciabatta and focaccia to mop up the juices. It could also include some hot crostini—rounds of toasted bread topped with melted cheese and various garnishes—or mini pizzas. Whatever the choice, a good quality olive oil is of the utmost importance.

Salads
Salads also feature in antipasti, but apart from the basic green salad, most can, by varying the portions, be served at any meal, as an appetizer, a side dish or even as a main course.

Soups
Soups are popular in Italy, although they are not usually eaten at the same meal as rice or pasta, as they often contain these ingredients. When soup is served as a separate course, however, it is in hearty portions. The most substantial soups are served as a main course as a light alternative to the main meal of the day.

Vegetables
Vegetables rarely accompany meat, chicken or game; a few potatoes and a green salad are considered plenty after a first course of pasta or rice. Instead, vegetables are usually eaten as a separate dish, either in small quantities as a first course, or in larger quantities as a main course. Many—green beans, artichoke hearts, peppers—are also popular ingredients in Italian salads.

Pasta and rice
Pasta, eaten in southern Italy, and rice, eaten in the north, are both traditionally served after the antipasto as a first course before the main course of fish or meat. But pasta and rice dishes can be eaten as any part of a meal and at any time of day.

Polenta
Polenta, another Italian staple, is normally eaten with a main course to soak up the juices or added to hearty dishes baked in the oven.

Cheese
Cheese, if it is eaten at all at a meal, is served after the main course. It is usually a small selection and is sometimes accompanied by a sweet pear or a ripe peach. It is also added to pizzas and some sauces, while grated Parmesan is frequently served with pasta dishes.

Desserts
Although Italians love sweets, everyday meals are normally concluded with fresh fruit. You are much more likely to see Italians eating cakes and pastries with a cup of coffee in the morning or afternoon. Elaborate desserts are kept for special occasions, often bought rather than made, and sensibly left to the skilled hands of the pastry cook.

Right: *In Italy it is the freshness of the vegetables, often bought at market on the day they are used, that makes the food so delicious.*

Equipment

Many of the utensils in the Italian kitchen are everyday items found in most kitchens, but some specialized ones are particularly useful. Pasta can be made by hand, but a pasta machine will make it much lighter work, and trying to serve spaghetti from the pan without a special spoon is very frustrating. If you are making pizzas, a cutting wheel will cut them into clean slices.

Colander
Indispensable for draining hot pasta and vegetables.

Cookie cutters
Usually used for cutting cookie dough into fancy shapes but equally good for cutting fresh pasta shapes.

Earthenware pot
Excellent for slow-cooking stews, soups or sauces. It can be used either in the oven or on top of the stove over low heat with a metal heat diffuser under it to prevent cracking. Many shapes and sizes are available. To season a terra-cotta pot before using it for the first time, immerse it in cold water overnight. Remove from the water and rub the unglazed bottom with a garlic clove. Fill with water and bring slowly to a boil. Discard the water. Repeat the process, changing the water, until the "earth" taste disappears.

Fluted pastry cutter
For cutting fresh pasta or pastry.

Hand food mill
Excellent for soups, sauces and tomato passata, the pulp passes through the holes, leaving the seeds and skin behind.

Ice cream scoop
Ideal for serving firm and well-frozen ice creams.

Italian ice cream scoop
Good for soft ices that are not too solid.

Meat mallet
Good for pounding cutlets. It can also be used to crush nuts and whole spices.

Mortar and pestle
For hand-grinding spices, coarse salt, pepper, herbs and bread crumbs.

Olive pitter
Can be used to pit olives or cherries.

Parmesan cheese knife
In Italy Parmesan is not cut with a conventional knife, but broken off the large cheese wheels using this kind of wedge. Insert the point and apply pressure.

Pasta machine
Many models are available, including sophisticated electric and industrial models. Most have an adjustable roller width and thin and wide noodle cutters.

Pasta rolling pin
A length of dowel 2 inches in diameter can also be used. Smooth the surface with fine sandpaper, rinse and dry before using for the first time.

Piping tips
For piping decorations, garnishes, etc. Use with a nylon or paper pastry bag.

Pizza cutting wheel
Useful for cutting slices, although a sharp knife may also be used.

Spaghetti spoon
The wooden "teeth" catch the spaghetti strands as they boil.

Spatula
Very useful for spreading and smoothing.

Whisk
Excellent for smoothing sauces and beating egg whites.

Wide vegetable peeler
Very easy to use for peeling all sizes of vegetable.

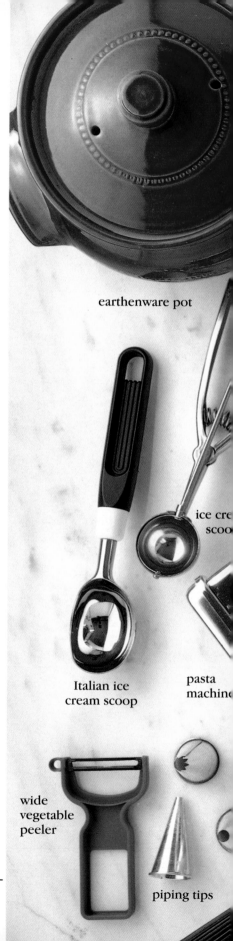

earthenware pot

ice cream scoop

pasta machine

Italian ice cream scoop

wide vegetable peeler

piping tips

mortar and pestle

pasta rolling pin

hand food mill

olive pitter

fluted pastry cutter

whisk

cookie cutters

meat mallet

colander

spaghetti spoon

Parmesan cheese knife

pizza cutting wheel

spatula

Basic Ingredients

Cured Meats

Cured meats are a popular ingredient of antipasti, and each region has its own specialties. A typical antipasto could consist of a plate of mixed prepared meats and sausages. Salamis, pancetta, air-dried bresaola, coppa and mortadella sausages are some of the meats most commonly used in Italy, often served with crusty bread and butter. Prosciutto crudo—raw prosciutto—is the most prized of all meats, and is delicious served thinly sliced with ripe melon or fresh figs.

Cheeses

An Italian meal is more likely to end with a selection of cheeses and fruit than a sweet dessert. Among the huge variety of cheeses, the following are some of the best known:

Gorgonzola
This creamy blue cheese is made in Lombardy. It has a mild flavor when young, which becomes stronger with maturity.

Mascarpone
This is a rich, triple-cream cheese with a mild flavor. It is often used in desserts as a substitute for whipped cream.

Mozzarella
Mozzarella is a fresh, white cheese made from water buffalo's or, more commonly, cow's milk. The texture is soft and chewy and the taste mild.

Parmesan
Parmesan is a long-aged, full-flavored cheese with a hard rind,
used for both grating and eating in slivers. The wheels are aged for between 18 and 36 months. Fresh Parmesan is superb, and is incomparably better than the ready-grated varieties sold pre-packed in jars.

Pecorino
There are two main types of Pecorino: Pecorino romano and Pecorino Toscano, both made from sheep's milk. This salted, sharp-flavored cheese is widely used for dessert eating, and for grating when mature.

Scamorza
A distinctively shaped cheese made from cow's milk. Its shape is the result of being hung from a string during aging.

Gorgonzola

Scamorza

Parmesan cheese

Parma ham

bresaola

mozzarella

pecorino

mortadella

cacciatoro

salami

pancetta

Pantry Ingredients

The following ingredients are all commonly used to give Italian dishes their characteristic flavors. They are good basics to keep in your pantry for use when you need them.

Amaretti cookies
Usually served with sweet wine, for dipping.

Authentic Balsamic vinegar
This has only recently become widely available outside Italy. Aged slowly in wooden barrels, the finest varieties are deliciously mellow and fragrant.

Capers
Aromatic buds pickled in jars of wine vinegar. They go well with garlic and lemon.

Dried beans
A typical Italian pantry will always contain a supply of dried natural ingredients. Dried beans and lentils should be stored in airtight containers for use in soups and stews.

Dried red chilies
Good for adding spicy flavor to all kinds of dishes.

Fennel seeds
These have a great affinity with fish, pork and poultry and can also be sprinkled on bread.

Juniper berries
These have a sweet, resinous flavor that goes well with hearty meat dishes.

Olive oil
Perhaps the single most important ingredient in a modern Italian kitchen is olive oil. The fruity flavor of a fine extra virgin olive oil perfumes any dish it is used in, from pesto sauce to the simplest salad dressing. Buy the best olive oil you can afford; one bottle goes a long way and makes a huge difference to any recipe.

Olives
These are one of Italy's most wonderful native ingredients. Unfortunately, fresh cured olives do not travel well, and many of the most delicious varieties are not available outside the Mediterranean. Sample canned or bottled olives before adding to sauces, as they sometimes acquire an unpleasant metallic taste that could spoil the flavor of the dish. Good-quality olives can be bought at the fresh food counters of supermarkets and delicatessens.

Pine nuts
These are very popular in the Mediterranean region and are an essential ingredient in pesto sauce. They have a delicate flavor and can be used in sweet and savory dishes.

Polenta
The coarsely ground yellow cornmeal is a staple of the northern Italian diet. Once cooked, it can be eaten hot or left to cool and set, then sliced and brushed with oil before broiling.

Porcini mushrooms
These mushrooms are found in the woods in various parts of Europe in autumn. They can be eaten cooked fresh, or sliced thinly and dried in the sun or in special ovens. A few dried porcini soaked in water add a deliciously woodsy flavor.

Rice
Another popular ingredient in northern Italy is rice, which is used to make risotto. Of the special varieties grown in the area for this purpose, the best known are arborio, vialone nano and carnaroli.

Sun-dried tomatoes
Packed in oil, they can be used straight from the jar in salads, sauces and stuffings.

white peppercorns

polenta

junip
berri

fennel seeds

green olives

bay leaves

salt cod

sun-dried
tomatoes

olive oil

authentic
balsamic vinegar

garlic

dried red chilies

arborio rice

green lentils

chickpeas

porcini
mushrooms

Great Northern
beans

pinto beans

capers

amaretti cookies

pine nuts

coffee beans

Fresh Produce

Italian cooking is based on the creative use of fresh, seasonal ingredients. Vegetables and herbs play central roles in almost every aspect of the menu. In the markets, there is a sense of anticipation at the beginning of each new season, heralded by the arrival, on the beautifully displayed stalls, of the year's first artichokes, olives, chestnuts or wild mushrooms. Seasonal recipes are always popular and make the most of available produce.

Regional differences

The cuisine of the hot south is typically Mediterranean: Vegetables feature in pasta dishes, on their own or in salads. In the cooler north, meat dishes are more plentiful, and there is a vast array of dairy products. Central Italy combines the best of both north and south. The one thing that all the regions have in common is that they take the best, freshest ingredients and cook them very simply. Italian cuisine is not a complicated or sophisticated style of cooking.

Vegetables

Many of the vegetables once considered exotically Mediterranean are now readily available in the markets and supermarkets of most countries. Fennel and eggplant, bell peppers, zucchini and radicchio are now increasingly present in pasta sauces, soups and pizzas, and they add a wonderful accent to meat and fish dishes too.

Wherever you shop, look for the freshest possible fruits and vegetables. Choose unblemished, firm, sun-ripened produce, preferably locally or organically grown.

Herbs

Many herbs grow freely in the Mediterranean climate, especially basil, parsley, thyme, marjoram, oregano, sage and rosemary, and they are used extensively in Italian cooking.

Fresh herbs such as basil, parsley and sage are easy to cultivate in window boxes and gardens and have an infinitely finer flavor than their dried counterparts.

If buying and using dried herbs, store them in a cool, dark place and don't keep them for too long, or they will become stale and musty.

Right, clockwise from top left: *Garlic cloves, artichokes, red onions, purple cauliflower, fennel, radicchio, fresh herbs (basil, thyme, parsley and sage), eggplants and green bell peppers.*

Fresh pasta

Sheets of lasagne, and long ribbon-like pasta – tagliarini, fettuccine and tagliatelle are most commonly found in the fresh pasta section of supermarkets or delicatessens. Manufacturers are constantly adding to their ranges and although there are many varieties of dried pasta, a wide choice of fresh pasta is now available.

Fresh pasta is not necessarily better than dried, but buying it fresh offers the opportunity to choose a ready-stuffed variety. Popular ready-filled types are ravioli, agnolotti ("little slippers"), tortellini, tortelloni and cappelletti ("little peaked hats"). Fillings include spinach and ricotta, ground beef and ham. Pasta is often made from flavored dough to complement the filling. If the filling looks quite rich, the calorie count can be kept down by combining the pasta with an uncomplicated sauce. Easier still, simply toss it in a little olive oil or low-fat margarine and sprinkle with some chopped fresh herbs.

Cooking fresh pasta usually takes much less time than for dried pasta, as fresh pasta still contains moisture. As with dried pasta, it is best to follow the cooking instructions given on the package since the ingredients may vary.

For the best fresh pasta of all, nothing beats making it yourself. Once you have mastered the technique for basic pasta dough, you can add delicious fresh ingredients like finely chopped spinach, tomato purée and herbs to the dough to give extra color and flavor.

Fresh pasta should always be stored in the fridge or freezer until ready for cooking. Make sure that you check the storage time on the package.

tagliarini

cappelletti

cheese and tomato agnolotti

mini ravioli

gemelli

fusilli

tortelloni

tortellini

tagliatelle

ravioli (small and large tomato)

egg mafaldane

Dried Pasta

This is a good standby that can be kept for months in an airtight container. Look for the words "semolina" on the packet, as this is top quality pasta which produces good results. Always follow the manufacturer's instructions when cooking dried pasta, and when calculating portions, remember that pasta can increase in volume as much as four times when cooked.

Anellini
Small pasta rings, sometimes serrated. They are good in soups and casseroles (1).

Campanelle
Twisted with frilled edges (2).

Cannelloni
Pasta tubes traditionally stuffed with a meat or cheese filling and baked in the oven (3).

Conchiglie
Pasta shells – they are smooth or ridged (rigate). The smaller shells are called conchigliette. The largest shells (conchiglioni) can be stuffed (4).

Elicoidali (rigatoni)
Good served with chunky sauces, or in baked dishes (5).

Farfalle (pasta bows)
Pasta in bow shapes, usually with decorated edges. They are ideal for "dressing up" a plain-looking salad (6).

Fettuccine
Long, narrow ribbons of pasta made from egg pasta. It is not as wide as tagliatelle (7).

Fusillata casareccia
These twists of pasta are good with tomato sauce (8).

Fusilli
Corkscrew-shaped pasta that works well with tomato and vegetable sauces (9).

Lasagne
Wide sheets of pasta, often layered between meat and vegetable sauces and baked. Usually the lasagne has to be cooked before baking, but pre-cooked varieties are available. Dried lasagne has smooth or wavy-edged sheets (10).

Macaroni
Hollow tubes of pasta – they are often served in baked dishes with a cheese sauce (11).

Mafaldine
Long wavy-edged strips of pasta (lasagnette) often eaten with soft cheeses such as Ricotta (12).

Pappardelle
Wide ribbons of egg pasta occasionally with wavy edges. They are a good accompaniment to meat or creamy sauces (13).

Penne
Quills of pasta in different sizes often with diagonal cuts for catching more sauce. They are available in both smooth and ridged varieties (14).

Pipe
Tubular pasta that comes either ridged (rigate) or plain (15).

Spaghetti
Long, very thin sticks of pasta – a traditional favorite in tomato or oily sauces (16).

Spirali
Short pasta spirals – they are versatile enough to be used in sauces or soups (17).

Stelline
These little pasta stars are often used in soups (18).

Tagliatelle
Long, flat strands of pasta that go well with creamy sauces. Tagliatelle verdi is green because it has had chopped spinach added to the dough. Squid-ink tagliatelle is manufactured by coloring pasta dough with the ink from squid (19).

Herbs and Spices

Herbs and spices are essential for seasoning pasta dishes and pizzas and improving their flavor. Fresh herbs should be used whenever possible. Buy growing herbs in pots if you can: this ensures the herbs are as fresh as possible and provides a continuous supply.

Basil
Intensely aromatic, basil has a distinctive peppery flavor. The leaves can be used to garnish pizzas and are also ideal as a main seasoning ingredient. Traditional basil pesto is the perfect partner for pasta.

Black peppercorns
Black peppercorns are best used freshly ground in a mill or crushed as the taste and aroma disappears quickly.

Chilies (fresh and dried chili products)
Fresh chilies vary in taste, from mild to fiery hot. Generally the large, round fleshy varieties are milder than the small, thin-skinned pointed ones. For a milder, spicy flavor, remove the seeds and veins.

Red chili flakes are made from dried, crushed chilies and are somewhat milder than fresh chilies. They can be heated with olive oil to make chili oil for brushing over pizza bases or used to add bite to pizza toppings and pasta sauces.

Mild chili powder is a commercially prepared mixture of chili, ground herbs and spices. It can be used to flavor more contemporary-style dishes.

Chives
A member of the onion family, the long, narrow green leaves can be used as a garnish or snipped and added to a pasta sauce or pizza dough.

Cilantro
The delicate light green leaves have an unusual flavor and distinctive aroma. Chopped leaves are sometimes used in Californian-style pizzas and to flavor pasta dough. The fresh leaves also make an attractive garnish.

Cumin
These seeds have a warm, earthy flavor and aromatic fragrance and are sold whole or ground. Use in pasta dishes and pizzas, especially those with chili and oregano, for a Mexican flavor.

Curly parsley
This provides color and gives a fresh, clean flavor.

Italian parsley
This variety has much more flavor than common curly parsley, but they can be used interchangeably.

Herbes de Provence
A dried herb mixture of thyme, savory, rosemary, marjoram and oregano. It is especially good added to pasta and pizza doughs or sprinkled over pizzas before they are cooked.

Nutmeg
Nutmeg has a sweetish, highly aromatic flavor which has an affinity for rich foods. It is used to great effect in stuffed pizzas, pizza toppings, and cheesy pasta dishes.

Oregano
An aromatic and highly flavored herb, oregano features very strongly in Italian cooking, where it perfectly complements tomato-based sauces.

Rosemary
Rosemary, with its pungent, dark green, needle-like leaves, can be overpowering, but when used judiciously, it can add a delicious flavor to vegetables for an unusual, aromatic pasta sauce or pizza topping.

Saffron
The dried stigmas of the saffron crocus, saffron is the most expensive spice in the world, but fortunately very little is needed in most recipes, sometimes as little as a pinch. Pungent with a brilliant yellow color, saffron is available as strands or ground.

Sage
Just a few leaves can deliciously flavor a sauce or topping, especially with a rich-tasting cheese like Gorgonzola; sage tends to overpower subtle flavors.

Salt
For seasoning, use sea salt flakes or refined table salt; the former has a slightly stronger flavor so use it sparingly. Salt also balances the action of yeast and is an integral part of making bread, and hence pizza dough.

Thyme
This is excellent chopped or crumbled, and stirred into tomato sauces or sprinkled on to pasta and pizza dishes. Whole sprigs can be used as a garnish.

saffron

red chili flakes

cilantro

mild chili powder

fresh red chilies

chives

thyme

curly parsley

Italian parsley

ground cumin

herbes de Provence

nutmeg

sage

rosemary

oregano

basil

black peppercorns

sea salt

Basic Pasta Dough

Serves 3–4

INGREDIENTS
1³/₄ cups all-purpose flour
pinch of salt
2 eggs
2 teaspoons of cold water

Making pasta on a work surface

1 Sift the flour and salt onto a clean work surface and make a well in the center with your hand.

2 Put the eggs and water into the well. Using a fork, beat the eggs gently together, then gradually draw in the flour from the sides, to make a thick paste.

3 When the mixture becomes too stiff to use a fork, use your hands to mix until dough is firm. Knead the dough for about 5 minutes, until smooth. (This can be done in an electric food mixer fitted with a dough hook.) Cover with plastic wrap to prevent it drying out and leave to rest for 20–30 minutes.

Making pasta in a bowl

1 Sift the flour and salt into a glass bowl and make a well in the center. Add the eggs and water.

2 Using a fork, beat the eggs gently together, then gradually draw in the flour from the sides, to make a thick paste.

3 When the mixture becomes too stiff to use a fork, use your hands to mix until dough is firm. Knead the dough for 5 minutes until smooth. (This can be done in an electric food mixer fitted with a dough hook.) Cover with plastic wrap to prevent it drying out and leave to rest for 20–30 minutes.

VARIATIONS

TOMATO: add 4 teaspoons of concentrated tomato purée to the eggs before mixing.
SPINACH: add 4 ounces frozen spinach, thawed and squeezed of excess moisture. Moisten with the eggs, before adding to the flour.
HERB: add 3 tablespoons finely chopped fresh herbs to the eggs before mixing the dough.
WHOLE WHEAT: use 5 ounces wholemeal flour and 2 ounces plain flour. Add an extra 2 teaspoons cold water (whole wheat flour will absorb more liquid than white flour).
PAPRIKA: use 1 teaspoon ground paprika sifted with the flour.

Rolling out pasta dough by hand

1 Cut the basic dough in quarters. Use one quarter at a time and cover the rest with plastic wrap, so it does not dry out. Flatten the dough and dust liberally with flour. Start rolling out the dough, making sure you roll it evenly.

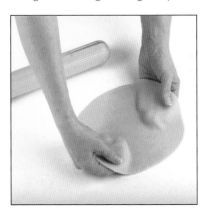

2 As the dough becomes thinner, keep on rotating it on the work surface by gently lifting the edges with your fingers and supporting it over the rolling pin. Make sure you don't tear the dough.

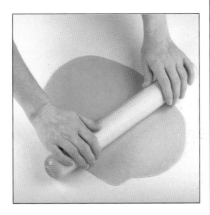

3 Continue rolling out the dough until it has reached the desired thickness, about ⅛-inch thick.

Rolling out dough using a pasta machine

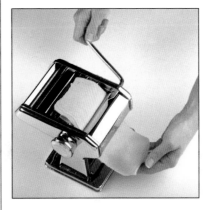

1 Cut the basic dough into quarters. Use one quarter at a time and cover the rest with plastic wrap, so it does not dry out. Flatten the dough and dust liberally with flour. Start with the machine set to roll at the thickest setting. Pass the dough through the rollers several times, dusting the dough from time to time with flour until it is smooth.

2 Fold the strip of dough into three, press the ends well together and pass through the machine again. Repeat the folding and rolling several times on each setting.

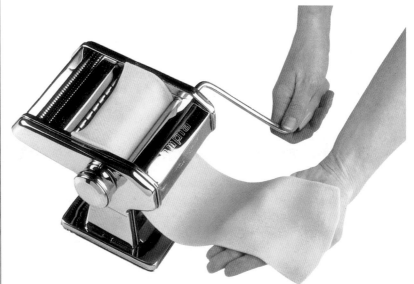

3 Guide the dough through the machine but don't pull or stretch it or the dough will tear. As the dough is worked through all the settings, it will become thinner and longer. Guide the dough over the back of your hand, as the dough is rolled out to a thin sheet. Pasta used for stuffing, such as ravioli or tortellini, should be used as soon as possible. Otherwise, lay the rolled sheets on a clean dish towel, lightly dusted with sifted flour, and leave to dry for 10 minutes before cutting. This makes it easier to cut and prevents the strands of pasta sticking together.

Cutting pasta shapes

Until you are confident at handling and shaping pasta dough, it is easier to work with small quantities. Always keep the dough well covered with plastic wrap to prevent it drying out, until you are ready to work with it.

Shaping ravioli

Cutting out spaghetti
To cut spaghetti, fit the appropriate attachment to the machine or move the handle to the appropriate slot. Cut the pasta sheets into 10-inch lengths and pass these through the machine. Guide the strands over the back of your hand as they appear out of the machine.

Cutting out tagliatelle
To cut tagliatelle, fit the appropriate attachment to the machine or move the handle to the appropriate slot. Cut the pasta sheets into 10-inch lengths and pass these through the machine as for spaghetti.

1 To make square ravioli, place spoonfuls of filling on a sheet of dough at intervals of 2–3 inches, leaving a 1-inch border. Brush the dough between the spoonfuls of filling with egg white.

Cutting out lasagne
Take a sheet of pasta dough and cut out neat rectangles about 7 x 3 inches to make sheets of lasagne. Lay on a clean dish towel to dry.

2 Lay a second sheet of pasta carefully over the top. Press around each mound of filling, removing any air pockets.

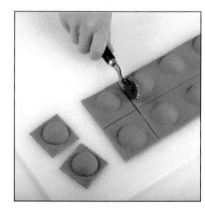

3 Using a fluted pastry wheel or a sharp knife, cut between the filling.

Making farfalle

Making tagliatelle

1 Lightly flour some spinach-flavored pasta dough and roll it up into a strip 12 x 4 inches.

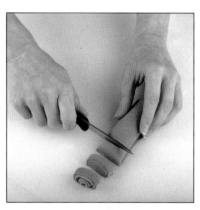

2 Using a sharp knife, cut straight across the roll.

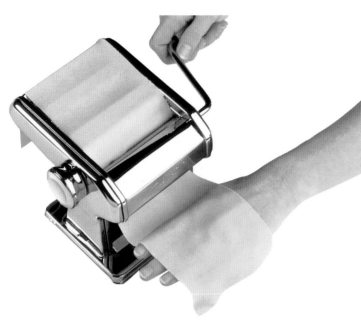

1 Roll the pasta dough through a pasta machine until the sheets are very thin. Then cut into long strips 1½-inches wide.

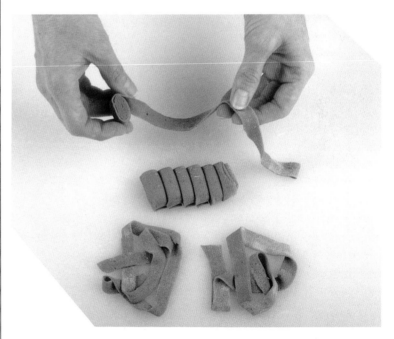

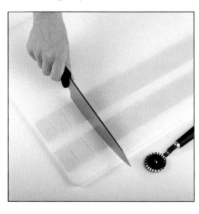

2 Cut the strips into small rectangles. Run a pastry wheel along the two shorter edges of the little rectangles – this will give the bows a decorative edge.

3 Moisten the center of the strips and using a finger and thumb, gently pinch each rectangle together in the middle to make little pasta bows.

3 Carefully unravel each little roll as you cut it to make ribbons of fresh tagliatelle.

Basic Pizza Dough

This simple bread base is rolled out thinly for a traditional pizza recipe.

MAKES
1 × 10–12 in round pizza
    base
4 × 5 in round pizza bases
1 × 12 × 7 in oblong pizza
    base

INGREDIENTS
1½ cups bread flour
¼ tsp salt
1 tsp rapid-rise dried yeast
½–⅔ cups lukewarm water
1 tbsp olive oil

1 Sift the flour and salt into a large mixing bowl.

2 Stir in the yeast.

3 Make a well in the center of the dry ingredients. Pour in the water and oil and mix with a spoon to a soft dough.

4 Knead the dough on a lightly floured surface for about 10 minutes until smooth and elastic.

5 Place the dough in a greased bowl and cover with plastic wrap. Let rise in a warm place for about 1 hour or until the dough has doubled in size.

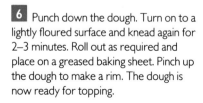

6 Punch down the dough. Turn on to a lightly floured surface and knead again for 2–3 minutes. Roll out as required and place on a greased baking sheet. Pinch up the dough to make a rim. The dough is now ready for topping.

Deep-dish Pizza Dough

This recipe produces a deep and spongy base.

MAKES
1 × 10 in deep-dish pizza base

INGREDIENTS
2 cups bread flour
½ tsp salt
1 tsp rapid-rise dried yeast
⅔ cup lukewarm water
2 tbsp olive oil

Follow the method for Basic Pizza Dough. When the dough has doubled in size, punch down and knead for 2–3 minutes. Roll out the dough to fit a greased 10 in deep-dish pizza pan or square cake pan. Let the dough prove for 10 minutes, then add the topping. Alternatively, shape and place on a greased baking sheet.

Whole Wheat Pizza Dough

INGREDIENTS
3 oz/¾ cup whole wheat flour
¾ cup bread flour
¼ tsp salt
1 tsp rapid-rise dried yeast
½–⅔ cup lukewarm water
1 tbsp olive oil

Follow the method for Basic Pizza Dough. You may have to add a little extra water to form a soft dough, depending on the absorbency of the flour.

Cornmeal Pizza Dough

INGREDIENTS
1½ cups bread flour
¼ cup cornmeal
¼ tsp salt
1 tsp rapid-rise dried yeast
½–⅔ cup lukewarm water
1 tbsp olive oil

Follow the method for Basic Pizza Dough.

Scone Pizza Dough

The joy of using a scone mixture is it's quick to make and uses pantry cupboard ingredients.

MAKES
1 × 10 in round pizza base
1 × 12 × 7 in oblong pizza
 base

INGREDIENTS
1 cup self-rising flour
1 cup self-rising whole wheat
 flour
pinch of salt
4 tbsp butter, diced
⅔ cup milk

1 Mix together the flours and salt in a mixing bowl. Rub in the butter until the mixture resembles fine bread crumbs.

2 Add the milk and mix with a wooden spoon to a soft dough.

3 Knead lightly on a lightly floured surface until smooth. The dough is now ready to use.

Superquick Pizza Dough

If you're really pressed for time, try a packaged pizza dough mix. For best results roll out the dough to a 10–12 in circle; this is slightly larger than stated on the package, but it does produce a perfect thin, crispy base. For a deep-dish version use two packets.

ALSO MAKES
4 × 5 in round pizza bases
1 × 12 × 7 in oblong pizza
 base

INGREDIENTS
1 × 5 oz package pizza base mix
½ cup lukewarm water

1 Empty the contents of the package into a mixing bowl.

2 Pour in the water and mix with a wooden spoon to a soft dough.

3 Turn the dough on to a lightly floured surface and knead for 5 minutes until smooth and elastic. The dough is now ready to use.

Using a Food Processor

For speed make the pizza dough in a food processor; let the machine do the mixing and kneading, then let the dough proof until doubled in size.

1 Put the flour, salt and yeast into a food processor. Process to mix for a few seconds.

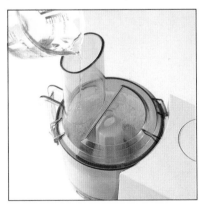

2 Measure the water into a bowl and add the oil. With the machine running, add the liquid and process until the dough forms a soft ball. Leave to rest for 2 minutes, then process for 1 minute more to knead the dough.

3 Remove the dough from the processor and shape into a neat round. Place in a greased bowl and cover with plastic wrap. Let rise in a warm place for about 1 hour until doubled in size. Punch down and knead the dough for 2–3 minutes. The dough is now ready to use.

Readymade Pizza Bases

Fortunately for the busy cook it is now possible to buy fresh, frozen or long-life pizza bases from most supermarkets. Many are enriched with additional ingredients like cheese, herbs and onions. Although they never seem to taste as good as a real homemade pizza base they can be very useful to keep on hand. All you have to do is add your chosen topping and bake in the usual way.

Basic Tomato Sauce for Pizza

Tomato sauce forms the basis of the topping in many pizza recipes. Make sure it is well seasoned and thick before spreading it over the crust. It will keep fresh in a covered container in the refrigerator for up to 3 days.

Covers one 10–12-inch round or 12 x 7-inch oblong pizza crust

INGREDIENTS
1 tablespoon olive oil
1 medium onion, finely chopped
1 garlic clove, finely chopped
1 can (14 ounces) chopped
    tomatoes
1 tablespoon tomato paste
1 tablespoon chopped fresh mixed
    herbs, such as parsley, thyme,
    basil and oregano
pinch of sugar
salt and ground black pepper

1 Heat the oil in a medium saucepan, add the onion and garlic and gently fry for about 5 minutes or until softened.

2 Add the tomatoes, tomato paste, herbs, sugar and seasoning.

3 Simmer, uncovered, stirring occasionally, for 15–20 minutes or until the tomatoes have reduced to a thick pulp. Let cool.

Basic Tomato Sauce for Pasta

Tomato sauce is without a doubt the most popular topping for pasta in Italy. This sauce is best made with fresh tomatoes of any variety, but also works well with canned plum tomatoes.

Serves 4

INGREDIENTS
¼ cup olive oil
1 medium onion, very finely
    chopped
1 garlic clove, finely chopped
1 pound tomatoes, fresh
    or canned, chopped, with
    their juice
salt and ground black pepper
a few fresh basil leaves or
    parsley sprigs

1 Heat the oil in a medium saucepan. Add the onion and cook, stirring occasionally, over medium heat for 5–8 minutes or until it is translucent.

2 Stir in the garlic, fresh tomatoes and 3 tablespoons water. If using canned tomatoes, add them with their juice instead of water and break them up with a wooden spoon. Season with salt and pepper and add the herbs. Cook for 20–30 minutes.

3 Pass the sauce through a food mill or purée in a food processor. To serve, reheat gently, adjust the seasoning, if necessary, and pour the sauce over the drained pasta.

Bolognese Meat Sauce

This great meat sauce is a specialty of Bologna. It is delicious with tagliatelle or short pasta such as penne or conchiglie, as well as spaghetti, and is indispensable in baked lasagne.

Serves 6

INGREDIENTS
2 tablespoons butter
¼ cup olive oil
1 medium onion, finely chopped
2 tablespoons finely chopped
    pancetta or unsmoked bacon
1 carrot, finely sliced
1 celery stalk, finely sliced
1 garlic clove, finely chopped
12 ounces lean ground beef
⅔ cup dry red wine
½ cup milk
1 can (14 ounces) plum
    tomatoes, chopped, with juice
1 bay leaf
¼ teaspoon fresh thyme leaves
salt and ground black pepper

butter   *olive oil*   *onion*

pancetta   *carrot*

garlic

ground beef   *milk*   *red wine*   *celery*

bay leaf   *thyme*   *canned tomatoes*

COOK'S TIP
This sauce keeps well in the refrigerator for several days and can also be frozen.

1 Heat the butter and oil in a heavy saucepan. Add the onion and cook gently for 3–4 minutes. Add the pancetta and cook until the onion is translucent. Stir in the carrot, celery and garlic. Cook for 3–4 minutes, until the vegetables are softened.

2 Add the beef and crumble it into the vegetables with a fork. Stir until the meat loses its red color. Season with salt and pepper. Pour in the wine, raise the heat slightly and cook for 3–4 minutes, until the liquid evaporates. Add the milk and cook until it evaporates.

3 Stir in the tomatoes with their juice and the herbs. Bring the sauce to a boil. Reduce the heat to low and simmer, uncovered, for 1½–2 hours, stirring occasionally. Adjust the seasoning, if necessary, and remove the bay leaf before serving.

Chopping herbs

Use this method to chop herbs until they are as coarse or as fine as desired.

1 Strip the leaves from the stalk and pile them on a cutting board.

2 Using a sharp knife, cut the herbs into small pieces, holding the tip of the blade against the board and rocking the blade back and forth.

Tomato and Fresh Basil Soup

A soup for late summer, when fresh tomatoes are at their most flavorful.

Serves 4–6

INGREDIENTS
1 tablespoon olive oil
2 tablespoons butter
1 medium onion, finely chopped
2 pounds ripe plum tomatoes, roughly chopped
1 garlic clove, roughly chopped
about 3 cups chicken or vegetable broth
½ cup dry white wine
2 tablespoons sun-dried tomato paste
2 tablespoons shredded fresh basil, plus a few whole sprigs to garnish
⅔ cup heavy cream
salt and pepper

olive oil *garlic* *chicken broth*

butter

onion

heavy cream

white wine

basil

plum tomatoes *sun-dried tomato paste*

VARIATION
The soup can also be served chilled. Pour it into a container after sieving and chill for at least 4 hours. Serve in chilled bowls.

1 Heat the oil and butter in a large saucepan over medium heat until foaming. Add the onion and cook gently for about 5 minutes, stirring frequently, until it is softened but not brown.

2 Stir in the chopped tomatoes and garlic, then add the broth, white wine and sun-dried tomato paste, with salt and pepper to taste. Bring to a boil, then lower the heat, half-cover the saucepan and simmer gently for 20 minutes, stirring occasionally to prevent the tomatoes from sticking to the bottom of the pan.

3 Purée the soup with the shredded basil in a blender or food processor, then press through a sieve into a clean pan.

4 Add the heavy cream and heat through, stirring. Do not allow the soup to approach boiling point. Check the consistency and add more broth if necessary, then adjust the seasoning. Pour into heated bowls and garnish with whole basil sprigs. Serve immediately.

Roasted Plum Tomatoes with Garlic

These are so simple to prepare, yet taste absolutely wonderful. Use a large, shallow earthenware dish that will allow the tomatoes to sear and char in a hot oven.

Serves 4

INGREDIENTS
8 plum tomatoes
12 garlic cloves
¼ cup extra virgin olive oil
3 bay leaves
salt and ground black pepper
3 tablespoons fresh oregano leaves,
   to garnish

olive oil

plum tomatoes   *garlic*

oregano   *bay leaves*

1 Preheat the oven to 450°F. Halve the plum tomatoes, leaving a small part of the green stem intact, if possible, for decoration.

2 Select an ovenproof dish that will hold all the tomatoes snugly in a single layer. Place the tomatoes in the dish with the cut side facing upward, and push the whole, unpeeled garlic cloves between them.

3 Brush the tomatoes with the oil, add the bay leaves and sprinkle black pepper over the top.

4 Bake for about 45 minutes, until the tomatoes have softened and are sizzling in the dish. They should be charred around the edges. Season with salt and a little more black pepper, if needed. Garnish with the fresh oregano leaves and serve immediately.

VARIATION
For a sweet alternative, use red or yellow bell peppers instead of the tomatoes. Cut each pepper in half and remove all the seeds before placing, cut side up, in an ovenproof dish.

COOK'S TIP
Select ripe, juicy tomatoes without any blemishes to get the best flavor out of this dish.

Consommé with Agnolotti

Serves 4–6

INGREDIENTS

75 g/3 oz cooked peeled prawns
75 g/3 oz canned crab meat, drained
5 ml/1 tsp fresh root ginger, peeled
   and finely grated
15 ml/1 tbsp fresh white
   breadcrumbs
5 ml/1 tsp light soy sauce
1 spring onion, finely chopped
1 garlic clove, crushed
1 quantity of basic pasta dough
egg white, beaten
400 g/14 oz can chicken or
   fish consommé
30 ml/2 tbsp sherry or vermouth
salt and ground black pepper
50 g/2 oz cooked, peeled prawns
   and fresh coriander leaves,
   to garnish

prawns

root ginger   *crab meat*

spring onion   *fresh coriander*

garlic

chicken consommé

flour

fresh white breadcrumbs

basic pasta dough

1 Put the prawns, crab meat, ginger, breadcrumbs, soy sauce, onion, garlic and seasoning into a food processor or blender and process until smooth.

2 Roll the pasta into thin sheets. Stamp out 32 rounds 5 cm/2 in in diameter, with a fluted pastry cutter.

3 Place a small teaspoon of the filling in the centre of half the pasta rounds. Brush the edges of each round with egg white and sandwich with a second round on top. Pinch the edges together firmly to stop the filling seeping out.

4 Cook the pasta in a large pan of boiling, salted water for 5 minutes (cook in batches to stop them sticking together). Remove and drop into a bowl of cold water for 5 seconds before placing on a tray. (You can make these pasta shapes a day in advance. Cover with clear film and store in the fridge.)

5 Heat the chicken or fish consommé in a pan with the sherry or vermouth. When piping hot, add the cooked pasta shapes and simmer for 1–2 minutes.

6 Serve in a shallow soup bowl. Garnish with extra peeled shrimp and fresh cilantro leaves.

Chicken Stellette Soup

Serves 4–6

INGREDIENTS

3³/₄ cups chicken stock
1 bay leaf
4 scallions, sliced
2 ounces stellette
8 ounces button
    mushrooms, sliced
1 cooked chicken breast
²/₃ cup dry white wine
1 tablespoon chopped parsley
salt and ground black pepper

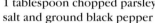

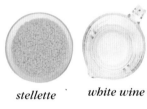
stellette   *white wine*

chicken stock

cooked chicken breast

scallions

parsley

bay leaf

mushrooms

1 Put the stock and bay leaf into a pan and bring to a boil.

2 Add the scallions and mushrooms to the stock.

3 Remove the skin from the chicken and slice thinly. Transfer to a plate and set aside.

4 Add the pasta to the pan, cover and simmer for 7–8 minutes. Just before serving, add the chicken, wine and parsley, heat through for 2–3 minutes.

Vegetable Minestrone with Anellini

Serves 6–8

INGREDIENTS
large pinch of saffron strands
1 onion, chopped
1 leek, sliced
1 stick celery, sliced
2 carrots, diced
2–3 garlic cloves, crushed
2½ cups chicken stock
2 x 14-ounce cans
    chopped tomatoes
½ cup frozen peas
2 ounces soup pasta (anellini)
1 teaspoon caster sugar
1 tablespoon chopped fresh parsley
1 tablespoon chopped fresh basil
salt and ground black pepper

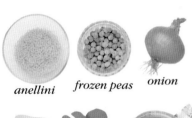
anellini *frozen peas* *onion*

saffron strands *basil* *stock*

parsley
chopped tomatoes

carrot *celery*
garlic *leek*

1 Soak the pinch of saffron strands in 1 tablespoon boiling water. Let stand for 10 minutes.

2 Meanwhile, put the prepared onion, leek, celery, carrots and garlic into a pan. Add the chicken stock, bring to a boil, cover and simmer for 10 minutes.

3 Add the canned tomatoes, the saffron with its liquid, and the peas. Bring back to a boil and add the anellini. Simmer for 10 minutes until tender.

4 Season with salt, pepper and sugar to taste. Stir in the chopped herbs just before serving.

Beet Soup with Ravioli

Serves 4–6

INGREDIENTS
1 recipe basic pasta dough
egg white, beaten, for brushing
flour, for dusting
1 small onion or shallot,
    finely chopped
2 garlic cloves, crushed
1 teaspoon fennel seeds
$2\frac{1}{2}$ cups chicken or vegetable stock
8 ounces cooked beets
2 tablespoons fresh orange juice
fennel or dill leaves, to garnish
crusty bread, to serve

FOR THE FILLING
4 ounces mushrooms,
    finely chopped
1 shallot or small onion,
    finely chopped
1–2 garlic cloves, crushed
1 teaspoon fresh thyme
1 tablespoon fresh parsley
6 tablespoons fresh white
    bread crumbs
large pinch ground nutmeg
salt and ground black pepper

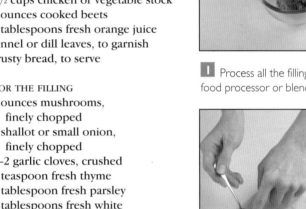

1 Process all the filling ingredients in a food processor or blender.

2 Roll the pasta into thin sheets. Lay one piece over a ravioli tray and put a teaspoonful of the filling into each depression. Brush around the edges of each ravioli with egg white. Cover with another sheet of pasta and press the edges together to seal. Transfer to a floured dish towel and rest for 1 hour before cooking.

3 Cook the ravioli in a large pan of boiling, salted water for 2 minutes. (Cook in batches to stop them from sticking together.) Remove and drop into a bowl of cold water for 5 seconds before placing on a tray. (You can make these pasta shapes a day in advance. Cover with clear film and store in the fridge.) Put the onion, garlic and fennel seeds into a pan with $\frac{2}{3}$ cup of the stock. Bring to a boil, cover and simmer for 5 minutes until tender. Peel and finely dice the beets. (Reserve 4 tbsp for the garnish.) Add the rest to the soup with the remaining stock and bring to a boil.

4 Add the orange juice and cooked ravioli and simmer for 2 minutes. Serve in shallow soup bowls, garnished with the reserved diced beets and fennel or dill leaves. Serve hot, with some crusty bread.

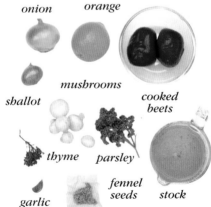

onion   orange

mushrooms

shallot   cooked beets

thyme   parsley

garlic   fennel seeds   stock   nutmeg   basic pasta dough   bread crumbs

dill

Garlic, Chick-pea and Spinach Soup

This delicious, thick and creamy soup is full flavored and perfect for vegetarians.

Serves 4

INGREDIENTS

2 tablespoons olive oil
4 garlic cloves, crushed
1 onion, roughly chopped
2 teaspoons ground cumin
2 teaspoons ground coriander
5 cups vegetable stock
12 ounces potatoes, peeled and
    finely chopped
1 can (15 ounces) chick-peas,
    drained
1 tablespoon cornstarch
²/₃ cup heavy cream
2 tablespoons light tahini (sesame
    seed paste)
½ pound spinach, shredded
cayenne pepper
salt and black pepper

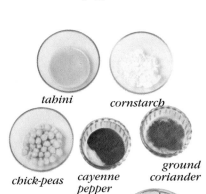
tahini   *cornstarch*

chick-peas   *cayenne   *ground
                pepper*   coriander*

*heavy
cream*   *garlic*
onions   *potatoes*   *vegetable   *ground   *olive
                               stock*   cumin*   oil*

1 Heat the oil in a large saucepan and cook the garlic and onions for 5 minutes or until they are softened and golden brown.

2 Stir in the cumin and coriander and cook for another minute.

3 Pour in the stock and add the potatoes. Bring to a boil and simmer for 10 minutes. Add the drained chick-peas and simmer for 5 more minutes, or until the potatoes and chick-peas are just tender.

4 Blend the cornstarch, cream, tahini and plenty of seasoning. Stir into the soup, with the spinach. Bring to a boil, stirring, and simmer for 2 more minutes. Adjust the seasoning with salt, black pepper and cayenne pepper to taste. Serve immediately, sprinkled with a little cayenne pepper.

Pasta Parcels

Serves 4–6

INGREDIENTS
1 quantity basic pasta dough
flour, for dusting
egg white, beaten
salt and pepper

FOR THE FILLING
1 small onion, finely chopped
1 garlic clove, crushed
$^2/_3$ cup chicken stock
8 ounces ground turkey meat
2–3 fresh sage leaves, chopped
2 canned anchovy fillets, drained

FOR THE SAUCE
$^2/_3$ cup chicken stock
7 ounces low-fat cream cheese
1 tablespoon lemon juice
1 teaspoon caster sugar
2 tomatoes, peeled, seeded and
    finely diced
$^1/_2$ purple onion, finely chopped
6 small cornichons, sliced

1 To make the filling, put the onion, garlic and stock into a pan. Bring to a boil, cover and simmer for 5 minutes until tender. Uncover and boil for about 5 minutes or until the stock is reduced to 2 tablespoons.

2 Add the ground turkey, and stir over the heat until no longer pink in color. Add the sage and anchovy fillets and season with salt and pepper. Cook uncovered for 5 minutes until all the liquid has been absorbed. Let cool.

3 Divide the pasta dough in half. Roll into thin sheets and cut into rectangles measuring 3$^1/_2$ x 2$^1/_2$ inches. Lay on a lightly floured dish towel and repeat with the remaining dough.

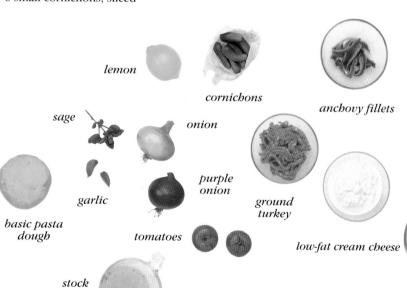

lemon

cornichons

anchovy fillets

sage

onion

garlic

purple onion

basic pasta dough

tomatoes

ground turkey

low-fat cream cheese

stock

4 Place a heaped teaspoon of the filling on the center of each rectangle, brush around the meat with beaten egg white and roll up the pasta, pinching in the ends. Set it aside onto a floured dish towel for 1 hour before cooking.

5 To make the sauce, put the stock, cream cheese, lemon juice and sugar into a pan. Heat gently and whisk until smooth. Add the diced tomatoes, onion and cornichons.

6 Cook the pasta in a large pan of boiling, salted water for 5 minutes. (Cook in batches to stop them from sticking together.) Remove with a slotted spoon, drain well and drop into the sauce. Repeat until all the bonbons are cooked. Simmer for 2–3 minutes. Serve in pasta bowls or soup plates and spoon over a little sauce.

Spinach Tagliarini with Asparagus

Serves 4–6

INGREDIENTS

2 chicken breasts, skinned
   and boned
1 tablespoon light soy sauce
2 tablespoon sherry
2 tablespoon cornstarch
8 scallions, trimmed and cut into
   1-inch diagonal slices
1–2 garlic cloves, crushed
finely grated zest of half a lemon
   and 2 tablespoons lemon juice
²/₃ cup chicken stock
1 teaspoon caster sugar
8 ounces slender asparagus spears,
   cut into 3-inch lengths
1 recipe of basic pasta dough, with 4
   ounces cooked, spinach added,
   or 1 pound fresh tagliarini pasta
salt and ground black pepper

scallions

asparagus

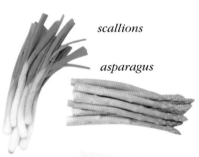

garlic

lemon

chicken breasts

soy
sauce

basic pasta
dough

stock

1 Place the chicken breasts between two sheets of plastic wrap and flatten to a thickness of ¹/₄-inch with a rolling pin.

2 Cut into 1-inch strips across the grain of the fillets. Put the chicken into a bowl with the soy sauce, sherry, cornstarch and seasoning. Toss to coat each piece.

3 In a large non-stick frying pan, put the chicken, scallions, garlic and the grated lemon rind. Add the stock and bring to the boil, stirring constantly until thickened. Add the lemon juice, sugar and asparagus. Simmer for 4-5 minutes until tender.

4 Meanwhile cook the pasta in a large pan of boiling, salted water for 2–3 minutes. Drain thoroughly. Arrange on serving plates and spoon over the chicken and asparagus sauce. Serve the dish immediately.

Sweet and Sour Peppers with Bows

Serves 4–6

INGREDIENTS

1 red, 1 yellow and 1 orange pepper
1 garlic clove, crushed
2 tablespoons capers
2 tablespoons raisins
1 teaspoon wholegrain mustard
rind and juice of 1 lime
1 teaspoon honey
2 tablespoons chopped
   fresh cilantro
8 ounces pasta bows (farfalle)
salt and ground black pepper
shavings of Parmesan cheese,
    to serve (optional)

lime *raisins*

red pepper *yellow pepper*

cilantro

orange pepper

pasta bows

Parmesan cheese

honey *garlic* *capers*

1 Quarter the peppers, and remove the stalk and seeds. Put into boiling water and cook for 10–15 minutes until tender. Drain and rinse under cold water. Peel away the skin and cut the flesh into strips lengthways.

2 Put the garlic, capers, raisins, mustard, lime rind and juice, honey, cilantro and seasoning into a bowl and whisk together.

3 Cook the pasta in a large pan of boiling, salted water for 10–12 minutes until tender. Drain thoroughly.

4 Return the pasta to the pan, add the reserved peppers and dressing. Heat gently and toss to mix. Transfer to a warm serving bowl. Serve with a few shavings of Parmesan cheese, if using.

Herbed Pasta Crescents

Serves 4–6

INGREDIENTS
1 recipe basic pasta dough, with 3
   tablespoons chopped fresh
   herbs added
egg white, beaten, for brushing
flour, for dusting
basil leaves, to garnish

FOR THE FILLING
8 ounces chopped frozen spinach
1 small onion, finely chopped
pinch of ground nutmeg
4 ounces low-fat cottage cheese
1 egg, beaten
1 ounce Parmesan cheese
salt and ground black pepper

FOR THE SAUCE
1¼ cups skim milk
1 ounce margarine
3 tablespoons plain flour
¼ teaspoon ground nutmeg
2 tablespoons chopped fresh herbs
   (chives, basil and parsley)

egg

low-fat
cottage cheese

spinach

chives

onion

Parmesan
cheese

nutmeg

parsley

basil

skim milk

basic pasta
dough

margarine

1 To make the filling, put the spinach and onion into a pan, cover and cook slowly to defrost. Remove the lid and increase the heat to boil off any water. Season with salt, pepper and nutmeg. Turn the spinach into a bowl and cool slightly. Add the cottage cheese, beaten egg and Parmesan cheese.

2 Roll the herb pasta into thin sheets. Cut into 3-inch rounds with a fluted pastry cutter.

3 Place a spoonful of filling in the centre of each round. Brush the edges with egg white. Fold each in half (to make crescents). Press the edges together to seal. Transfer to a floured dish towel and let rest for 1 hour before cooking the pasta.

4 Put all the sauce ingredients (except the herbs) into a pan. With a whisk, thicken over medium heat until smooth. Season with salt, pepper and nutmeg to taste. Stir in the herbs.

5 Cook the pasta in a large pan of boiling, salted water for 3 minutes (cook in batches to stop them from sticking together). Drain thoroughly.

6 Serve the crescents on warmed serving plates and pour over the herb sauce. Garnish with basil leaves and serve at once.

Minestrone

A classic substantial winter soup originally from Milan, but found in various versions around the Mediterranean coasts of Italy and France. Cut the vegetables as roughly or as small as you like. Add freshly grated Parmesan cheese just before serving.

Serves 6–8

INGREDIENTS
2 cups dried white beans
2 tbsp olive oil
2 oz bacon, diced
2 large onions, sliced
2 garlic cloves, crushed
2 medium carrots, diced
3 celery sticks, sliced
14 oz canned chopped tomatoes
10 cups beef stock
12 oz potatoes, diced
1½ cups small pasta shapes
    (macaroni, stars, shells, etc)
½ lb green cabbage, thinly sliced
6 oz fine green beans, sliced
¾ cup frozen peas
3 tbsp chopped fresh parsley
salt and pepper
freshly grated Parmesan cheese,
    to serve

1 Cover the beans with cold water and leave to soak overnight.

2 Heat the oil in a large saucepan and add the bacon, onions, and garlic. Cover and cook gently for 5 minutes, stirring occasionally, until soft.

3 Add the carrots and celery and cook for 2–3 minutes until softening.

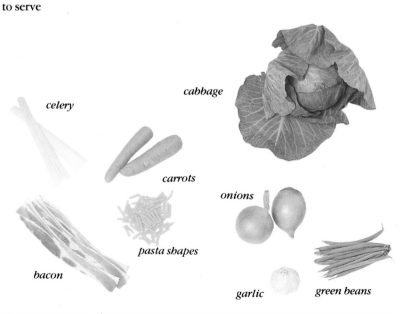
celery

cabbage

carrots

onions

pasta shapes

bacon

garlic   green beans

4 Drain the beans and add to the pan with the tomatoes and stock. Cover and simmer for 2–2½ hours, until the beans are tender.

5 Add the potatoes 30 minutes before the soup is finished.

VARIATION

To make Soupe au Pistou from the South of France, stir in a basil, garlic and pine nut sauce (pesto or pistou) just before serving.

6 Add the pasta, cabbage, beans, peas, and parsley 15 minutes before the soup is ready. Season to taste and serve with a bowl of freshly grated Parmesan cheese.

Italian Bean and Pasta Soup

A thick and hearty soup which, followed by bread and cheese, makes a substantial lunch.

Serves 6

INGREDIENTS
1½ cups dried white beans, soaked
   overnight in cold water
7½ cups chicken stock or water
1 cup medium pasta shells
4 tbsp olive oil, plus extra to serve
2 garlic cloves, crushed
4 tbsp chopped fresh parsley
salt and pepper

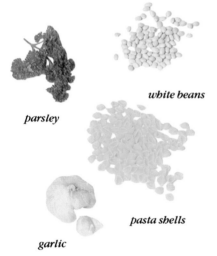

parsley

white beans

pasta shells

garlic

1 Drain the beans and place in a large saucepan with the stock or water. Simmer, half-covered, for 2–2½ hours or until tender.

2 Liquidize half the beans and a little of their cooking liquid, then stir into the remaining beans in the pan.

3 Add the pasta and simmer gently for 15 minutes until tender. (Add extra water or stock if the soup seems too thick.)

4 Heat the oil in a small pan and fry the garlic until golden. Stir into the soup with the parsley and season well with salt and pepper. Ladle into individual bowls and drizzle each with a little extra olive oil.

Zucchini Soup with Small Pasta Shells

A pretty, fresh-tasting soup which could be made using cucumber instead of zucchini.

Serves 4–6

INGREDIENTS
4 tbsp olive or sunflower oil
2 medium onions, finely chopped
6¼ cups chicken stock
2 lb zucchini
1 cup small soup pasta
fresh lemon juice
salt and pepper
2 tbsp chopped fresh chervil
sour cream, to serve

zucchini

onion

soup pasta

chervil

1 Heat the oil in a large saucepan and add the onions. Cover and cook gently for about 20 minutes until very soft but not colored, stirring occasionally.

2 Add the stock and bring to the boil.

3 Meanwhile grate the zucchini and stir into the boiling stock with the pasta. Turn down the heat and simmer for 15 minutes until the pasta is tender. Season to taste with lemon juice, salt, and pepper.

4 Stir in the chervil and add a swirl of sour cream before serving.

COOK'S TIP

If no fresh stock is available, instead of using a stock cube, use canned chicken or beef consommé.

Chicken Vermicelli Soup with Egg Shreds

This soup is very quick and easy – you can add all sorts of extra ingredients to vary the taste, using up lurking leftovers such as scallions, mushrooms, a few shrimp, chopped salami and so on.

Serves 4–6

INGREDIENTS
3 large eggs
2 tbsp chopped fresh cilantro or parsley
6¼ cups good chicken stock or canned consommé
1 cup dried vermicelli or angel hair pasta
¼ lb cooked chicken breast, sliced
salt and pepper

vermicelli

chicken breast

eggs

cilantro

THAI CHICKEN SOUP

To make a Thai variation, use Chinese rice noodles instead of pasta. Stir ½ tsp dried lemon grass, 2 small whole fresh chilies and 4 tbsp coconut milk into the stock. Add 4 sliced scallions and plenty of chopped fresh cilantro.

1 First make the egg shreds. Whisk the eggs together in a small bowl and stir in the cilantro or parsley.

2 Heat a small nonstick skillet and pour in 2–3 tbsp egg, swirling to cover the base evenly. Cook until set. Repeat until all the mixture is used up.

3 Roll each pancake up and slice thinly into shreds. Set aside.

4 Bring the stock to a boil and add the pasta, breaking it up into short lengths. Cook for 3–5 minutes until the pasta is almost tender, then add the chicken, salt, and pepper. Heat through for 2–3 minutes, then stir in the egg shreds. Serve immediately.

Creamy Parmesan and Cauliflower Soup with Pasta Bows

A silky smooth, mildly cheesy soup that isn't overpowered by the cauliflower. It is an elegant dinner party soup served with the crisp melba toast.

Serves 6

INGREDIENTS
1 large cauliflower
5 cups chicken or vegetable stock
1½ cups pasta bows (farfalle)
⅔ cup light cream or milk
freshly grated nutmeg
pinch of cayenne pepper
4 tbsp freshly grated Parmesan cheese
salt and pepper

MELBA TOAST
3–4 slices day-old white bread
freshly grated Parmesan cheese, for
    sprinkling
¼ tsp paprika

cauliflower

pasta bows

Parmesan cheese

nutmeg

1 Cut the leaves and central stalk away from the cauliflower and discard. Divide the cauliflower into florets.

2 Bring the stock to a boil and add the cauliflower. Simmer for about 10 minutes or until very soft. Remove the cauliflower with a perforated spoon and place in a food processor.

3 Add the pasta to the stock and simmer for 10 minutes until tender. Drain, reserve the pasta, and pour the liquid over the cauliflower in the food processor. Add the cream or milk, nutmeg, and cayenne to the cauliflower. Blend until smooth, then press through a strainer. Stir in the cooked pasta. Reheat the soup and stir in the Parmesan. Taste and adjust the seasoning.

4 Meanwhile make the melba toast. Preheat the oven to 350°F. Toast the bread lightly on both sides. Quickly cut off the crusts and split each slice in half horizontally. Scrape off any doughy bits and sprinkle with Parmesan and paprika. Place on a baking sheet and bake in the oven for 10–15 minutes or until uniformly golden. Serve with the soup.

Pasta, Melon and Shrimp Salad

Orange-fleshed cantaloupe or Charentais melon looks spectacular in this salad. You could also use a mixture of honeydew, cantaloupe and watermelon.

Serves 4–6

INGREDIENTS

1½ cups pasta shapes
½ lb frozen shrimp, thawed and
    drained
1 large or 2 small melons
4 tbsp olive oil
1 tbsp tarragon vinegar
2 tbsp chopped fresh chives or parsley
sprigs of herbs, to garnish
Napa cabbage, to serve

melons

pasta shapes

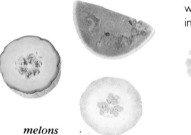

shrimp

Napa cabbage

1 Cook the pasta in boiling salted water according to the manufacturer's instructions. Drain well and allow to cool.

2 Peel the shrimp and discard the shells.

3 Halve the melon and remove the seeds with a teaspoon. Carefully scoop the flesh into balls with a melon baller and mix with the shrimp and pasta.

4 Whisk the oil, vinegar, and chopped herbs together. Pour on to the shrimp mixture and toss to coat. Cover and chill for at least 30 minutes.

5 Meanwhile shred the Napa cabbage and use to line a shallow bowl or the empty melon halves.

6 Pile the shrimp mixture onto the Napa cabbage and garnish with herbs.

Warm Pasta Salad with Ham, Egg, and Asparagus

In the summer months when the weather is hot, try serving your pasta *calda*, as a warm salad. Here it is served with ham, eggs, and asparagus. A mustard dressing made from the thick part of asparagus provides a rich accompaniment.

Serves 4

INGREDIENTS
1 lb asparagus
salt
1 lb dried tagliatelle
½ lb sliced cooked ham,
   ¼ in thick, cut into fingers
2 eggs, hard-cooked and sliced
2 oz Parmesan cheese, shaved

DRESSING
2 oz cooked potato
5 tbsp olive oil, preferably Sicilian
1 tbsp lemon juice
2 tsp Dijon mustard
½ cup vegetable stock

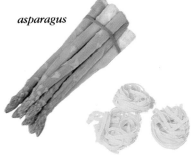

asparagus

tagliatelle

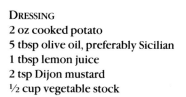

eggs

Parmesan cheese

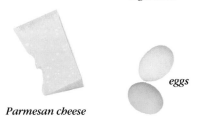

ham

1 Bring a saucepan of salted water to the boil. Trim and discard the tough woody part of the asparagus. Cut the asparagus in half and boil the thicker halves for 12 minutes. After 6 minutes throw in the tips. Refresh under cold water until warm, then drain.

2 Finely chop 5 oz of the asparagus middle section. Place in a food processor with the dressing ingredients and process until smooth. Season to taste.

3 Boil the pasta in a large saucepan of salted water according to the packet instructions. Refresh under cold water until warm, and drain. Dress with the asparagus sauce and transfer to 4 pasta plates. Top with the ham, hard-cooked eggs, and asparagus tips. Finish with Parmesan cheese.

Chicken and Pasta Salad

This is a delicious way to use up leftover cooked chicken, and makes a great appetizer.

Serves 4

INGREDIENTS
8 oz tri-colored pasta twists
2 tbsp bottled pesto sauce
1 tbsp olive oil
1 beefsteak tomato
12 pitted black olives
8 oz cooked green beans
12 oz cooked chicken, cubed
salt and freshly ground black pepper
fresh basil, to garnish

tomato

green beans

olive oil

chicken

pesto sauce

basil

pasta twists

black olives

1 Cook the pasta in plenty of boiling, salted water until *al dente* (for about 12 minutes or as directed on the package).

2 Drain the pasta and rinse in plenty of cold running water. Put into a bowl and stir in the pesto sauce and olive oil.

3 Skin the tomato by placing in boiling water for about 10 seconds and then into cold water, to loosen the skin.

4 Cut the tomato into small cubes and add to the pasta with the black olives, seasoning and green beans cut into 1½ in lengths. Add the cubed chicken. Toss gently together and transfer to a serving platter. Garnish with fresh basil.

Avocado, Tomato, and Mozzarella Pasta Salad with Pine Nuts

A salad made from ingredients representing the colors of the Italian flag – a sunny cheerful dish!

Serves 4

INGREDIENTS
1½ cups pasta bows (farfalle)
6 ripe red tomatoes
½ lb mozzarella cheese
1 large ripe avocado
2 tbsp pine nuts, toasted
1 sprig fresh basil, to garnish

DRESSING
6 tbsp olive oil
2 tbsp wine vinegar
1 tsp balsamic vinegar (optional)
1 tsp whole-grain mustard
pinch of sugar
salt and pepper
2 tbsp chopped fresh basil

olive oil

avocado

tomatoes

basil

mozzarella cheese

pine nuts   *pasta bows*

1 Cook the pasta in plenty of boiling salted water according to the manufacturer's instructions. Drain well and cool.

2 Slice the tomatoes and mozzarella cheese into thin rounds.

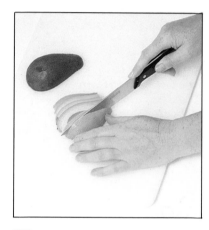

3 Halve the avocado, remove the pit, and peel off the skin. Slice the flesh lengthwise.

4 Whisk all the dressing ingredients together in a small bowl.

5 Arrange the tomato, mozzarella, and avocado in overlapping slices around the edge of a flat plate.

6 Toss the pasta with half the dressing and the chopped basil. Pile into the center of the plate. Pour over the remaining dressing, scatter over the pine nuts, and garnish with a sprig of fresh basil. Serve immediately.

Whole-wheat Pasta, Asparagus, and Potato Salad with Parmesan

A meal in itself, this is a real treat when made with fresh asparagus just in season.

Serves 4

INGREDIENTS
½ lb whole-wheat pasta shapes
4 tbsp extra-virgin olive oil
salt and pepper
12 oz baby new potatoes
½ lb fresh asparagus
¼ lb piece fresh Parmesan cheese

olive oil

asparagus

pasta shapes

Parmesan cheese

new potatoes

1 Cook the pasta in boiling salted water according to the manufacturer's instructions. Drain well and toss with the olive oil, salt, and pepper while still warm.

2 Wash the potatoes and cook in boiling salted water for 12–15 minutes or until tender. Drain and toss with the pasta.

3 Trim any woody ends off the asparagus and halve the stalks if very long. Blanch in boiling salted water for 6 minutes until bright green and still crunchy. Drain. Plunge into cold water to stop them cooking and allow to cool. Drain and dry on paper towels.

4 Toss the asparagus with the potatoes and pasta, season, and transfer to a shallow bowl. Using a rotary vegetable peeler, shave the Parmesan cheese over the salad.

White Bean and Celery Salad

This simple bean salad is a delicious alternative to the potato salad that seems to appear at every picnic spread. If you do not have time to soak and cook dried beans, use canned ones.

Serves 4

INGREDIENTS

1 lb dried white beans (haricot, canellini, navy, or butter beans) or 3 × 14 oz cans white beans
4½ cups vegetable stock, made from a cube
3 stalks celery, cut into ½ in strips
½ cup French Dressing
3 tbsp chopped fresh parsley
salt and pepper

parsley

white beans

celery

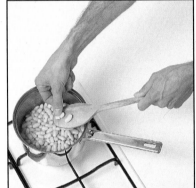

1 If using dried beans, cover with plenty of cold water and soak for at least 4 hours. Discard the soaking water, then place the beans in a heavy saucepan. Cover with fresh water, bring to a boil, and simmer without a lid for 1½ hours, or until the skins are broken. Cooked beans will squash readily between a thumb and forefinger. Drain the beans. If using canned beans, drain, rinse, and use from this stage in the recipe.

COOK'S TIP

Dried beans that have been kept for longer than 6 months will need soaking overnight to lessen their cooking time. As a rule, the less time beans have been kept, the shorter the soaking and cooking time they need. The times given here are suited to freshly purchased beans.

2 Place the cooked beans in a large saucepan. Add the vegetable stock and celery, bring to a boil, cover, and simmer for 15 minutes. Drain thoroughly. Toss the beans with the dressing and leave to cool.

3 Add the chopped parsley and season to taste with salt and pepper.

Mediterranean Salad with Basil

This pasta salad conjures up all the sunny flavors of the Mediterranean.

Serves 4

INGREDIENTS
½ lb chunky pasta shapes
6 oz fine green beans
2 large ripe tomatoes
2 oz fresh basil leaves
7 oz can tuna fish in oil, drained
2 hard-cooked eggs, shelled and sliced or quartered
2 oz can anchovies, drained
capers and black olives

DRESSING
6 tbsp extra-virgin olive-oil
2 tbsp white-wine vinegar or lemon juice
2 garlic cloves, crushed
½ tsp Dijon mustard
2 tbsp chopped fresh basil
salt and pepper

tomatoes

olive oil

garlic

basil

pasta

egg

anchovies

green beans

tuna fish

1 Whisk all the ingredients for the dressing together and leave to infuse while you make the salad.

2 Cook the pasta in plenty of boiling salted water according to the manufacturer's instructions. Drain well and cool.

3 Trim the beans and blanch in boiling salted water for 3 minutes. Drain and refresh in cold water.

4 Slice or quarter the tomatoes and arrange on the bottom of a bowl. Toss with a little dressing and cover with a quarter of the basil leaves. Then cover with the beans. Toss with a little more dressing and cover with a third of the remaining basil.

5 Cover with the pasta tossed in a little more dressing, half the remaining basil and the roughly flaked tuna.

6 Arrange the eggs on top, then finally scatter over the anchovies, capers and black olives. Pour over the remaining dressing and garnish with the remaining basil. Serve immediately. Don't be tempted to chill this salad – all the flavor will be dulled.

Arugula, Pear, and Parmesan Salad

For a sophisticated start to an elaborate meal, try this simple salad of honey-rich pears, fresh Parmesan, and aromatic leaves of arugula. Enjoy with a young Beaujolais or chilled Lambrusco wine.

Serves 4

INGREDIENTS
3 ripe pears, Williams or Packhams
2 tsp lemon juice
3 tbsp hazelnut or walnut oil
4 oz arugula
3 oz Parmesan cheese
black pepper
open-textured bread, to serve

arugula

Parmesan cheese

pears

1 Peel and core the pears and slice thickly. Toss with lemon juice to keep the flesh white.

2 Combine the nut oil with the pears. Add the arugula leaves and toss.

3 Transfer the salad to 4 small plates and top with shavings of Parmesan cheese. Season with freshly ground black pepper and serve.

COOK'S TIP
If you are unable to buy arugula easily, you can grow your own from early spring to late summer.

Melon and Prosciutto Salad with Strawberry Salsa

Sections of cool fragrant melon wrapped with slices of air-dried ham make a delicious salad starter. If strawberries are in season, serve with a savory-sweet strawberry salsa and watch it disappear.

Serves 4

INGREDIENTS
1 large melon, cantaloupe, Spanish or
    charentais
6 oz prosciutto, thinly sliced

SALSA
½ lb strawberries
1 tsp superfine sugar
2 tbsp peanut or sunflower oil
1 tbsp orange juice
½ tsp finely grated orange zest
½ tsp finely grated fresh ginger
salt and black pepper

2 To make the salsa, hull the strawberries and cut them into large dice. Place in a small mixing bowl with the sugar and crush lightly to release the juices. Add the oil, orange juice, zest, and ginger. Season with salt and a generous twist of black pepper.

3 Arrange the melon on a serving plate, lay the ham over the top, and serve with a bowl of salsa.

1 Halve the melon and take the seeds out with a spoon. Cut the rind away with a paring knife, then slice the melon thickly. Chill until ready to serve.

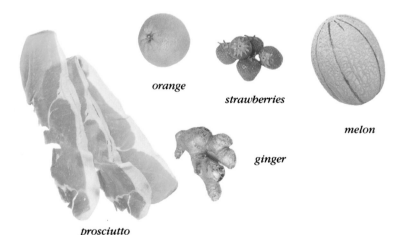

orange

strawberries

melon

ginger

prosciutto

Grilled Chicken Salad with Polenta and Sweet Herbs

Lavender may seem like an odd salad ingredient, but its delightful scent has a natural affinity with sweet garlic, orange, and other wild herbs. A serving of cornmeal polenta makes this salad both filling and delicious.

Serves 4

INGREDIENTS
4 boneless chicken breasts
3¾ cups light chicken stock
1 cup fine polenta or cornmeal
2 oz butter
1 lb young spinach
6 oz lamb's lettuce
8 sprigs fresh lavender
8 small tomatoes, halved
salt and pepper

LAVENDER MARINADE
6 fresh lavender flowers
2 tsp finely grated orange zest
2 cloves garlic, crushed
2 tsp clear honey
salt
2 tbsp olive oil, French or Italian
2 tsp chopped fresh thyme
2 tsp chopped fresh marjoram

1 To make the marinade, strip the lavender flowers from the stems and combine with the orange zest, garlic, honey, and salt. Add the olive oil and herbs. Score the chicken deeply, spread the mixture over the chicken, and leave to marinate in a cool place for at least 20 minutes.

2 To make the polenta, bring the chicken stock to a boil in a heavy saucepan. Add the cornmeal in a steady stream, stirring all the time until thick: this will take 2–3 minutes. Turn the cooked polenta out on to a 1-in-deep buttered tray and allow to cool.

3 Heat the broiler to a moderate temperature. (If using a barbecue, let the embers settle to a steady glow.) Broil the chicken for 15 minutes, turning once.

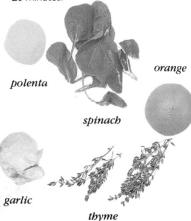

4 Cut the polenta into 1 in cubes with a wet knife. Heat the butter in a large skillet and fry the polenta until golden.

polenta

orange

spinach

garlic

thyme

lavender   *chicken breasts*

COOK'S TIP

Lavender marinade is a delicious flavoring for fish as well as chicken. Try it over broiled cod, haddock, halibut, sea bass, and bream.

5 Wash the salad leaves and spin dry, then divide between 4 large plates. Slice each chicken breast and lay over the salad. Place the polenta among the salad, decorate with sprigs of lavender and tomatoes, season and serve.

Grapefruit Salad with Campari and Orange

The bittersweet flavor of Campari combines especially well with citrus fruit. Because of its alcohol content, this dish is not suitable for young children.

Serves 4

INGREDIENTS
3 tbsp superfine sugar
4 tbsp Campari
2 tbsp lemon juice
4 grapefruit
5 oranges
4 sprigs fresh mint

COOK'S TIP

When buying citrus fruit, choose brightly colored varieties that feel heavy for their size.

grapefruit

oranges

mint

lemon juice

Campari

1 Bring ⅔ cup water to a boil in a small saucepan, add the sugar, and simmer until dissolved. Cool in a metal tray, then add the Campari and lemon juice. Chill until ready to serve.

2 Cut the peel from the top, bottom, and sides of the grapefruit and oranges with a serrated knife. Segment the fruit into a bowl by slipping a small paring knife between the flesh and the membranes. Combine the fruit with the Campari syrup and chill.

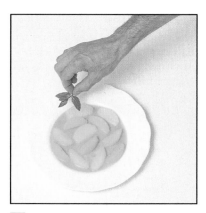

3 Spoon the salad into 4 dishes and finish with a sprig of fresh mint.

Fresh Spinach and Avocado Salad

Young, tender spinach leaves make a change from lettuce and are delicious served with avocado, cherry tomatoes and radishes in a tofu sauce.

Serves 2–3

INGREDIENTS
1 large avocado
juice of 1 lime
8 oz fresh baby spinach leaves
4 oz cherry tomatoes
4 scallions, sliced
1/2 cucumber
2 oz radishes, sliced

FOR THE DRESSING
4 oz soft silken tofu
3 tbsp milk
2 tsp prepared mustard
1/2 tsp white wine vinegar
pinch of cayenne
salt and freshly ground black pepper

tofu   scallions

spinach leaves

cherry tomatoes

avocado

white wine vinegar

mustard

cayenne

lime

cucumber

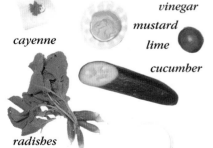

radishes

1 Cut the avocado in half, remove the pit, and strip off the skin. Cut the flesh into slices. Transfer to a plate, drizzle over the lime juice, and set aside.

2 Wash and dry the spinach leaves. Put them in a mixing bowl.

COOK'S TIP
Use soft silken tofu rather than the block variety. It can be found in most supermarkets in the vegetable or refrigerated sections.

3 Cut the larger cherry tomatoes in half, and add all the tomatoes to the mixing bowl, with the scallions. Cut the cucumber into chunks, and add to the bowl with the sliced radishes.

4 Make the dressing. Put the tofu, milk, mustard, wine vinegar and cayenne in a food processor or blender. Add salt and pepper to taste. Process for 30 seconds until smooth. Scrape the dressing into a bowl, and add a little extra milk if you like a thinner dressing. Sprinkle with a little extra cayenne, and garnish with radish roses and herb sprigs, if desired.

Broiled Bell Pepper Salad

Broiled bell peppers are delicious served hot with a sharp dressing. You can also eat them cold.

Serves 2

INGREDIENTS
1 red bell pepper
1 green bell pepper
1 yellow or orange bell pepper
½ radicchio, separated into leaves
½ frisée, separated into leaves
1½ tsp white wine vinegar
2 tbsp extra virgin olive oil
6 oz goat cheese
salt and freshly ground black pepper

frisée

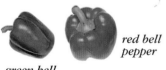

red bell pepper

green bell pepper

yellow bell pepper

goat cheese

white wine vinegar

radicchio

1 Preheat the broiler. Cut all the bell peppers in half. Cut each half into pieces.

2 Put the pepper pieces on a rack set over a broiler pan. Broil for 10 minutes.

3 Meanwhile, divide the radicchio and frisée leaves between two plates. Chill until required.

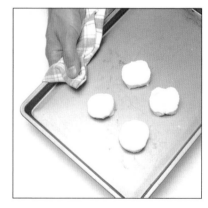

4 Mix the vinegar and olive oil in a jar. Add salt and pepper to taste. Close the jar tightly, and shake well.

5 Slice the goat cheese, and place on a baking sheet. Broil for 1 minute.

6 Arrange the peppers and broiled goat cheese on the salads. Pour over the dressing, and grind a little extra black pepper over each.

COOK'S TIP
Broil the bell peppers until they just start to blacken around the edges – don't let them burn.

Beef Stew with Red Wine

This rich, hearty dish should be served with mashed potatoes or polenta.

Serves 6

INGREDIENTS

5 tablespoons olive oil
2½ pounds lean stewing beef, cut
    into 1½-inch cubes
1 medium onion, very finely sliced
2 carrots, chopped
3 tablespoons finely chopped
    fresh parsley
1 garlic clove, chopped
1 bay leaf
a few fresh thyme sprigs, or pinch
    of dried thyme
pinch of grated nutmeg
1 cup dry red wine
1 can (14 ounces) plum tomatoes,
    chopped, with their juice
½ cup beef or chicken broth
about 15 black olives, pitted
    and halved
1 large red bell pepper, seeded and
    cut into strips
salt and ground black pepper

1 Preheat the oven to 350°F. Heat 3 tablespoons of the oil in a large, heavy, flameproof casserole. Brown the meat, a little at a time, turning it to color on all sides. Remove each batch to a plate while the remaining meat is being browned.

2 When all the meat cubes have been browned and removed, add the remaining oil, the onion and the carrots. Cook over low heat until the onion softens. Add the parsley and garlic and cook for 3–4 more minutes.

garlic

stewing beef

nutmeg

bay leaf

onion

parsley

red wine

carrots

thyme

black olives

canned plum tomatoes

chicken broth

olive oil

red bell pepper

3 Return the meat to the pan, raise the heat and stir well to mix the vegetables with the meat. Stir in the bay leaf, thyme and nutmeg. Add the wine, bring to a boil and cook, stirring, for 4–5 minutes. Stir in the tomatoes, broth and olives and mix well. Season with salt and pepper. Cover the casserole and place in the middle of the oven. Bake for 1½ hours.

4 Remove the casserole from the oven. Stir in the strips of red pepper. Return the casserole to the oven and cook, uncovered, for 30 more minutes, or until the beef is tender. Serve hot.

Calf's Liver with Balsamic Vinegar

This sweet-and-sour liver dish is a specialty of Venice. Serve it very simply, with green beans sprinkled with browned bread crumbs.

Serves 2

INGREDIENTS

1 tablespoon all-purpose flour
½ teaspoon finely chopped fresh sage
4 thin slices calf's liver, cut into serving pieces
3 tablespoons olive oil
2 tablespoons butter
2 small red onions, sliced and separated into rings
⅔ cup dry white wine
3 tablespoons balsamic vinegar
pinch of sugar
salt and ground black pepper
fresh sage sprigs, to garnish
green beans sprinkled with browned bread crumbs, to serve

flour

olive oil

butter

red onions

white wine

bread crumbs

green beans

sugar

balsamic vinegar

sage

calf's liver

1 Spread out the flour in a shallow bowl. Season it with the sage and plenty of salt and pepper. Turn the liver in the flour until well coated.

2 Heat 2 tablespoons of the oil with half the butter in a wide, heavy saucepan or frying pan until foaming. Add the onion rings and cook gently, stirring frequently, for about 5 minutes, until softened but not colored. Remove with a spatula and set aside.

3 Heat the remaining oil and butter in the pan until foaming, add the liver and cook over medium heat for 2–3 minutes on each side. Transfer to heated dinner plates and keep hot.

4 Add the wine and vinegar to the pan and stir to mix with the pan juices and any browned bits in the pan. Add the onions and sugar and heat through, stirring. Spoon the sauce over the liver, garnish with sage sprigs and serve immediately with the green beans sprinkled with bread crumbs.

Chicken with Chianti

Together, the robust, full-flavored red wine and tomato pesto give this sauce a rich color and almost spicy flavor, while the grapes add a delicious sweetness. Serve the stew with grilled polenta or crusty bread, and accompany with arugula leaves for a contrasting hint of bitterness.

Serves 4

INGREDIENTS
3 tablespoons olive oil
4 bone-in chicken breast halves, skinned
1 medium red onion
2 tablespoons tomato pesto
1¼ cups Chianti
1¼ cups water
1 small bunch red grapes, halved lengthwise and seeded if necessary
salt and ground black pepper
chopped fresh parsley, to garnish
arugula leaves, to serve

chicken breasts

olive oil

Chianti

tomato pesto

arugula leaves

parsley

red onion

red grapes

COOK'S TIP

Use bone-in chicken breast halves in preference to boneless chicken for this dish, as they have a better flavor. Chicken thighs or drumsticks could also be cooked in this way.

1 Heat 2 tablespoons of the oil in a wide, heavy saucepan or large frying pan, add the chicken breasts and sauté over medium heat for about 5 minutes, until they have changed color on all sides. Remove with a slotted spoon and drain on paper towels. Cut the onion in half through the root. Trim off the root, then slice the onion halves lengthwise to create thin wedges.

2 Heat the remaining oil in the pan, add the onion wedges and pesto and cook gently, stirring constantly, for about 3 minutes, until the onion is softened but not browned.

4 Reduce the heat, then cover the pan and simmer gently for about 20 minutes, or until the chicken is tender and cooked through, stirring occasionally.

3 Add the Chianti and water to the pan and bring to a boil, stirring, then return the chicken to the pan and add salt and pepper to taste.

VARIATION

Use plain pesto instead of tomato, and substitute a dry white wine such as Pinot Grigio for the Chianti, then finish with seedless green grapes. A few spoonfuls of mascarpone cheese can be added at the end, if desired, to enrich the sauce.

5 Add the grapes to the pan and cook over low heat until heated through. Taste the sauce and adjust the seasoning if necessary. Serve the chicken hot with the arugula leaves and garnished with chopped parsley.

Polpette with Mozzarella and Tomato

These Italian meat patties are made with beef and topped with mozzarella cheese and fresh tomato.

Serves 6

INGREDIENTS
½ slice white bread, crust removed
3 tablespoons milk
1½ pounds ground beef
1 egg, beaten
⅔ cup dried bread crumbs
vegetable oil, for frying
2 beefsteak or other tomatoes, sliced
1 tablespoon chopped fresh oregano
8 ounces mozzarella cheese, cut into 6 slices
6 canned anchovy fillets, drained and cut in half lengthwise
salt and ground black pepper

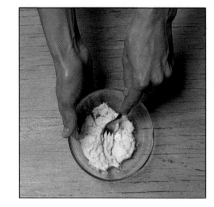

1 Preheat the oven to 400°F. Put the bread and milk into a small saucepan and heat very gently until the bread absorbs all the milk. Transfer the bread to a bowl, mash it to a pulp and let cool.

bread

milk

ground beef

bread crumbs

oregano

egg

beefsteak tomatoes

vegetable oil

anchovy fillets

mozzarella cheese

2 Put the ground beef in a bowl with the bread mixture, the egg and seasoning. Mix well, then shape the mixture into six patties. Sprinkle the bread crumbs onto a plate and dredge the patties, coating them thoroughly.

3 Heat about ¼ inch oil in a large frying pan. Add the patties and fry for 2 minutes on each side, until brown. Transfer to a greased ovenproof dish, in a single layer.

4 Lay a slice of tomato on top of each patty, sprinkle with oregano and season with salt and pepper. Place a mozzarella slice on top of each. Arrange two strips of anchovy, placed in a cross, on top of each slice of cheese.

5 Bake for 10–15 minutes, until the cheese has melted and the patties are cooked through. Serve hot, straight from the dish.

Pork Chops with Gremolata

Gremolata is a popular Italian garnish of garlic, citrus zest and parsley.

Serves 4

INGREDIENTS

2 tablespoons olive oil
4 center-cut pork chops
1 medium onion, chopped
2 garlic cloves, finely chopped
2 tablespoons tomato paste
1 can (14 ounces) chopped tomatoes
⅔ cup dry white wine
1 bouquet garni
3 canned anchovy fillets, drained
    and chopped
salt and ground black pepper
salad greens, to serve

FOR THE GREMOLATA

3 tablespoons chopped fresh parsley
grated zest of ½ lemon and 1 lime
1 garlic clove, chopped

onion
pork chops
garlic
tomato paste
white wine
canned tomatoes
bouquet garni
anchovy fillets
lime
parsley
lemon
olive oil
salad greens

1 Heat the oil in a large, flameproof casserole, add the pork chops and brown on both sides. Remove the chops from the casserole and set aside.

2 Add the onion to the casserole and cook until soft and beginning to brown. Add the garlic and cook for 1–2 minutes, then stir in the tomato paste, chopped tomatoes with their liquid and white wine. Add the bouquet garni. Bring to a boil, then boil rapidly for 3–4 minutes to reduce and thicken slightly.

3 Return the pork to the casserole, then cover and cook for about 30 minutes. Stir in the chopped anchovies. Cover the casserole and cook for another 15 minutes, or until the pork is tender and cooked through.

4 Meanwhile, to make the gremolata, combine the chopped fresh parsley, lemon and lime zests and garlic. Mix well and set aside.

5 Remove the pork chops and discard the bouquet garni. Reduce the sauce over high heat, if it has not already thickened. Taste the sauce and add salt and pepper as necessary.

6 Return the pork chops to the casserole, then sprinkle with the gremolata. Cover and cook for another 5 minutes. Serve hot with salad greens.

Veal with Tomatoes and White Wine (*Osso Bucco*)

This famous Milanese dish is rich and hearty. It is traditionally served with risotto alla Milanese, but Tomato Risotto would go equally well.

Serves 4

INGREDIENTS
2 tablespoons all-purpose flour
4 veal shank crosscuts
2 small onions
2 tablespoons olive oil
1 large celery stalk, finely chopped
1 medium carrot, finely chopped
2 garlic cloves, finely chopped
1 can (14 ounces) chopped tomatoes
1¼ cups dry white wine
1¼ cups chicken broth or veal stock
1 strip of thinly pared lemon zest
2 bay leaves, plus extra for garnishing
salt and ground black pepper

FOR THE GREMOLATA
2 tablespoons finely chopped fresh flat-leaf parsley
finely grated zest of 1 lemon
1 garlic clove, finely chopped

COOK'S TIP
Veal shanks are available at large supermarkets and good butchers. Choose pieces about ¾ inch thick.

1 Preheat the oven to 325°F. Season the flour with salt and pepper and spread it out in a shallow dish. Add the veal shanks and turn them in the flour until evenly coated. Shake off any excess flour.

4 Add the chopped tomatoes with their liquid, wine, broth or stock, lemon zest and bay leaves, then season with salt and pepper. Bring to a boil, stirring.

onions *celery* *carrot*
olive oil
canned tomatoes
bay leaves *garlic* *flour*
chicken broth *lemon* *parsley* *white wine*

2 Slice one of the onions into rings. Heat the oil in a large flameproof casserole, then add the veal, with the onion rings, and brown the veal on both sides over medium heat. Remove the veal with tongs and set aside to drain.

5 Return the veal shanks to the pan and coat thoroughly with the sauce. Cover and bake for 2 hours, or until the veal feels tender when pierced with a fork.

3 Chop the remaining onion and add to the pan with the celery, carrot and garlic. Stir the bottom of the pan to mix in the juices and brown bits. Cook gently, stirring frequently, for about 5 minutes, until the vegetables soften slightly.

6 Meanwhile, make the gremolata. Combine the parsley, lemon zest and garlic. Remove the casserole from the oven and discard the lemon zest and bay leaves. Taste the sauce for seasoning. Serve hot, sprinkled with the gremolata and garnished with extra bay leaves.

Garlic Chicken on a Bed of Vegetables

This is the perfect after-work dinner-party dish: It is quick to prepare and full of sunshiny flavors.

Serves 4

INGREDIENTS

4 bone-in chicken breast halves,
    2 pounds total weight
1 cup soft cheese with garlic and
    herbs (e.g. Boursin)
1 pound zucchini
2 red bell peppers, seeded
1 pound plum tomatoes
4 celery stalks
3 tablespoons olive oil
2 small onions, roughly chopped
3 garlic cloves, crushed
8 sun-dried tomatoes in oil, drained
    and roughly chopped
1 teaspoon dried oregano
2 tablespoons balsamic vinegar
1 teaspoon paprika
salt and ground black pepper
olive ciabatta or crusty bread,
    to serve

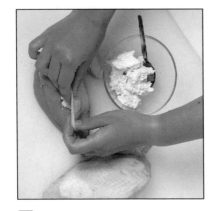

1 Preheat the oven to 375°F. Loosen the skin of each chicken breast, without removing it, to make a pocket. Divide the cheese into quarters and push one quarter underneath the skin of each chicken breast, spreading it in an even layer.

2 Cut the zucchini and bell peppers into similar-size chunks. Quarter the tomatoes and thickly slice the celery stalks.

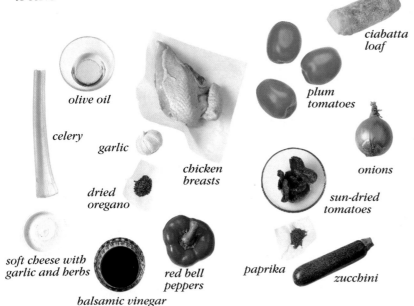

olive oil

ciabatta loaf

plum tomatoes

celery

garlic

chicken breasts

onions

dried oregano

sun-dried tomatoes

soft cheese with garlic and herbs

red bell peppers

paprika

zucchini

balsamic vinegar

3 Heat 2 tablespoons of the oil in a large, shallow, flameproof casserole. Cook the onions and garlic for 4 minutes, until the onions are soft and golden, stirring frequently.

4 Add the chopped zucchini, peppers and celery and cook for 5 more minutes.

5 Stir in the plum tomatoes, sun-dried tomatoes, oregano and balsamic vinegar. Season well with salt and pepper.

6 Place the chicken on top, drizzle with the remaining olive oil and season with salt and paprika. Bake for 35–40 minutes, or until the chicken is golden and cooked through. Serve with plenty of olive ciabatta or crusty bread.

Meat-stuffed Cabbage Rolls

Stuffed cabbage leaves are a good way of using up cooked meats and make a satisfying luncheon dish.

Serves 4–5

INGREDIENTS

1 head Savoy cabbage
4-6 slices white bread
a little milk
12 ounces lean ground beef or cold cooked meat, very finely chopped
1 egg, beaten
2 tablespoons finely chopped fresh parsley
1 garlic clove, finely chopped
½ cup freshly grated Parmesan cheese
pinch of grated nutmeg
5 tablespoons olive oil
1 medium onion, finely chopped
1 cup dry white wine
salt and ground black pepper

white wine

Savoy cabbage

ground beef

milk

egg *garlic*

onion

nutmeg

white bread

Parmesan cheese *olive oil* *parsley*

1 Cut the leaves from the cabbage, reserving the innermost part for a soup. Blanch the leaves, a few at a time, in a large pan of boiling water for 4–5 minutes. Refresh under cold water. Spread the leaves out on clean dish towels to dry.

2 Cut the crust from the bread and discard. Dice the bread and soak it in a little milk for about 5 minutes. Squeeze out the excess moisture with your hands.

3 In a mixing bowl, combine the ground or chopped meat with the egg and soaked bread. Stir in the parsley, garlic and Parmesan cheese. Season with nutmeg, salt and pepper to taste.

4 Divide any very large cabbage leaves in half, discarding the rib. Lay the leaves out on a flat surface. Form little sausage-shaped mounds of stuffing and place them at the edge of each leaf. Roll up the leaves, tucking the ends in as you roll. Squeeze each roll lightly in the palm of your hand to help the leaves stick.

VARIATION

Serve the cabbage rolls with a tomato sauce, spooned on top just before serving.

5 In a large pan big enough to hold all the rolls in one layer, heat the olive oil. Add the onion and cook gently until it softens. Raise the heat slightly and add the rolls, turning them with a wooden spoon as they begin to cook.

6 Pour in half the wine. Cook over low to medium heat, until the wine has evaporated. Add the rest of the wine, cover the pan and cook for 10–15 more minutes. Remove the lid and cook until all the liquid has evaporated. Remove from the heat and let rest for 5 minutes before serving.

Beef Fillet with Anchovies

This pungent sauce is one of the rare cases where fish marries well with beef. The saltiness of the anchovies has been diffused by the olives, oil and garlic.

Serves 4

INGREDIENTS
3 lb trimmed fillet of beef
large bunch of fresh rosemary
4 garlic cloves, crushed
1¼ cups olive oil
salt and freshly ground black pepper

For the tapenade
2 oz canned anchovies
¾ cup pitted black olives
2 garlic cloves
2 egg yolks
⅔ cup olive oil
2 tsp lemon juice

egg

rosemary

beef fillet

black olives

garlic

anchovies

1 In a non-metallic dish cover the beef with the rosemary, garlic cloves, oil and seasoning. Leave to marinate for at least 2 hours in the refrigerator.

2 For the tapenade, drain the anchovies and leave them to soak in a bowl of cold water for about 20 minutes.

3 In a food processor fitted with a metal blade, roughly chop the anchovies, olives and garlic cloves.

4 Add the egg yolks and gradually pour in the oil while the blades are still running.

5 Stir in the lemon juice and season to taste. Chill for 30 minutes.

6 Spread the tapenade over the beef and cook in an oven preheated to 375°F for 45 minutes. Serve sliced with a crisp green salad.

Barbecued Lamb with Potato Slices

A traditional mixture of fresh herbs adds a really summery flavor in this simple lamb dish. A leg of lamb is easier to cook evenly on the barbecue if it's boned out, or "butterflied" first, and it's so much easier to carve!

Serves 4

1 leg of lamb, about 4½ lb
1 garlic clove, sliced thinly
handful of fresh flat-leaved
  parsley
handful of fresh sage
handful of fresh rosemary
handful of fresh thyme
6 tbsp dry sherry
4 tbsp walnut oil
1¼ lb medium-size potatoes
salt and freshly ground black
  pepper

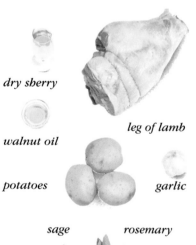

dry sherry

walnut oil

leg of lamb

potatoes

garlic

sage   *rosemary*

flat-leaved parsley   *thyme*

COOK'S TIP

If you have a spit-roasting attachment, the lamb can be rolled and tied with herbs inside and spit roasted for 1–1½ hours. You can cook larger pieces of lamb on the spit.

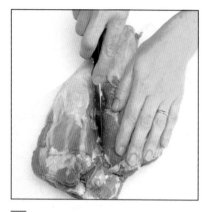

1 Place the lamb on a board, smooth side downwards so that you can see where the bone lies. Using a sharp knife, make a long cut through the flesh down to the bone.

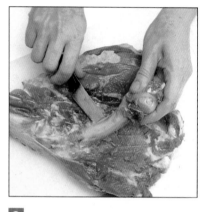

2 Scrape away the meat from the bone on both sides, until the bone is completely exposed. Remove the bone and cut away any gristle and excess fat.

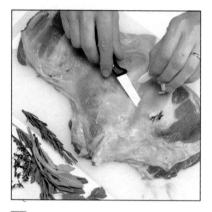

3 Cut through the thickest part of the meat to enable it to open out as flat as possible. Make several cuts in the lamb, with a sharp knife, and push slivers of garlic and sprigs of herbs into them.

4 Place the meat in a bowl and pour over the sherry and oil. Chop about half the remaining herbs and scatter over the meat. Cover and allow to marinate in the refrigerator for at least 30 minutes.

5 Remove the lamb from the marinade and season, place on a medium-hot barbecue and cook for 30–35 minutes, turning occasionally and basting with the reserved marinade.

6 Scrub the potatoes, then cut them in thick slices. Brush them with the marinade and place them around the lamb. Cook for about 15–20 minutes, turning occasionally, until they are golden brown.

Parmesan Chicken Bake

The tomato sauce may be made the day before and left to cool. Serve with crusty bread and salad.

Serves 4

INGREDIENTS
4 boned and skinned chicken breasts
4 tbsp all-purpose flour
4 tbsp olive oil
salt and freshly ground black pepper

FOR THE TOMATO SAUCE
1 tbsp olive oil
1 onion, finely chopped
1 stalk celery, finely chopped
1 red pepper, seeded and diced
1 garlic clove, crushed
1 × 14 oz can chopped tomatoes
⅔ cup fresh or canned chicken stock
1 tbsp tomato paste
2 tsp superfine sugar
1 tbsp chopped basil
1 tbsp chopped parsley

TO ASSEMBLE
8 oz mozzarella cheese, sliced
4 tbsp grated Parmesan cheese
2 tbsp fresh bread crumbs

1 First make the tomato sauce. Heat 1 tbsp of the oil in a frying pan and gently cook the onion, celery, pepper and garlic clove in the oil until tender.

2 Add the tomatoes with their juice, the stock, paste, sugar and herbs. Season to taste and bring to a boil. Simmer for 30 minutes until thick, stirring occasionally.

3 Divide each chicken breast into two natural fillets, place between sheets of plastic wrap and flatten to a thickness of ¼ in with a rolling pin.

4 Season the flour with salt and pepper. Toss the chicken breasts in the flour to coat, shaking to remove the excess.

5 Preheat the oven to 350°F. Heat the remaining oil in a large frying pan and then cook the chicken quickly in batches for about 3–4 minutes until colored. Remove and keep warm while frying the rest of the chicken.

chicken breasts

tomatoes

onion

garlic

tomato paste

olive oil

Parmesan

celery

mozzarella

flour

parsley

pepper

basil

bread crumbs

6 To assemble, layer the chicken pieces with the cheeses and thick tomato sauce, finishing with a layer of cheese and bread crumbs. Bake uncovered for 20–30 minutes or until golden brown.

Herbed Beef Pasta

Serves 6

INGREDIENTS
1 pound beef fillet
1 pound fresh tagliatelle with
    sun-dried tomatoes and herbs
4 ounces cherry tomatoes
½ cucumber

FOR THE MARINADE
1 tablespoon soy sauce
1 tablespoon sherry
1 tablespoon fresh ginger, grated
1 garlic clove, crushed

FOR THE HERB DRESSING
2–3 tablespoons horseradish
⅔ cup low-fat yogurt
1 garlic clove, crushed
2–3 tablespoons chopped fresh
    herbs (chives, parsley, thyme)
salt and ground black pepper

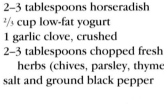
cherry tomatoes

cucumber
fillet beef

fresh ginger

garlic
tagliatelle

thyme

low-fat yogurt

horseradish sauce

parsley

soy sauce

chives

1 Mix all the marinade ingredients together in a shallow dish, put the beef in and turn it over to coat it. Cover with plastic wrap and leave for 30 minutes to allow the flavors to penetrate the meat.

2 Preheat the grill. Lift the fillet out of the marinade and pat it dry with paper towels. Place on a broiler rack and broil for 8 minutes on each side, basting with the marinade during cooking.

3 Transfer to a plate, cover with foil and leave to stand for 20 minutes.

4 Put all the dressing ingredients into a bowl and mix together thoroughly. Cook the pasta according to the directions on the package, drain thoroughly, rinse under cold water and leave to dry.

5 Cut the cherry tomatoes in half. Cut the cucumber in half lengthways, scoop out the seeds with a teaspoon and slice thinly into crescents.

6 Put the pasta, cherry tomatoes, cucumber and dressing into a bowl and toss to coat. Slice the beef thinly and arrange on a plate with the pasta salad.

Roast Monkfish with Garlic and Fennel

In the past monkfish was sometimes used as a substitute for lobster meat because it is very similar in texture. It is now appreciated in its own right and is delicious quickly roasted.

Serves 4

INGREDIENTS
2½ pounds monkfish tail
8 garlic cloves
1 tablespoon olive oil
2 fennel bulbs, sliced
juice and zest of 1 lemon
bay leaves
salt and ground black pepper

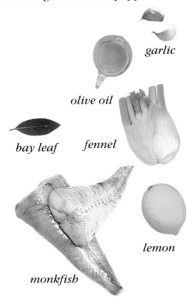

garlic

olive oil

bay leaf   *fennel*

lemon

monkfish

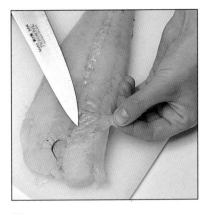

1 Preheat the oven to 425°F. With a filleting knife, cut away the thin membrane covering the outside of the monkfish.

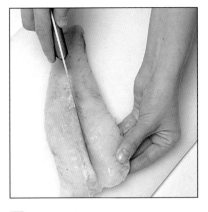

2 Cut along one side of the central bone to remove the fillet. Repeat on the other side.

3 Tie the separated fillets together with string to reshape as a tailpiece.

4 Peel and slice the garlic cloves and cut incisions into the monkfish flesh. Place the garlic slices into the incisions.

5 Heat the oil in a large, heavy saucepan and quickly cook the monkfish on all sides.

6 Remove the monkfish from the saucepan and place in a roasting pan together with the fennel slices, lemon juice, 1 bay leaf and seasoning. Roast for about 20 minutes, until tender and cooked through. Serve immediately, garnished with bay leaves and lemon zest.

COOK'S TIP
The anise-like flavor of fennel goes particularly well with fish. The feathery tops can be used as a garnish if desired.

Grilled Squid

If you like your food hot, chop some—or all—of the chili seeds with the flesh. If not, cut the chilies in half lengthwise, scrape out the seeds and discard them before chopping the flesh.

Serves 2

INGREDIENTS
2 whole prepared squid,
   with tentacles
5 tablespoons olive oil
2 tablespoons balsamic vinegar
¾ cup raw arborio rice
2 fresh red chilies, finely chopped
¼ cup dry white wine
salt and ground black pepper
fresh parsley sprigs, to garnish

squid

olive oil

white wine

balsamic vinegar

red chilies

parsley

rice

1 Make a cut down the body of each squid, then open out flat. Score the flesh with the tip of a sharp knife. Chop the tentacles. Place the squid in a glass dish. Whisk oil and vinegar. Add seasoning and pour over the squid. Cover and marinate for 1 hour. Meanwhile, cook the rice in salted water until tender.

2 Heat a cast-iron grill pan. Add the body of one of the squid. Cook over medium heat for 2–3 minutes per side, pressing with a spatula. Place on a plate. Cook the other body in the same way.

3 Cut the squid bodies into diagonal strips. Pile the hot rice in the center of heated soup plates and arrange the strips of squid on top. Keep hot.

4 Put the tentacles and chilies in a heavy frying pan. Toss over medium heat for 2 minutes. Stir in the wine, then drizzle the mixture over the squid and rice. Garnish with parsley and serve.

Shrimp in Tomato Sauce

The tomato sauce base can be sharpened up by adding hot chilies.

Serves 6

INGREDIENTS

6 tablespoons olive oil
1 medium onion, finely chopped
1 celery stalk, finely chopped
1 small red bell pepper, seeded
  and chopped
½ cup dry red wine
1 tablespoon wine vinegar
1 can (14 ounces) plum tomatoes,
  chopped, with their juice
2¼ pounds uncooked medium
  shrimp, in their shells
2–3 garlic cloves, finely chopped
3 tablespoons finely chopped
  fresh parsley
1 dried red chili, crumbled or
  chopped (optional)
salt and ground black pepper

olive oil

onion

red wine

red bell pepper

canned plum tomatoes

celery

wine vinegar

garlic

shrimp

parsley

dried red chili

1 In a heavy saucepan, heat half the oil. Add the onion and cook over low heat until soft. Stir in the celery and bell pepper and cook for 5 minutes. Raise the heat and add the wine, vinegar and tomatoes. Bring to a boil and cook for 5 minutes. Lower the heat, cover the pan and simmer for about 30 minutes, until the vegetables are soft.

2 Allow the mixture to cool a little, then purée through a food mill.

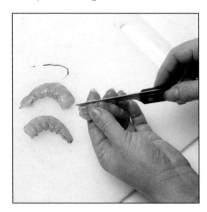

3 Shell the shrimp. Make a shallow incision with a small sharp knife down the center of the back and remove the long, black vein with the tip of a knife.

4 Heat the remaining oil in a clean, heavy saucepan. Stir in the chopped garlic and parsley, plus the chili, if using. Cook over medium heat, stirring, until the garlic is golden. Add the prepared tomato sauce and bring to a boil.

5 Stir in the shrimp. Bring the sauce back to a boil. Reduce the heat slightly and simmer until the shrimp are pink and firm. This will take 6–8 minutes, depending on their size. Season to taste and serve on warmed plates.

Pan-Fried Red Mullet with Basil and Citrus

Red mullet is popular all over the Mediterranean. This Italian recipe combines it with oranges and lemons, which grow in abundance there.

Serves 4

INGREDIENTS

4 red mullet, about
    8 ounces each, filleted
6 tablespoons olive oil
10 black peppercorns, crushed
2 oranges, 1 peeled and sliced and
    1 squeezed
1 lemon
2 tablespoons all-purpose flour
1 tablespoon butter
2 canned anchovy fillets, drained
    and chopped
¼ cup shredded fresh basil
salt and ground black pepper

basil　　*lemon*

flour　*peppercorns*　*butter*

anchovy fillets　*orange*　*olive oil*

red mullet

COOK'S TIP

If you prefer, use other fish fillets for this dish, such as striped bass or red snapper.

1 Place the fish fillets in a shallow dish in a single layer. Pour the olive oil over them and sprinkle with the crushed peppercorns. Lay the orange slices on top of the fish. Cover the dish and let marinate in the refrigerator for at least 4 hours.

2 Halve the lemon, then remove the skin and pith from one half using a small, sharp knife and slice thinly. Squeeze the juice from the other half.

3 Lift the fish out of the marinade and pat dry with paper towels. Reserve the marinade and orange slices. Season the fish with salt and pepper and dust lightly with flour.

4 Heat 3 tablespoons of the marinade in a frying pan. Add the fish and fry for 2 minutes on each side. Remove from the pan and keep warm. Discard the marinade that is left in the pan.

5 Melt the butter in the pan with any of the remaining original marinade. Add the anchovies and cook until they are completely softened.

6 Stir in the orange and lemon juice, then check the seasoning and simmer until slightly reduced. Stir in the basil. Place the fish on a warmed serving plate, pour the sauce on top and garnish with the reserved orange slices and the lemon slices. Serve immediately.

Baked Mussels and Potatoes

This dish originated in Puglia, which is noted for its imaginative baked casseroles.

Serves 2–3

INGREDIENTS

1½ pounds large mussels, in their shells
8 ounces potatoes, unpeeled
5 tablespoons olive oil
2 garlic cloves, finely chopped
8 fresh basil leaves, torn into pieces
8 ounces tomatoes, peeled and thinly sliced
3 tablespoons dried bread crumbs
salt and ground black pepper

mussels

basil

potatoes

olive oil

garlic

bread crumbs

tomatoes

1 Cut the "beards" off the mussels. Scrub well and soak in several changes of cold water. Discard any with broken shells. Place the mussels with a cupful of water in a large saucepan, covered, over medium heat. As soon as they open, lift them out. (Discard any that do not open.) Remove and discard the empty half-shells, leaving the mussels in the other half. Strain any liquid in the pan through a layer of paper towels and reserve.

2 Boil the potatoes in salted water until they are almost cooked but still firm, then peel and slice them thinly.

3 Preheat the oven to 350°F. Spread 2 tablespoons of the olive oil in the bottom of a shallow ovenproof dish. Cover with the potato slices in one layer. Add the mussels in their half-shells in one layer. Sprinkle with garlic and pieces of basil.

4 Cover with a layer of the tomato slices. Sprinkle with bread crumbs and salt and pepper, the strained mussel liquid and the remaining olive oil. Bake for about 20 minutes, or until the tomatoes are soft and the bread crumbs are golden. Serve directly from the baking dish.

Sea Bass en Papillote

A dramatic presentation to delight your guests. Bring the unopened packages to the table and let them unfold their own fish to release the delicious aroma.

Serves 4

INGREDIENTS
8 tablespoons (1 stick) butter
1 pound fresh leaf spinach
3 shallots, finely chopped
4 small sea bass, gutted
¼ cup dry white wine
bay leaves
salt and ground black pepper
new potatoes and glazed carrots,
    to serve

butter

bay leaves

white wine

spinach

shallots

sea bass

new potatoes

carrots

1 Preheat the oven to 350°F. Melt 3 tablespoons of the butter in a large, heavy saucepan, add the spinach and cook gently until almost a purée. Let cool.

2 Melt another 3 tablespoons of the butter in a clean, heavy saucepan and add the shallots. Gently sauté for 5 minutes, until the shallots are soft but not browned. Add the shallots to the spinach and let cool.

3 Season the fish both inside and outside, then stuff the insides with the spinach and shallot filling.

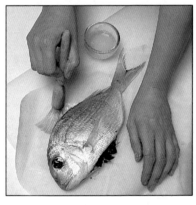

4 For each package, fold a large sheet of parchment or waxed paper in half and cut around the fish laid on one half to make a heart shape when unfolded. It should be at least 2 inches larger than the fish all around. Melt the remaining butter and brush a little onto the paper. Set the fish on one side of the paper.

5 Add a little wine and a bay leaf to each fish package.

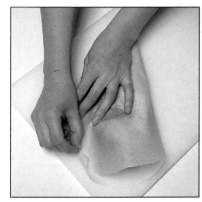

6 Fold the other side of the paper over the fish and make small pleats to seal the two edges, starting at the curve of the heart. Brush the outsides with butter. Transfer the packages to a baking sheet and bake for 20–25 minutes, until the packages are brown. Serve with new potatoes and glazed carrots.

Fresh Tuna and Tomato Stew

A deliciously simple dish that relies on good basic ingredients. For real Italian flavor, serve with polenta or pasta.

Serves 4

INGREDIENTS

12 baby onions, peeled
2 pounds ripe tomatoes
1½ pounds fresh tuna
3 tablespoons olive oil
2 garlic cloves, finely chopped
3 tablespoons chopped fresh herbs
2 bay leaves
½ teaspoon sugar
2 tablespoons sun-dried tomato paste
⅔ cup dry white wine
salt and ground black pepper
baby zucchini and fresh herbs,
  to garnish

herbs

baby onions

garlic *bay leaves* *olive oil*

tomatoes

sugar

white wine *tuna*

sun-dried tomato paste *baby zucchini*

1 Leave the onions whole and cook in a pan of boiling water for 4–5 minutes, until softened. Drain.

2 Slit the tomato skins and plunge the tomatoes into boiling water for 30 seconds. Refresh them in cold water. Peel away the skins and chop roughly.

VARIATION

Two large mackerel make a less expensive alternative to the tuna. Fillet them and cut into chunks or simply lay the whole fish over the sauce and cook, covered with a lid, until the mackerel is cooked through. Sage, rosemary and oregano all go extremely well with this dish. Choose whichever herb you prefer, or use a mixture.

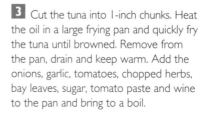

3 Cut the tuna into 1-inch chunks. Heat the oil in a large frying pan and quickly fry the tuna until browned. Remove from the pan, drain and keep warm. Add the onions, garlic, tomatoes, chopped herbs, bay leaves, sugar, tomato paste and wine to the pan and bring to a boil.

4 Reduce the heat and simmer gently for 5 minutes, breaking up the tomatoes with a wooden spoon. Return the fish to the pan and cook for another 5 minutes. Remove the bay leaves, season and serve hot, garnished with baby zucchini and fresh herbs.

Stuffed Flounder Rolls

Sun-dried tomatoes, pine nuts and anchovies make a flavorful combination for the stuffing mixture.

Serves 4

INGREDIENTS

4 flounder fillets, about 8 ounces
    each, skinned
6 tablespoons butter
1 small onion, chopped
1 celery stalk, finely chopped
2 cups fresh white bread crumbs
3 tablespoons chopped fresh parsley
2 tablespoons pine nuts, toasted
3–4 pieces sun-dried tomatoes in
    oil, drained and chopped
1 can (2 ounces) anchovy fillets,
    drained and chopped
5 tablespoons fish or vegetable broth
ground black pepper

flounder   *anchovy fillets*

fish stock   *onion*

celery

pine nuts   *sun-dried tomatoes*   *butter*

white bread crumbs   *parsley*

1 Preheat the oven to 350°F. Using a sharp knife, cut each fish fillet in half lengthwise to make eight smaller fillets. Melt the butter in a frying pan and add the onion and celery. Cover and cook over low heat for about 15 minutes, until softened. Do not let brown.

2 Combine the bread crumbs, parsley, pine nuts, sun-dried tomatoes and anchovies in a large bowl. Stir in the softened vegetables with the buttery juices and season with pepper to taste.

3 Divide the stuffing into eight portions. Taking one portion at a time, form the stuffing into balls, then roll up each one inside a fish fillet. Secure each roll with a toothpick.

4 Place the rolls in a buttered ovenproof dish. Pour in the stock and cover the dish with buttered foil. Bake for 20 minutes, or until the fish flakes. Remove the toothpicks. Serve the fish with some cooking juice drizzled on top.

Tuscan Tuna and Beans

A great kitchen-cupboard dish, which is especially good for children as there are no bones.

Serves 4

INGREDIENTS
1 red onion, finely chopped
2 tbsp smooth French mustard
1¼ cups olive oil
4 tbsp white wine vinegar
2 tbsp chopped fresh parsley, plus
    extra to garnish
2 tbsp chopped fresh chives
2 tbsp chopped fresh tarragon or
    chervil
1 × 14 oz can navy beans
1 × 14 oz can kidney beans
8 oz canned tuna in oil, drained and
    lightly flaked

kidney beans

mustard

chives

parsley

navy beans

tuna

red onion

tarragon

1 Chop the onion finely.

2 In a small bowl, beat the mustard, oil, vinegar, parsley, chives and tarragon or chervil together.

3 Rinse and drain the canned beans.

4 Mix the red onion, beans and dressing together thoroughly, toss well and serve.

Haddock Fillets in a Polenta Crust

Polenta is sometimes called cornmeal. Use the instant polenta if you can as it will give a better crunchy coating.

Serves 4

INGREDIENTS
8 small haddock fillets
finely grated rind of 1 lemon
2 cups polenta
2 tbsp olive oil
1 tbsp butter
salt and freshly ground black pepper
2 tbsp mixed fresh herbs such as
    parsley, chervil and chives
steamed spinach, to serve
toasted pine nuts

fresh herbs

haddock fillets

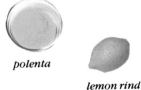

polenta

lemon rind

I Make four cuts in each fillet to stop the fish curling when it cooks.

2 Sprinkle the seasoning and lemon rind over the fish.

3 Press the polenta onto the fillets. Chill for 30 minutes.

4 Heat the oil and butter in a large frying pan and gently fry the fillets on either side for 3–4 minutes. Serve with steamed spinach and garnish with toasted pine nuts and the mixed fresh herbs. ·

Mackerel with Tomatoes, Pesto and Onions

This rich oily fish needs the sharp tomato sauce. The aromatic pesto is excellent drizzled over the top of the fish. Serve with mashed potato to mop up those delicious juices.

Serves 4

INGREDIENTS

For the pesto sauce
2 oz pine nuts
2 tbsp fresh basil leaves
2 garlic cloves, crushed
2 tbsp freshly grated Parmesan
   cheese
⅔ cup extra virgin olive oil
salt and freshly ground
   black pepper

For the fish
4 mackerel, gutted
2 tbsp olive oil
4 oz onion, roughly chopped
1 lb tomatoes, roughly chopped

tomato

pine nuts

Parmesan cheese

mackerel

onion

basil

1 For the pesto sauce, place the nuts, basil leaves and garlic cloves in a food processor fitted with a metal blade. Process until the mixture forms a rough paste. Add the Parmesan cheese and whilst the blades are still running, gradually add the oil. Set aside until required.

2 Heat the broiler until very hot. Season the mackerel well, and cook for 10 minutes on either side.

3 Meanwhile, heat the oil in a large, heavy-based saucepan and sauté the onions until soft.

4 Stir in the tomatoes and cook for 5 minutes. Serve the warm fish on top of the tomato mixture and top with a dollop of pesto sauce.

Pan-fried Garlic Sardines

Lightly fry a sliced clove of garlic to garnish the fish. This dish could also be made with smelts or fresh anchovies if available.

Serves 4

INGREDIENTS
2½ lb fresh sardines
2 tbsp olive oil
4 garlic cloves
finely grated rind of 2 lemons
2 tbsp chopped fresh parsley
salt and freshly ground black pepper

For the tomato bread
8 slices crusty bread, toasted
2 large ripe tomatoes

olive oil

garlic

tomato

lemon

sardines

parsley

bread

1 Gut and clean the sardines thoroughly.

2 Heat the oil in a frying pan and add the garlic cloves. Cook until soft.

3 Add the sardines and fry for 4–5 minutes. Sprinkle over the lemon rind, parsley and seasoning.

4 Cut the tomatoes in half and rub them onto the toast, discard the skins. Serve the sardines with the tomato toast.

Stuffed Sardines

This tasty dish doesn't take a lot of preparation and is a meal in itself. Just serve with a crisp green salad tossed in a fresh lemon vinaigrette to make it complete.

Serves 4

INGREDIENTS
2 lb fresh sardines
2 tbsp olive oil
½ cup wholewheat bread
    crumbs
¼ cup raisins
½ cup pine nuts
2 oz canned anchovy fillets,
    drained
4 tbsp chopped fresh parsley
1 onion, finely chopped
salt and freshly ground black pepper
lemon wedges, to garnish

raisins

pine nuts

onion

sardines

olive oil

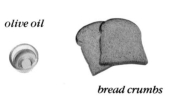

bread crumbs

parsley

1 Preheat the oven to 400°F. Gut the sardines and wipe out thoroughly with paper towels. Heat the oil in a frying pan and fry the bread crumbs until golden.

2 Add the raisins, pine nuts, anchovies, parsley, onion and seasoning and mix well.

3 Stuff each sardine with the mixture. Close the fish firmly and place, closely packed together in an ovenproof dish.

4 Scatter any remaining filling over the sardines and drizzle over the remaining olive oil. Bake for 30 minutes in the preheated oven and serve garnished with fresh lemon wedges.

Baked Tuna with a Peppercorn Crust

Fresh tuna is very meaty and filling. Barbecue this dish if you can to give a charcoal-grilled flavor.

Serves 4

INGREDIENTS
For the salsa
1 mango, peeled, pit removed and cut into dice
finely grated rind and juice of 1 lime
½ red chili, deseeded and finely chopped

finely grated rind of 1 lemon
1 tsp black peppercorns
½ small onion, finely chopped
2 tbsp chopped fresh coriander
4 × 6 oz fresh tuna steaks
½ cup olive oil

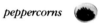
peppercorns

mango

lime

red chili

tuna steak

onion

lemon

1 To make mango salsa, mix the mango, lime juice, rind and chili in a bowl and leave to marinate for at least 1 hour.

2 Mix together the lemon rind, black peppercorns, onion and coriander in a coffee grinder to make a coarse paste.

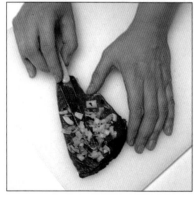

3 Spoon onto one side of each tuna steak pressing on well.

4 Heat the olive oil in a heavy based frying pan until it begins to smoke. Add the tuna, paste-side down, and fry until a crust forms. Lower the heat and turn the steaks to cook for a minute more. Pat off any excess oil onto absorbent paper towels and serve with the mango salsa.

Salmon with Spicy Pesto

This is a great way to serve boned salmon steaks as a solid piece of fish. It's also cheaper than buying fillet if you have to pay for the fishmonger boning it. The pesto is unusual because it uses sunflower kernels and chili as its flavoring rather than the classic basil and pine nuts.

Serves 4

INGREDIENTS
4 × ½ lb salmon steaks
2 tbsp sunflower oil
finely grated rind and juice of 1 lime
salt and freshly ground black pepper

For the pesto
6 mild fresh red chilies
2 garlic cloves
2 tbsp pumpkin or sunflower
  seeds
finely grated rind and juice of 1 lime
5 tbsp olive oil

red chilli

salmon

lime

garlic

pumpkin seeds

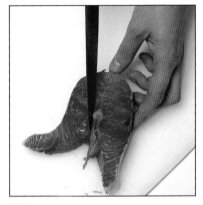

1 Insert a very sharp knife closely to the top of the bone. Working closely to the bone, cut your way to the end of the steak so one side of the steak has been released and one side is still attached. Repeat with the other side. Pull out any extra visible bones with a pair of tweezers.

2 Sprinkle a little salt on the surface and take hold of the end of the salmon piece skin-side down. Insert a small sharp knife under the skin and, working away from you, cut off the skin keeping as close to the skin as possible. Repeat with the other pieces of fish.

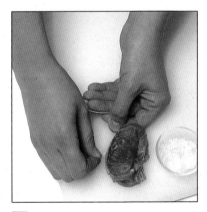

3 Wrap each piece of fish into a circle, with the thinner end wrapped around the fatter end. Secure tightly with a length of string.

4 Rub the sunflower oil into the boneless fish rounds. Add the lime juice and rind and marinate in the refrigerator for 2 hours.

5 For the pesto, de-seed the chilies, and place them together with the garlic cloves, pumpkin seeds, lime juice, rind and seasoning into a food processor fitted with a metal blade. Process until well mixed. Pour the olive oil gradually over the moving blades until the sauce has thickened and emulsified. Drain the salmon from its marinade. Broil the fish steaks for 5 minutes either side and serve with the spicy pesto.

Monkfish with Peppered Citrus Marinade

Monkfish is a firm, meaty fish that cooks well on the barbecue and keeps its shape well. Serve with a green salad.

Serves 4

2 monkfish tails,
    about 12 oz each
1 lime
1 lemon
2 oranges
handful of fresh thyme sprigs
1 tbsp mixed peppercorns,
    roughly crushed
2 tbsp olive oil
salt and freshly ground black
    pepper

monkfish tails

lemon

lime

oranges

olive oil

thyme sprigs

mixed peppercorns

VARIATION
You can also use this marinade for monkfish kabobs.

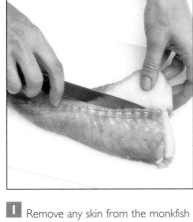

1 Remove any skin from the monkfish tails. Cut carefully down one side of the backbone, sliding the knife between the bone and flesh, to remove the fillet on one side. You can ask your fish seller to do this for you.

2 Turn the fish and repeat on the other side, to remove the second fillet. Repeat on the second tail. Lay the four fillets out flat.

3 Cut two slices from each of the citrus fruits and arrange them over two of the fillets. Add a few sprigs of thyme and sprinkle with salt and pepper. Finely grate the rind from the remaining fruit and sprinkle it over the fish.

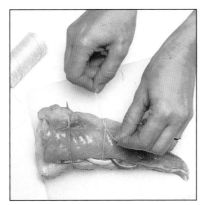

4 Lay the other two fillets on top and tie them firmly at intervals, with fine cotton string, to hold them in shape. Place in a wide dish.

5 Squeeze the juice from the citrus fruits and mix it with the oil and more salt and pepper. Spoon over the fish. Cover and allow to marinate for about an hour, turning occasionally and spooning the marinade over it.

6 Drain the monkfish, reserving the marinade, and sprinkle with the crushed peppercorns. Cook on a medium-hot barbecue for 15–20 minutes, basting it with the marinade and turning it occasionally, until it's evenly cooked.

Calamari with Two-tomato Stuffing

Calamari, or baby squid, are quick to cook, but do turn and baste them often and don't overcook them.

Serves 4

1¼ lb baby squid, cleaned
1 garlic clove, crushed
3 plum tomatoes, skinned and chopped
8 sun-dried tomatoes in oil, drained and chopped
4 tbsp chopped fresh basil, plus extra, to serve
4 tbsp fresh white bread crumbs
3 tbsp olive oil
1 tbsp red wine vinegar
salt and freshly ground black pepper
lemon juice, to serve

baby squid

garlic

bread crumbs

plum tomatoes

sun-dried tomatoes in oil

olive oil

basil

red wine vinegar

I Remove the tentacles from the squid and roughly chop them; leave the main part of the squid whole.

2 Mix together the garlic, plum tomatoes, sun-dried tomatoes, basil and breadcrumbs. Stir in 1 tbsp of the oil and the vinegar. Season well with salt and pepper. Soak the wooden tooth-picks in water for 10 minutes before use, to prevent them from burning.

3 With a tsp, fill the squid with the stuffing mixture. Secure the open ends with the wooden toothpicks.

4 Brush the squid with the remaining oil and cook over a medium-hot barbecue for 4–5 minutes, turning often. Sprinkle with lemon juice and extra basil to serve.

Tiger Shrimp Skewers with Walnut Pesto

An unusual starter or main course, which can be prepared in advance and kept in the refrigerator until you're ready to cook it.

Serves 4

12–16 large, raw shell-on tiger
  shrimp
1/2 cup walnut pieces
4 tbsp chopped fresh flat-leaved
  parsley
4 tbsp chopped fresh basil
2 garlic cloves, chopped
3 tbsp grated fresh Parmesan
  cheese
2 tbsp extra-virgin olive oil
2 tbsp walnut oil
salt and freshly ground black
  pepper

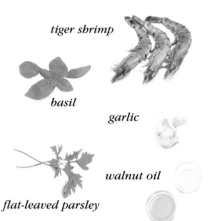

tiger shrimp

basil

garlic

walnut oil

flat-leaved parsley

extra-virgin olive oil

Parmesan cheese

walnut pieces

1 Peel the shrimp, removing the head but leaving on the tail section. Devein and then put the shrimp in a large bowl.

2 To make the pesto, place the walnuts, parsley, basil, garlic, Parmesan and oils in a blender or food processor and process until very finely chopped. Season with salt and pepper.

3 Add half the pesto to the shrimp, toss them well and then cover and chill for a minimum of an hour; or leave them overnight.

4 Thread the shrimp on to skewers and cook them on a hot barbecue for 3–4 minutes, turning once. Serve with the remaining pesto and a green salad.

Grilled Tuna with Fiery Pepper Purée

Tuna is an oily fish that grills well and is meaty enough to combine successfully with quite strong flavors – even hot chili, as in this red pepper purée, which is excellent served with fresh, crusty bread.

Serves 4

4 tuna steaks, about 6 oz each
finely grated zest and juice of
  1 lime
2 tbsp olive oil
salt and freshly ground black
  pepper

FOR THE PEPPER PURÉE
2 red bell peppers, seeded and
  halved
1 small onion
2 garlic cloves, crushed
2 red chilies
1 slice white bread without
  crusts, diced
3 tbsp olive oil, plus extra for
  brushing
lime wedges, to serve

lime

tuna steaks

olive oil

red chilies

red peppers   *garlic*

onion   *diced white bread*

COOK'S TIP

The pepper purée can be made in advance, by cooking the peppers and onion under a hot grill; keep it in the refrigerator until you cook the fish.

1 Trim any skin from the tuna and place the steaks in one layer in a wide dish. Sprinkle over the lime zest and juice, oil, salt and pepper. Cover and refrigerate until required.

2 To make the pepper purée, brush the pepper halves with a little oil and cook them, skin-side down, on a hot barbecue, until the skin is blackened. Place the onion in its skin on the barbecue and cook until browned, turning it occasionally.

3 Allow to cool slightly, covered with a clean cloth, and then remove the skins from the peppers and the onion.

4 Place the peppers, onion, garlic, chilies, bread and oil in a food processor. Process until smooth. Add salt to taste.

5 Lift the tuna steaks from the marinade and cook them on a hot barbecue for 8–10 minutes, turning once, until golden brown. Serve with the pepper purée and crusty bread.

Fish Parcels

Sea bass is good for this recipe, but you could also use small whole trout, or white fish fillet such as cod or haddock.

Serves 4

4 pieces sea bass fillet or
  4 whole small sea bass,
  about 1 lb each
oil for brushing
2 shallots, thinly sliced
1 garlic clove, chopped
1 tbsp capers
6 sun-dried tomatoes, finely
  chopped
4 black olives, pitted and thinly
  sliced
grated rind and juice of
  1 lemon
1 tsp paprika
salt and freshly ground black
  pepper

COOK'S TIP

These parcels can also be baked in the oven: place them on a baking sheet and cook at 400°F for 15–20 minutes.

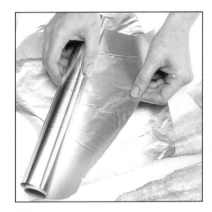

1 Clean the fish if whole. Cut four large squares of double-thickness foil, large enough to enclose the fish; brush with a little oil.

2 Place a piece of fish in the center of each piece of foil and season well with salt and pepper.

3 Scatter over the shallots, garlic, capers, tomatoes, olives and grated lemon rind. Sprinkle with the lemon juice and paprika.

paprika

shallots

lemon

garlic

sun-dried tomatoes

capers

black olives

sea bass fillets

4 Fold the foil over to enclose the fish loosely, sealing the edges firmly so none of the juices can escape. Place on a moderately-hot barbecue and cook for 8–10 minutes. Then open up the tops of the parcels and serve.

MEAT AND FISH PASTA DISHES

Traditionally in Italy pasta dishes are served before the main course, often simply prepared with a dash of olive oil or butter. Nowadays there are no set rules and classic meat and fish pasta dishes have come to the forefront of Italian cuisine, drawing from the abundance of wonderful ingredients available throughout mainland Italy.

Lasagne

Serves 6–8

INGREDIENTS
1 large onion, chopped
2 garlic cloves, crushed
1¼ lb ground turkey meat
1 pound carton tomato sauce
1 teaspoon mixed dried herbs
8 ounces frozen leaf spinach,
    defrosted
7 ounces lasagne verde
7 ounces low-fat cottage cheese

FOR THE SAUCE
1 ounce low-fat margarine
1 ounce plain flour
1¼ cups skim milk
¼ teaspoon ground nutmeg
1 ounce grated Parmesan cheese
salt and ground black pepper
mixed greens, to serve

1 Put the onion, garlic and ground turkey into a non-stick saucepan. Brown quickly for 5 minutes, stirring with a wooden spoon to separate the pieces.

2 Add the tomato sauce, herbs and seasoning. Bring to a boil, cover and simmer for 30 minutes.

3 For the sauce: put all the sauce ingredients, except the Parmesan cheese, into a saucepan. Heat to thicken, whisking constantly until bubbling and smooth. Adjust the seasoning, add the cheese to the sauce and stir.

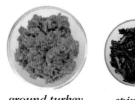

ground turkey

spinach

garlic

nutmeg

Parmesan cheese

lasagne verdi

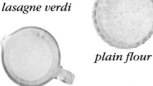

plain flour

skim milk

onion

low-fat margarine

low-fat cottage cheese

tomato sauce

4 Preheat the oven to 375°F. Lay the spinach leaves on paper towels and pat dry.

5 Layer the turkey mixture, dried lasagne, cottage cheese and spinach in a 8-cup ovenproof dish, starting and ending with a layer of turkey.

6 Spoon the sauce over the top to cover and bake for 45-50 minutes or until bubbling. Serve with a mixed salad.

Spaghetti with Meatballs

No Italian menu would be complete without succulent meatballs served on a bed of spaghetti. Accompany this dish with a light green salad and some warm, crusty bread.

Serves 4

INGREDIENTS
12 ounces spaghetti
salt and ground black pepper
fresh rosemary sprigs, to garnish
freshly grated Parmesan cheese,
    to serve

FOR THE MEATBALLS
1 medium onion, chopped
1 garlic clove, chopped
12 ounces ground lamb
1 egg yolk
1 tablespoon chopped fresh parsley
1 tablespoon olive oil

FOR THE SAUCE
1 ¼ cups passata (see Cook's Tip)
2 tablespoons chopped fresh basil
1 garlic clove, chopped

spaghetti

rosemary   *basil*

fresh parsley

Parmesan cheese

onion   *egg*   *garlic*

passata   *olive oil*   *ground lamb*

1 To make the meatballs, combine the onion, garlic, lamb, egg yolk, parsley and seasoning until well blended.

2 Divide the mixture into 20 pieces and mold into balls. Place on a baking sheet, cover with plastic wrap and chill for 30 minutes.

3 Heat the oil in a large frying pan and place the meatballs in it.

4 Fry the meatballs for about 10 minutes, turning occasionally, until browned on all sides. Spoon off any excess fat, without removing the meatballs.

5 For the sauce, add the passata, basil and garlic and seasoning to the pan and bring to a boil. Cover and simmer for 20 minutes, until the meatballs are tender.

COOK'S TIP

Passata is available in jars, cans or cartons at specialty Italian grocery stores and most large supermarkets. It is made from sieved tomatoes, so if you cannot find any, drain and sieve canned tomatoes instead.

The meatballs can be made a day in advance. Place them on a baking sheet, cover with plastic wrap and chill.

6 Meanwhile, bring a large pot of salted water to a boil. Add the pasta and cook according to the package instructions until it is just al dente. Drain thoroughly and divide it among four plates. Spoon on the meatballs and some of the sauce. Garnish each portion with a fresh rosemary sprig and serve immediately with plenty of freshly grated Parmesan cheese.

Baked Seafood Spaghetti

In this dish, each portion is baked and served in an individual package, which is then opened at the table. Use baking parchment or aluminum foil to make the packages.

Serves 4

INGREDIENTS

1 pound mussels, in their shells
½ cup dry white wine
¼ cup olive oil
2 garlic cloves, finely chopped
1 pound tomatoes, peeled and
   finely chopped
14 ounces spaghetti or other
   long pasta
8 ounces uncooked medium
   shrimp, peeled and deveined
2 tablespoons chopped fresh parsley
salt and ground black pepper

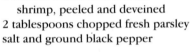
mussels   *white wine*

1 Scrub the mussels well under cold running water, cutting off the "beards" with a small, sharp knife. Place the mussels and the wine in a large saucepan and heat, covered, until the mussels open.

olive oil   *tomatoes*

2 Lift out the mussels with a slotted spoon and set aside. (Discard any that do not open.) Strain the cooking liquid through paper towels and reserve until needed. Preheat the oven to 300°F.

garlic   *spaghetti*
shrimp   *parsley*

3 In a medium saucepan, heat the oil and garlic together for 1–2 minutes. Add the tomatoes and cook over medium to high heat until they soften. Stir in ¾ cup of the cooking liquid from the mussels. Bring a large pot of salted water to a boil. Add the pasta and cook according to the package instructions until it is just al dente.

4 Just before draining the pasta, add the shrimp and the chopped parsley to the tomato sauce. Cook for 2 minutes, or until the shrimp are firm. Taste one and adjust the seasoning if necessary, then remove from the heat.

5 Prepare four pieces of baking parchment or foil measuring about 18 x 12 inches. Place each sheet in the center of a shallow bowl. (The bowl under the paper will prevent the sauce from spilling while the packages are being closed.) Transfer the drained pasta to a bowl. Add the tomato sauce and mix well. Stir in the mussels.

COOK'S TIP

Bottled mussels or clams may be substituted for fresh shellfish in this recipe: Add them to the tomato sauce with the shrimp. Canned tomatoes may be used instead of fresh ones.

6 Divide the pasta and seafood mixture among the four pieces of paper or foil, placing a mound in the center of each and twisting the ends together to make a closed package. Arrange on a large baking sheet and place in the middle of the oven. Bake for 8–10 minutes. Place one unopened package on each individual serving plate.

Cannelloni

Serves 4

INGREDIENTS

2 garlic cloves, crushed
2 x 14 ounce cans
   chopped tomatoes
2 teaspoons brown sugar
1 tablespoon fresh basil
1 tablespoon fresh marjoram
1 pound chopped frozen spinach
large pinch ground nutmeg
4 ounces cooked, ground lean ham
7 ounces low-fat cottage cheese
12–14 cannelloni tubes
2 ounces low-fat mozzarella
   cheese, diced
1 ounce sharp Cheddar
   cheese, grated
1 ounce fresh white bread crumbs
salt and ground black pepper
flat-leaf parsley, to garnish

1 To make the sauce put the garlic, canned tomatoes, sugar and herbs into a pan, bring to the boil and cook, uncovered, for 30 minutes, stirring occasionally, until fairly thick.

2 To make the filling put the spinach into a pan, cover and cook slowly until defrosted. Break up with a fork, then increase the heat to remove excess water. Season with salt, pepper and nutmeg. Transfer the spinach to a bowl, cool slightly, then add the ground ham and cottage cheese.

3 Pipe the filling into each tube of uncooked cannelloni. It is easiest to hold them upright with one end flat on a chopping board, while piping from the other end.

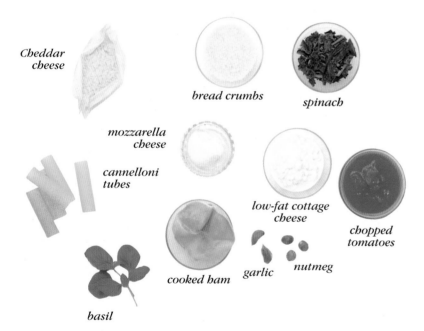

Cheddar
cheese

bread crumbs

spinach

mozzarella
cheese

cannelloni
tubes

low-fat cottage
cheese

chopped
tomatoes

cooked ham

garlic

nutmeg

basil

4 Preheat the oven to 350°F. Spoon half of the tomato sauce into the bottom of an 8-inch square ovenproof dish. Lay two rows of filled cannelloni on top of the sauce.

5 Sprinkle with the diced mozzarella and cover with the rest of the sauce.

6 Sprinkle with the Cheddar cheese and bread crumbs. Bake in a preheated oven for 30–40 minutes. Place under broiler to brown, if necessary. Garnish with flat-leaf parsley.

Ravioli with Bolognese Sauce

Serves 6

INGREDIENTS

8 ounces low-fat cottage cheese
2 tablespoons grated Parmesan cheese, plus extra for serving
1 egg white, beaten, including extra for brushing
1/4 teaspoon ground nutmeg
1 recipe pasta dough
flour, for dusting
1 medium onion, finely chopped
1 garlic clove, crushed
2/3 cup beef stock
12 ounces extra lean ground beef
1/2 cup red wine
2 tablespoons tomato paste
14 ounce can chopped tomatoes
1/2 tsp chopped fresh rosemary
1/4 tsp ground allspice
salt and ground black pepper

nutmeg

onion   ground beef   stock

tomato purée   low-fat cottage cheese   red wine

Parmesan cheese   chopped tomatoes

egg   rosemary

garlic

1 To make the filling mix the cottage cheese, grated Parmesan, egg white, seasoning and nutmeg together thoroughly.

2 Roll the pasta into thin sheets and place a small teaspoon of filling along the pasta in rows 2 inches apart.

3 Moisten between the filling with beaten egg white. Lay a second sheet of pasta lightly over the top and press between each pocket to remove any air and seal firmly.

4 Cut into rounds with a fluted ravioli or pastry cutter. Transfer to a floured cloth and let rest for at least 30 minutes before cooking.

5 To make the Bolognese sauce cook the onion and garlic in the stock for 5 minutes or until all the stock is reduced. Add the beef and cook quickly to brown, breaking up the meat with a fork. Add the wine, tomato paste, chopped tomatoes, rosemary and allspice, bring to a boil and simmer for 1 hour. Adjust the seasoning to taste.

6 Cook the ravioli in a large pan of boiling, salted water for 4–5 minutes. (Cook in batches to stop them from sticking together.) Drain thoroughly. Serve topped with Bolognese sauce. Serve grated Parmesan cheese separately.

Spaghetti alla Carbonara

Serves 4

INGREDIENTS
5 ounces smoked turkey bacon
1 medium onion, chopped
1–2 garlic cloves, crushed
²/₃ cup chicken stock
²/₃ cup dry white wine
7 ounces low-fat cream cheese
1 pound chili and garlic-
    flavored spaghetti
2 tablespoons chopped
    fresh parsley
salt and ground black pepper
shavings of Parmesan cheese,
    to serve

garlic

*flavored
spaghetti*

parsley

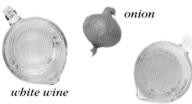
*smoked turkey
bacon*

*low-fat cream
cheese*

onion

white wine

stock

1 Cut the turkey bacon into ½-inch strips. Fry quickly in a non-stick pan for 2–3 minutes. Add the onion, garlic and stock to the pan. Bring to a boil, cover and simmer for 5 minutes until tender.

2 Add the wine and boil rapidly until reduced by half. Whisk in the cream cheese until smooth.

3 Meanwhile cook the spaghetti in a large pan of boiling, salted water for 10–12 minutes. Drain thoroughly.

4 Return to the pan with the sauce and parsley, toss well and serve immediately with shavings of Parmesan cheese.

Pasta Shells with Tomato and Tuna Sauce

Serves 6

INGREDIENTS

1 medium onion, finely chopped
1 stick celery, finely chopped
1 red bell pepper, seeded and diced
1 garlic clove, crushed
²/₃ cup chicken stock
14 ounce can chopped tomatoes
1 tablespoon tomato paste
2 teaspoons caster sugar
1 tablespoon chopped fresh basil
1 tablespoon chopped fresh parsley
1 pound dried pasta shells
14 ounce canned tuna packed in
    water, drained
2 tablespoons capers in
    vinegar, drained
salt and ground black pepper

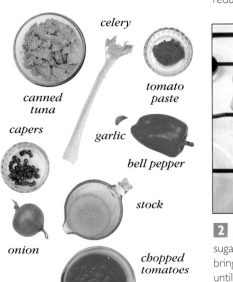

canned tuna

celery

capers

garlic

tomato paste

bell pepper

stock

onion

chopped tomatoes

basil

parsley

1 Put the chopped onion, celery, pepper and garlic into a non-stick pan. Add the stock, bring to a boil and cook for 5 minutes or until the stock is reduced almost completely.

2 Add the tomatoes, tomato paste, sugar and herbs. Season to taste and bring to a boil. Simmer for 30 minutes until thick, stirring occasionally.

3 Meanwhile cook the pasta in a large pan of boiling, salted water according to package instructions. Drain thoroughly and transfer to a warm serving dish.

4 Flake the tuna into large chunks and add to the sauce with the capers. Heat gently for 1–2 minutes, pour over the pasta, toss gently and serve at once.

Shrimp and Pasta Salad with Green Dressing

Serves 4–6

INGREDIENTS

4 anchovy fillets, drained
4 tablespoons skim milk
8 ounces squid
1 tablespoon chopped capers
1 tablespoon chopped cornichons
1–2 garlic cloves, crushed
²/₃ cup low-fat plain yogurt
2–3 tablespoons reduced-fat
  mayonnaise
squeeze of lemon juice
2 ounces watercress, finely chopped
2 tablespoons chopped fresh parsley
2 tablespoons chopped fresh basil
12 ounces fusilli
12 ounces peeled shrimp
salt and ground black pepper

squid *anchovy fillets*

cornichons and capers

watercress

parsley

low-fat plain yogurt

shrimp

fusilli *reduced-fat mayonnaise*

garlic *lemon*

basil

1 Put the anchovies into a small bowl and cover with the skim milk. Leave to soak for 10 minutes to remove the oil and strong salty flavor. Pull the head from the body of each squid and remove the quill. Peel outer speckled skin from the bodies. Cut the tentacles from the heads and rinse under cold water. Cut into ¹/₄-inch rings.

2 To make the dressing, mix the capers, cornichons, garlic, yogurt, mayonnaise, lemon juice and fresh herbs in a bowl. Drain and chop the anchovies. Add to the dressing with the seasoning.

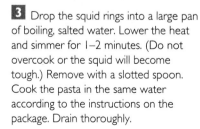

3 Drop the squid rings into a large pan of boiling, salted water. Lower the heat and simmer for 1–2 minutes. (Do not overcook or the squid will become tough.) Remove with a slotted spoon. Cook the pasta in the same water according to the instructions on the package. Drain thoroughly.

4 Mix the shrimp and squid into the dressing in a large bowl. Add the pasta, toss and serve warm or cold as a salad.

Spaghetti Bolognese

Serves 8

INGREDIENTS

1 medium onion, chopped
2–3 garlic cloves, crushed
1¼ cups beef or chicken stock
1 lb extra lean ground turkey
   or beef
2 x 14 ounce cans chopped
   tomatoes
1 teaspoon dried basil
1 teaspoon dried oregano
4 tablespoons concentrated
   tomato paste
1 pound button mushrooms,
   quartered or sliced
⅔ cup red wine
1 pound spaghetti
salt and ground black pepper

garlic

mushrooms

stock

spaghetti

onion

ground turkey

red wine

chopped tomatoes

tomato paste

1 Put the chopped onion and garlic into a non-stick pan with half of the stock. Bring to a boil and cook for 5 minutes until the onions are tender and the stock is reduced completely.

2 Add the turkey or beef and cook for 5 minutes breaking the meat up with a fork. Add the tomatoes, herbs and tomato paste, bring to the boil, cover and simmer for about 1 hour.

3 Meanwhile put the mushrooms into a non-stick pan with the wine, bring to a boil and cook for 5 minutes or until the wine has evaporated. Add the mushrooms to the meat.

4 Cook the pasta in a large pan of boiling, salted water for 8–10 minutes until tender. Drain thoroughly. Serve topped with meat sauce.

Pasta with Scallops in Warm Green Tartare Sauce

Serves 4

INGREDIENTS
½ cup low-fat sour cream
2 teaspoons coarse-grained mustard
2 garlic cloves, crushed
2–3 tablespoons fresh lime juice
4 tablespoons chopped fresh parsley
2 tablespoons snipped chives
12 ounces black tagliatelle
12 large scallops
4 tablespoons white wine
⅔ cup fish stock
salt and ground black pepper
lime wedges and parsley sprigs,
    to garnish

chives

lime

parsley

*black
tagliatelle*

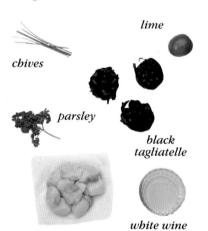

white wine

scallops

fish stock

*low-fat sour
cream*

garlic

1 To make the tartare sauce, mix the sour cream, mustard, garlic, lime juice, herbs and seasoning together in a bowl.

2 Cook the pasta in a large pan of boiling, salted water until *al dente*. Drain thoroughly.

3 Slice the scallops in half, horizontally. Put the white wine and fish stock into a saucepan. Heat to simmering point. Add the scallops and cook very gently for 3–4 minutes (no longer or they will become tough).

4 Remove the scallops. Boil the wine and stock to reduce by half and add the green sauce to the pan. Heat gently to warm, replace the scallops and cook for 1 minute. Spoon over the pasta and garnish with lime wedges and parsley.

Garlic and Herb Pasta

A tasty pasta dish served with plenty of fresh Parmesan cheese, this recipe makes a wonderful supper.

Serves 4

INGREDIENTS

9 ounces mixed egg and
    spinach tagliatelle
3 garlic cloves, crushed
2 canned anchovy fillets, rinsed
    and drained
2 tablespoons drained capers,
    finely chopped
1 teaspoon Dijon mustard
1/4 cup olive oil
1/4 cup mixed chopped fresh chives,
    parsley and oregano
1/3 cup pine nuts, toasted
1 tablespoon lemon juice
salt and pepper
freshly shaved Parmesan cheese,
    to serve

oregano

capers

chives

anchovies   olive oil

pine nuts

Dijon mustard

tagliatelle   garlic

lemon juice   Parmesan cheese   parsley

1 Cook the pasta in boiling, salted water, according to the package instructions, until just tender.

2 In a mortar and pestle, pound the garlic and anchovy, until combined. Transfer to a bowl, add the capers and mustard and mix well.

3 Gradually drizzle in the olive oil, mixing until thoroughly combined. Stir in the herbs, pine nuts and lemon juice. Season well.

4 Drain the pasta and toss with the herb dressing, until well combined. Serve, sprinkled with plenty of shaved Parmesan cheese.

Saffron Pappardelle

Serves 4

INGREDIENTS

large pinch of saffron strands
4 sun-dried tomatoes, chopped
1 teaspoon fresh thyme
12 large shrimp in their shells
8 ounces baby squid
8 ounces monkfish fillet
2–3 garlic cloves, crushed
2 small onions, quartered
1 small bulb fennel, trimmed
    and sliced
²⁄₃ cup white wine
8 ounces pappardelle
salt and ground black pepper
2 tablespoons chopped fresh
    parsley, to garnish

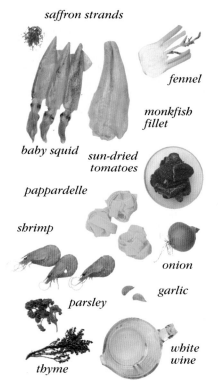

saffron strands

fennel

monkfish
fillet

baby squid

sun-dried
tomatoes

pappardelle

shrimp

onion

garlic

parsley

thyme

white
wine

1 Put the saffron, sun-dried tomatoes and thyme into a bowl with 4 tablespoons hot water. Let soak for 30 minutes.

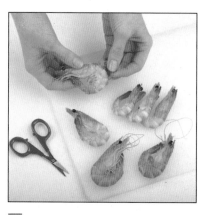

2 Wash the shrimp and carefully remove the shells, leaving the heads and tails intact. Pull the head from the body of each squid and remove the quill. Cut the tentacles from the head and rinse under cold water. Pull off the outer skin and cut into ¼-inch rings. Cut the monkfish into 1-inch cubes.

3 Put the garlic, onions and fennel into a pan with the wine. Cover and simmer for 5 minutes until tender.

4 Add the monkfish, saffron, tomatoes and thyme in their liquid. Cover and cook for 3 minutes. Then add the shrimp and squid. Cover and cook gently for 1–2 minutes. (Do not overcook or the squid will become tough.)

5 Meanwhile cook the pasta in a large pan of boiling, salted water until *al dente*. Drain thoroughly.

6 Divide the pasta among four serving dishes and top with the fish and shellfish sauce. Sprinkle with parsley and serve at once.

Rolled Stuffed Cannelloni

Serves 4

INGREDIENTS
12 sheets lasagne
fresh basil leaves, to garnish

FOR THE FILLING
2–3 garlic cloves, crushed
1 small onion, finely chopped
²/₃ cup white wine
1 pound ground turkey
1 tablespoon dried basil
1 tablespoon dried thyme
1½ ounces fresh white bread
    crumbs

FOR THE SAUCE
1 ounce low-fat margarine
1 ounce flour
1¼ cups skim milk
4 sun-dried tomatoes, chopped
1 tablespoon chopped fresh herbs
    (basil, parsley, marjoram)
2 tablespoons grated
    Parmesan cheese
salt and ground black pepper

skim milk

*sliced
white bread*

lasagne

*sun-dried
tomatoes*

*ground
turkey*

parsley

*grated
Parmesan
cheese*

*white
wine*

onion

flour

*low-fat
margarine*

basil

1 Put the garlic, onion and half the wine into a pan. Cover and cook for about 5 minutes until tender. Increase the heat, add the turkey and break up the pieces with a wooden spoon. Cook quickly until all the liquid has evaporated and the turkey begins to brown.

2 Lower the heat, add the remaining wine, seasoning and dried herbs. Cover and cook for 20 minutes. Remove from the heat and stir in the bread crumbs. Leave to cool.

3 Cook the lasagne sheets in a large pan of boiling, salted water until *al dente*. Cook in batches to prevent them from sticking together. Drain thoroughly and rinse in cold water. Pat dry on a clean dish towel.

4 Lay the lasagne on a chopping board. Spoon the turkey mixture along one short edge and roll it up to encase the filling. Cut the tubes in half.

5 Preheat the oven to 400°F. Put the margarine, flour and skim milk into a pan, heat and whisk until smooth. Add the chopped tomatoes, fresh herbs and seasoning.

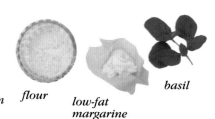

6 Spoon a thin layer of the sauce into a shallow ovenproof dish and arrange a layer of cannelloni on top. Spoon over a layer of sauce and cover with more cannelloni and sauce. Sprinkle with grated Parmesan and bake for 10–15 minutes until lightly browned. Serve at once, garnished with fresh basil leaves.

Pipe Rigate with Spicy Ground Beef

Serves 6

INGREDIENTS

1 pound extra lean ground beef
    or turkey
1 onion, finely chopped
2–3 garlic cloves, crushed
1–2 red chilies, seeded and
    finely chopped
14-ounce can chopped tomatoes
3 tablespoons tomato paste
1 teaspoon mixed dried herbs
1³/₄ cups water
1 pound pipe rigati
14-ounce can red kidney beans,
    drained
salt and ground black pepper

onion   *red chili*

garlic

red kidney beans   *tomato paste*   *pipe rigati*

chopped tomatoes   *ground beef*

1 Cook the ground beef or turkey in a non-stick saucepan, breaking up any large pieces with a wooden spoon until browned all over.

2 Add the onion, garlic and chilies, cover with a lid and cook gently for 5 minutes.

3 Add the tomatoes, tomato paste, herbs, water and seasoning. Bring to a boil and simmer for 1¹/₂ hours. Leave to cool slightly.

4 Cook the pasta in a large pan of boiling, salted water until *al dente*. Drain thoroughly. Skim off any fat that rises to the surface. Add the red kidney beans and heat for 5–10 minutes. Pour over the cooked pasta, and serve.

Turkey and Pasta Casserole

Serves 4

INGREDIENTS

10 ounces ground turkey
5 ounces smoked turkey
  bacon, chopped
1–2 garlic cloves, crushed
1 onion, finely chopped
2 carrots, diced
2 tablespoons concentrated
  tomato paste
1¼ cups chicken stock
8 ounces rigatoni
2 tablespoons grated
  Parmesan cheese
salt and ground black pepper

turkey bacon   *carrots*   *onion*

rigatoni

garlic

*tomato
purée*

*Parmesan
cheese*

ground turkey   *stock*

1 Brown the ground turkey in a non-stick saucepan, breaking up any large pieces with a wooden spoon, until well browned all over.

2 Add the chopped turkey bacon, garlic, onion, carrots, paste, stock and seasoning. Bring to a boil, cover and simmer for 1 hour until tender.

3 Preheat the oven to 350°F. Cook the pasta in a large pan of boiling, salted water until *al dente*. Drain thoroughly and mix with the turkey sauce.

4 Transfer to a shallow ovenproof dish and sprinkle with grated Parmesan cheese. Bake in the preheated oven for 20–30 minutes until lightly browned.

Ham-filled Paprika Ravioli

Serves 4

INGREDIENTS
8 ounces cooked smoked ham
4 tablespoons mango chutney
1 recipe basic pasta dough, with
	1 teaspoon ground paprika
	added
egg white, beaten
flour, for dusting
1–2 garlic cloves, crushed
1 stick celery, sliced
2 ounces sun-dried tomatoes
1 red chili, seeded and chopped
²⁄₃ cup red wine
14-ounce can chopped tomatoes
1 teaspoons chopped fresh thyme,
	plus extra to garnish
2 teaspoons sugar
salt and ground black pepper

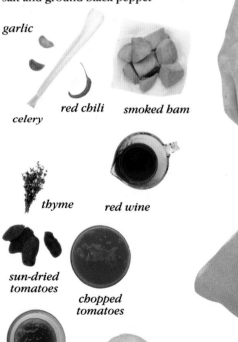

garlic

celery   red chili   smoked ham

thyme   red wine

sun-dried
tomatoes   chopped
tomatoes

mango
chutney   basic pasta
dough   paprika

1 Remove all traces of fat from the ham, place it with the mango chutney in a food processor or blender and mince the mixture finely.

2 Roll the pasta into thin sheets and lay one piece over a ravioli tray. Put a teaspoonful of the ham filling into each of the depressions.

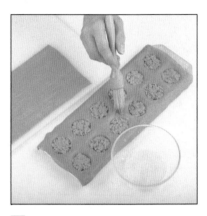

3 Brush around the edges of each ravioli with egg white. Cover with another sheet of pasta and press the edges together to seal.

5 Put the garlic, celery, sun-dried tomatoes, chili, wine, canned tomatoes and thyme into a pan. Cover and cook for 15–20 minutes. Season with salt, pepper and sugar.

4 Using a rolling pin, roll over the top of the dough to cut and seal each pocket. Transfer to a floured dish towel and let rest for 1 hour before cooking.

6 Cook the ravioli in a large pan of boiling, salted water for 4–5 minutes. Drain thoroughly. Spoon a little of the sauce onto a serving plate and arrange the ravioli on top. Sprinkle with fresh thyme and serve at once.

Fava Bean and Ham Lasagne

Serve this tasty lasagne with a salad and bread.

Serves 6

INGREDIENTS

2 teaspoons olive oil
3 cups sliced leeks
1 garlic clove, crushed
3 cups mushrooms, sliced
2 zucchini, sliced
12 ounces baby fava beans
2 cups diced lean smoked ham
5 tablespoons chopped fresh
  parsley
2 tablespoons chopped fresh chives
4 tablespoons reduced-fat spread
½ cup whole-wheat flour
2½ cups skim milk
1¼ cups vegetable stock, cooled
6 ounces low-fat cheese
1 teaspoon smooth mustard
8 ounces instant no-boil
  whole-wheat lasagne
½ cup fresh whole-wheat
  bread crumbs
1 tablespoon grated Parmesan
salt and ground black pepper
fresh herb sprigs, to garnish

 Preheat the oven to 350°F. Heat the oil in a saucepan, add the leeks and garlic and cook, stirring, for 3 minutes. Add the mushrooms and zucchini and cook, stirring, for 5 minutes.

 *garlic*

olive oil

leeks

 mushrooms

zucchini

 baby fava beans

 *smoked ham*

fresh parsley

 fresh chives

reduced-fat spread

whole-wheat flour

 skim milk

 vegetable stock

 mustard

 low-fat cheese

 fresh whole-wheat bread crumbs

salt

black pepper

 whole-wheat lasagne

 Parmesan cheese

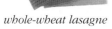

2 Remove the pan from the heat and stir in the fava beans, ham and herbs. Set aside.

3 Make the cheese sauce. Put the reduced-fat spread, flour, milk and stock in a saucepan and heat gently, whisking constantly, until the sauce comes to a boil and thickens. Simmer gently for 3 minutes, stirring. Grate the cheese.

4 Remove the pan from the heat, add the mustard and grated cheese and stir until the cheese has melted and is well blended. Season to taste. Reserve ½ cup of cheese sauce and set aside. Mix the remaining sauce with the ham and vegetables.

5 Spoon half the ham mixture over the bottom of a shallow ovenproof dish or baking pan. Cover with half the pasta. Repeat these layers with the remaining ham mixture and pasta, then pour the reserved cheese sauce over the pasta to cover it completely.

6 Mix together the bread crumbs and Parmesan cheese and sprinkle over the lasagne. Bake for 45–60 minutes, until cooked and golden brown on top. Garnish with fresh herb sprigs and serve immediately.

Duck Breast Rigatoni

Serves 6

INGREDIENTS
2 duck breasts, boned
1 teaspoon coriander seeds, crushed
12 ounces rigatoni
²/₃ cup fresh orange juice
1 tablespoon lemon juice
2 teaspoons honey
1 shallot, finely chopped
1 garlic clove, crushed
1 stalk celery, chopped
3 ounces dried cherries
3 tablespoons port
1 tablespoon chopped fresh mint,
    plus extra for garnish
2 tablespoons chopped fresh
    cilantro, plus extra for garnish
1 apple, diced
2 oranges, segmented
salt and ground black pepper

rigatoni   port   coriander
cilantro
duck breasts
1
orange
apple
shallot   garlic
mint
dried cherries
celery

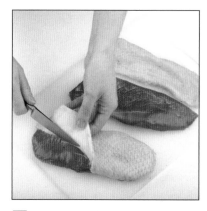

1 Remove the skin and fat from the duck breasts and season with salt and pepper. Rub with crushed coriander seeds. Cook under a preheated broiler for 7–10 minutes depending on size. Wrap in foil and leave for 20 minutes.

2 Cook the pasta in a large pan of boiling, salted water until *al dente*. Drain thoroughly and rinse under cold running water. Let to cool.

3 To make the dressing, put the orange juice, lemon juice, honey, shallot, garlic, celery, cherries, port, mint and fresh cilantro into a bowl, whisk together and leave to marinate for 30 minutes.

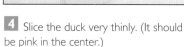

4 Slice the duck very thinly. (It should be pink in the center.)

5 Put the pasta into a bowl, add the dressing, diced apple and segments of orange. Toss well to coat the pasta. Transfer the salad to a serving plate with the duck slices and garnish with the extra coriander and mint.

Macaroni and Cheese

Serves 4

INGREDIENTS
1 medium onion, chopped
²/₃ cup vegetable or chicken stock
1 ounce low-fat margarine
1½ ounces plain flour
¼ cup skim milk
2 ounces reduced-fat Cheddar
  cheese, grated
1 teaspoon mustard
8 ounces quick-cook macaroni
4 smoked turkey bacon slices,
  cut in half
2–3 firm tomatoes, sliced
a few fresh basil leaves
1 tablespoon grated Parmesan
  cheese
salt and ground black pepper

tomatoes

smoked turkey
bacon

onion

basil   Parmesan
                 cheese

low-fat
margarine

macaroni

flour

stock

Cheddar
cheese

skim milk

1 Put the onion and stock into a non-stick frying pan. Bring to a boil, stirring occasionally and cook for 5–6 minutes or until the stock has reduced entirely and the onions are transparent.

2 Put the margarine, flour, milk, and seasoning into a pan and whisk together over the heat until thickened and smooth. Remove from the heat and add the cheeses, mustard and onions.

3 Cook the macaroni in a large pan of boiling, salted water for 6 minutes or according to the instructions on the package. Drain thoroughly and stir into the sauce. Transfer the macaroni to a shallow ovenproof dish.

4 Layer the turkey bacon and tomatoes on top of the macaroni and cheese, sprinkling the basil leaves over the tomatoes. Lightly sprinkle with Parmesan cheese and broil to lightly brown the top.

Fettuccine with Broccoli and Garlic

Serves 4

INGREDIENTS
3–4 garlic cloves, crushed
12 ounces broccoli florets
⅔ cup chicken stock
4 tablespoons white wine
2 tablespoons chopped fresh basil
4 tablespoons grated
    Parmesan cheese
12 ounces fettuccine or tagliatelle
salt and pepper
fresh basil leaves, to garnish

garlic

broccoli

basil

white wine

fettuccine

chicken stock

*grated
Parmesan cheese*

1 Put the garlic, broccoli and stock into a saucepan. Bring to a boil and cook for 5 minutes until tender, stirring from time to time.

2 Mash with a fork or potato masher, until roughly chopped. Return to the pan with the white wine, basil and Parmesan cheese. Season to taste.

3 Cook the fettuccine in a large pan of boiling, salted water until *al dente*. Drain thoroughly.

4 Return to the pan with half the broccoli sauce, toss to coat the pasta and transfer to serving plates. Top with the remaining broccoli sauce and garnish with basil leaves.

Penne with Spinach

Serves 4

INGREDIENTS

8 ounces fresh spinach
1 garlic clove, crushed
1 shallot or small onion,
    finely chopped
$\frac{1}{2}$ small red bell pepper, seeded and
    finely chopped
1 small red chili, seeded
    and chopped
$\frac{2}{3}$ cup stock
12 ounces penne
5 ounces smoked turkey bacon
3 tablespoons low-fat sour cream
2 tablespoons grated
    Parmesan cheese
shavings of Parmesan cheese,
    to garnish

red bell pepper

*grated
Parmesan cheese*

red chilies

shallot

*smoked turkey
bacon*

penne

stock

*low-fat sour
cream*

garlic

spinach

1 Wash the spinach and remove the hard central stems. Shred finely.

2 Put the garlic, shallot or small onion, pepper and chili into a large frying pan. Add the stock, cover and cook for about 5 minutes until tender. Add the prepared spinach and cook quickly for another 2–3 minutes until it has wilted.

3 Cook the pasta in a large pan of boiling, salted water until *al dente*. Drain thoroughly.

4 Fry the smoked turkey bacon, cool a little, and chop finely.

5 Stir the sour cream and grated Parmesan into the pasta with the spinach, and toss carefully together.

6 Transfer to serving plates and sprinkle with chopped turkey and shavings of Parmesan cheese.

Pasta Spirals with Pepperoni and Tomato Sauce

A warming supper dish, perfect for cold winter nights. All types of sausage are suitable, but if using raw sausages, make sure that they go in with the onion to cook thoroughly.

Serves 4

INGREDIENTS
1 medium onion
1 red bell pepper
1 green bell pepper
2 tbsp olive oil, plus extra for tossing
   the pasta
1¾ lb canned chopped tomatoes
2 tbsp tomato paste
2 tsp paprika
6 oz pepperoni or chorizo (spicy
   sausage)
3 tbsp chopped fresh parsley
salt and pepper
1 lb pasta spirals (fusilli)

pasta spirals

pepperoni

bell peppers

onion

parsley

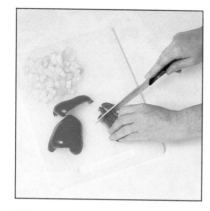

1 Chop the onion. Halve and seed the bell peppers, removing the cores, then cut the flesh into dice.

2 Heat the oil in a medium saucepan, add the onion, and cook for 2–3 minutes until beginning to color. Stir in the bell peppers, tomatoes, tomato paste, and paprika, bring to a boil and simmer, uncovered, for 15–20 minutes until reduced and thickened.

3 Slice the pepperoni and stir into the sauce with 2 tbsp chopped parsley. Season to taste.

4 While the sauce is simmering, cook the pasta in plenty of boiling salted water according to the manufacturer's instructions. Drain well. Toss the pasta with the remaining parsley and a little extra olive oil. Divide between warmed bowls and top with the sauce.

Spaghetti with Tomato and Clam Sauce

Small sweet clams make this a delicately succulent sauce. Mussels would make a good substitute, but don't be tempted to use seafood pickled in vinegar – the result will be inedible!

Serves 4

INGREDIENTS

2 lb live small clams, or 2 × 14 oz
   cans clams in brine, drained
6 tbsp olive oil
2 garlic cloves, crushed
1 lb 5 oz canned chopped tomatoes
3 tbsp chopped fresh parsley
salt and pepper
1 lb spaghetti

spaghetti

olive oil

parsley

garlic

clams

1 If using live clams, place them in a bowl of cold water and rinse several times to remove any grit or sand. Drain.

2 Heat the oil in a saucepan and add the clams. Stir over a high heat until the clams open. Throw away any that do not open. Transfer the clams to a bowl with a perforated spoon.

3 Reduce the clam juice left in the pan to almost nothing by boiling fast; this will also concentrate the flavor. Add the garlic and fry until golden. Pour in the tomatoes, bring to a boil, and cook for 3–4 minutes until reduced. Stir in the clam mixture or canned clams, and half the parsley and heat through. Season.

4 Cook the pasta in plenty of boiling salted water according to the manufacturer's instructions. Drain well and transfer to a warm serving dish. Pour over the sauce and sprinkle with the remaining parsley.

Rigatoni with Spicy Sausage and Tomato Sauce

This is really a shortcut to Bolognese sauce, using the wonderful fresh spicy sausages sold at every Italian grocers.

Serves 4

INGREDIENTS
1 lb fresh spicy Italian sausage
2 tbsp olive oil
1 medium onion, chopped
2 cups tomato coulis (strained, crushed tomatoes)
⅔ cup dry red wine
6 sun-dried tomatoes in oil, drained
salt and pepper
1 lb rigatoni or similar pasta
freshly grated Parmesan cheese, to serve

rigatoni

Italian sausage

Parmesan cheese

onion

sun-dried tomatoes

1 Squeeze the sausages out of their skins into a bowl and break up the meat.

2 Heat the oil in a medium saucepan and add the onion. Cook for 5 minutes until soft and golden. Stir in the sausage meat, browning it all over and breaking up the lumps with a wooden spoon. Pour in the coulis and the wine. Bring to a boil.

3 Slice the sun-dried tomatoes and add to the sauce. Simmer for 3 minutes until reduced, stirring occasionally. Season to taste.

4 Cook the pasta in plenty of boiling salted water according to the manufacturer's instructions. Drain well and top with the sauce. Serve with grated Parmesan cheese.

Pasta with Fresh Tomato and Smoky Bacon Sauce

A wonderful sauce to prepare in mid-summer when the tomatoes are ripe and sweet.

Serves 4

INGREDIENTS
2 lb ripe tomatoes
6 slices bacon
4 tbsp butter
1 medium onion, chopped
salt and pepper
1 tbsp chopped fresh oregano or 1 tsp
    dried oregano
1 lb pasta, any variety
freshly grated Parmesan cheese, to
    serve

pasta

oregano

tomatoes

onion

bacon

Parmesan cheese

1 Plunge the tomatoes into boiling water for 1 minute, then into cold water to stop them from becoming mushy. Slip off the skins. Halve the tomatoes, remove the seeds and cores, and roughly chop the flesh.

2 Remove the rind and roughly chop the bacon.

3 Melt the butter in a saucepan and add the bacon. Fry until lightly brown, then add the onion and cook gently for 5 minutes until softened. Add the tomatoes, salt, pepper, and oregano. Simmer gently for 10 minutes.

4 Cook the pasta in plenty of boiling salted water according to the manufacturer's instructions. Drain well and toss with the sauce. Serve with grated Parmesan cheese.

Pasta with Shrimp and Goat Cheese

This dish combines the richness of fresh shrimp with the tartness of goat cheese.

Serves 4

INGREDIENTS
1 lb medium raw shrimp
6 scallions
4 tbsp butter
8 ounces goat cheese
salt and pepper
small bunch fresh chives
1 lb penne, garganelle, or rigatoni

penne

scallions

goat cheese

chives

shrimp

1 Remove the heads from the shrimp by twisting and pulling off. Peel the shrimp and discard the shells. Chop the scallions.

2 Melt the butter in a skillet and stir in the shrimp. When they turn pink, add the scallions and cook gently for 1 minute.

3 Cut the cheese into ½-inch cubes.

4 Stir the goat cheese into the shrimp mixture and season with black pepper.

5 Cut the chives into 1 in lengths and stir half into the shrimp.

6 Cook the pasta in plenty of boiling salted water according to the manufacturer's instructions. Drain well, pile into a warmed serving dish, and top with the sauce. Scatter with the remaining chives and serve.

Tagliatelle with Prosciutto and Parmesan

A really simple dish, prepared in minutes from the best ingredients.

Serves 4

INGREDIENTS
¼ lb prosciutto
1 lb tagliatelle
salt and pepper
6 tbsp butter
½ cup freshly grated Parmesan
    cheese
few fresh sage leaves, to garnish

tagliatelle

sage

prosciutto

Parmesan cheese

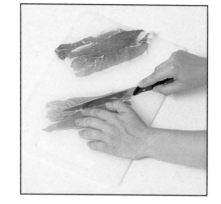

1 Cut the prosciutto into strips the same width as the tagliatelle. Cook the pasta in plenty of boiling salted water according to manufacturer's instructions.

2 Meanwhile, melt the butter gently in a saucepan, stir in the prosciutto strips and heat through, but do not fry.

3 Drain the tagliatelle well and pile into a warm serving dish.

4 Sprinkle over all the Parmesan cheese and pour over the buttery prosciutto. Season well with black pepper and garnish with the sage leaves.

Pasta with Spinach and Anchovy Sauce

Deliciously earthy, this would make a good entree or light supper dish. Add golden raisins for something really special.

Serves 4

INGREDIENTS

2 lb fresh spinach or 1¼ lb frozen leaf
 spinach, thawed
1 lb angel hair pasta
salt
4 tbsp olive oil
3 tbsp pine nuts
2 garlic cloves, crushed
6 canned anchovy fillets or whole
 salted anchovies, drained and
 chopped
butter, for tossing the pasta

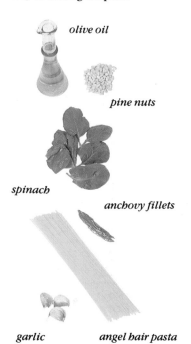

olive oil

pine nuts

spinach

anchovy fillets

garlic   *angel hair pasta*

1 Wash the spinach well and remove the tough stalks. Drain thoroughly. Place in a large saucepan with only the water that still clings to the leaves. Cover with a lid and cook over a high heat, shaking the pan occasionally, until the spinach is just wilted and still bright green. Drain.

2 Cook the pasta in plenty of boiling salted water according to the manufacturer's instructions.

3 Heat the oil in a saucepan and fry the pine nuts until golden. Remove with a perforated spoon. Add the garlic to the oil in the pan and fry until golden. Add the anchovies.

4 Stir in the spinach, and cook for 2–3 minutes or until heated through. Stir in the pine nuts. Drain the pasta, toss in a little butter, and transfer to a warmed serving bowl. Top with the sauce and fork through roughly.

Cannelloni al Forno

A lighter alternative to the usual beef-filled, béchamel-coated version. Fill with ricotta, onion, and mushroom for a vegetarian recipe.

Serves 4–6

INGREDIENTS
4 cups boneless, skinned chicken
　　breast, cooked
½ lb mushrooms
2 garlic cloves, crushed
2 tbsp chopped fresh parsley
1 tbsp chopped fresh tarragon
1 egg, beaten
salt and pepper
fresh lemon juice
12–18 cannelloni tubes
1 recipe Napoletana Sauce
½ cup freshly grated Parmesan
　　cheese
1 sprig fresh parsley, to garnish

cannelloni tubes　　　*parsley*

garlic

egg

Parmesan cheese　　*chicken*

1 Preheat the oven to 400°F. Place the chicken in a food processor and blend until finely ground. Transfer to a bowl.

2 Place the mushrooms, garlic, parsley, and tarragon in the food processor and blend until finely minced.

3 Beat the mushroom mixture into the chicken with the egg, salt and pepper, and lemon juice to taste.

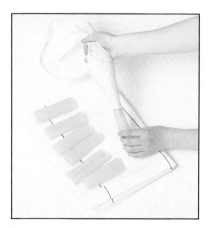

4 If necessary, cook the cannelloni in plenty of salted boiling water according to the manufacturer's instructions. Drain well on a clean dish towel.

5 Place the filling in a pastry bag fitted with a large plain tip. Use this to fill each tube of cannelloni.

6 Lay the filled cannelloni tightly together in a single layer in a buttered shallow ovenproof dish. Spoon over the tomato sauce and sprinkle with Parmesan cheese. Bake in the oven for 30 minutes, or until brown and bubbling. Serve garnished with a sprig of parsley.

Tagliatelle with Milanese Sauce

Serves 4

INGREDIENTS

1 onion, finely chopped
1 stalk celery, finely chopped
1 red bell pepper, seeded and diced
1–2 garlic cloves, crushed
$^{2}/_{3}$ cup vegetable stock
14 ounce can tomatoes
1 tbsp tomato paste
2 teaspoons sugar
1 teaspoon mixed dried herbs
12 ounces tagliatelle
4 ounces button mushrooms, sliced
4 tablespoons white wine
4 ounces lean cooked ham, diced
salt and ground black pepper
1 tablespoon chopped fresh parsley, to garnish

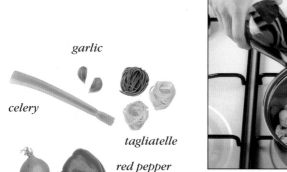

garlic

celery

tagliatelle

red pepper

onion

lean cooked ham

button mushrooms

parsley

tomato paste

vegetable stock

tomatoes

white wine

1 Put the chopped onion, celery, pepper and garlic into a non-stick pan. Add the stock, bring to a boil and cook for 5 minutes or until tender.

2 Add the tomatoes, tomato paste, sugar and herbs. Season with salt and pepper. Bring to a boil, simmer for 30 minutes until thick. Stir occasionally.

3 Cook the pasta in a large pan of boiling, salted water until *al dente*. Drain thoroughly.

4 Put the mushrooms into a pan with the white wine, cover and cook for 3–4 minutes until tender and all the wine has evaporated.

5 Add the mushrooms and diced ham to the tomato sauce. Reheat gently.

6 Transfer the pasta to a warmed serving dish and spoon on the sauce. Garnish with parsley.

VEGETARIAN PASTA DISHES

Pasta forms the basis of so many of the world's most popular vegetarian dishes. With its seemingly endless supply of fresh Mediterranean produce, it is little wonder that Italy is home to some of the best-loved vegetarian recipes.

Pasta Primavera

Serves 4

INGREDIENTS
8 ounces thin asparagus spears, cu
   in half
4 ounces snow peas, trimmed
4 ounces whole baby corn
8 ounces whole baby
   carrots, trimmed
1 small red bell pepper, seeded
   and chopped
8 scallions, sliced
8 ounces torchietti or rotini
²/₃ cup low-fat cottage cheese
²/₃ cup low-fat yogurt
1 tablespoon lemon juice
1 tablespoon chopped parsley
1 tablespoon snipped chives
skim milk (optional)
salt and ground black pepper
sun-dried tomato bread, to serve

scallions

red
pepper

baby corn

parsley

baby
carrots

lemon

chives

torchietti

snow peas

asparagus
spears

low-fat
yogurt

low-fat
cottage cheese

1 Cook the asparagus spears in a pan of boiling, salted water for 3–4 minutes. Add the snow peas halfway through the cooking time. Drain and rinse both under cold water.

2 Cook the baby corn, carrots, red pepper and spring onions in the same way until tender. Drain and rinse.

3 Cook the pasta in a large pan of boiling, salted water until *al dente*. Drain thoroughly.

4 Put the cottage cheese, yogurt, lemon juice, parsley, chives and seasoning into a food processor or blender and process until smooth. Thin the sauce with skim milk, if necessary. Put into a large pan with the pasta and vegetables, heat gently and toss carefully. Transfer to a serving plate and serve with sun-dried tomato bread.

Pasta with Mushrooms

The mushroom sauce is quick to make and the pasta cooks very quickly; both need to be cooked as near to serving as possible, so careful coordination is required.

Serves 4

INGREDIENTS
about 4 tablespoons butter
8–12 ounces chanterelles
1 tablespoon all-purpose flour
⅔ cup milk
6 tablespoons crème fraîche
1 tablespoon chopped fresh parsley
10 ounces fresh or dried tagliatelle
olive oil, for tossing
salt and ground black pepper

butter
flour
chanterelles
milk
crème fraîche
parsley
olive oil
tagliatelle

COOK'S TIP
Chanterelles are a little tricky to wash, as they are so delicate. However, since these are woodland mushrooms, it's important to clean them thoroughly. Hold each one by the stalk and let cold water run under the gills to dislodge hidden dirt. Shake gently to dry.

1 Melt 3 tablespoons of the butter in a frying pan and fry the mushrooms for 2–3 minutes over low heat until the juices begin to run, then increase the heat and cook until the liquid has almost evaporated. Transfer the cooked mushrooms to a bowl using a slotted spoon.

2 Stir the flour into the pan, adding a little more butter if necessary, and cook for about 1 minute, then gradually stir in the milk to make a smooth sauce.

3 Add the crème fraîche, mushrooms, parsley and seasoning and stir well. Cook very gently to heat through and then keep warm while cooking the pasta.

4 Bring a large pot of salted water to a boil. Add the pasta and cook according to the package instructions until it is just al dente. Drain well, toss with a little olive oil and then transfer to a warmed serving plate. Pour the mushroom sauce on top and serve immediately while it is hot.

VARIATION
If chanterelles are unavailable, use other wild mushrooms of your choice.

Vegetarian Lasagne

Serves 6–8

INGREDIENTS

1 small eggplant
1 large onion, finely chopped
2 garlic cloves, crushed
²⁄₃ cup vegetable stock
8 ounces mushrooms, sliced
14 ounce can chopped tomatoes
2 tablespoons tomato paste
²⁄₃ cup red wine
¼ teaspoon ground ginger
1 teaspoon mixed dried herbs
10–12 sheets lasagne
1 ounce low-fat margarine
1 ounce flour
1¼ cups skim milk
large pinch of grated nutmeg
7 ounces low-fat cottage cheese
1 egg, beaten
½ ounce grated Parmesan cheese
1 ounce reduced-fat Cheddar
   cheese, grated
salt and ground black pepper

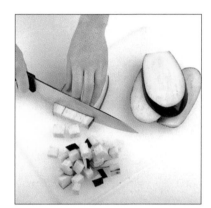

1 Wash the eggplant and cut it into 1-inch cubes. Put the onion and garlic into a saucepan with the stock, cover and cook for about 5 minutes or until tender.

2 Add the diced eggplant, sliced mushrooms, tomatoes, tomato paste, wine, ginger, seasoning and herbs. Bring to a boil, cover and cook for 15–20 minutes. Remove the lid and cook rapidly to reduce the liquid by half.

3 To make the sauce, put the margarine, flour, skim milk and nutmeg into a pan. Whisk together over the heat until thickened and smooth. Season to taste.

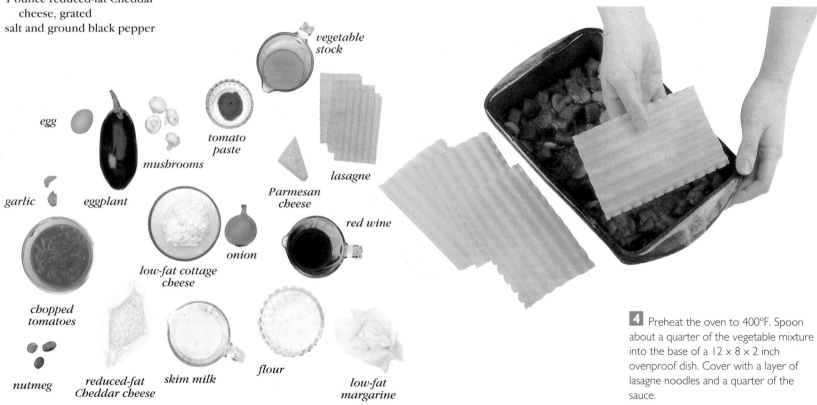

vegetable stock

egg

mushrooms

tomato paste

lasagne

garlic   *eggplant*

Parmesan cheese

red wine

low-fat cottage cheese

onion

chopped tomatoes

nutmeg   *reduced-fat Cheddar cheese*   *skim milk*   *flour*   *low-fat margarine*

4 Preheat the oven to 400°F. Spoon about a quarter of the vegetable mixture into the base of a 12 × 8 × 2 inch ovenproof dish. Cover with a layer of lasagne noodles and a quarter of the sauce.

5 Repeat with two more layers, then cover with the cottage cheese. Beat the egg into the remaining sauce and pour over the top. Sprinkle with the two grated cheeses.

6 Bake for 25–30 minutes or until the top is golden brown.

Crescent Spinach Ravioli

Serves 4–6

INGREDIENTS
1 bunch of scallions, finely chopped
1 carrot, coarsely grated
2 garlic cloves, crushed
7 ounces low-fat cottage cheese
1 tablespoon chopped dill
4 halves sun-dried tomatoes,
    finely chopped
1 ounce grated Parmesan cheese
1 recipe basic pasta dough, with
    4 ounces frozen spinach, thawed
    and chopped added
egg white, beaten, for brushing
flour, for dusting
salt and ground black pepper
2 halves sun-dried tomatoes, finely
    chopped, and fresh dill,
    to garnish

carrot

sun-dried tomatoes

dill

garlic

scallions

Parmesan cheese

spinach

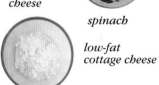

low-fat cottage cheese

1 Put the scallions, carrot, garlic and cottage cheese into a bowl. Add the chopped dill, tomatoes, seasoning and Parmesan cheese.

2 Roll the spinach pasta into thin sheets, cut into 3-inch rounds with a fluted pastry cutter.

3 Place a small spoonful of filling in the center of each circle. Brush the edges with egg white.

4 Fold each in half to make crescents. Press the edges together to seal. Transfer to a floured dish towel to let rest for 1 hour before cooking.

5 Cook the pasta in a large pan of boiling, salted water for 5 minutes. (Cook in batches to stop them sticking together.) Drain well.

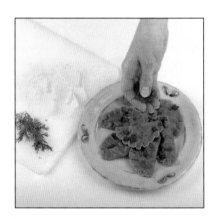

6 Serve the crescents on warmed serving plates and garnish with sun-dried tomatoes and dill.

Vegetarian Cannelloni

Serves 4–6

INGREDIENTS

1 onion, finely chopped
2 garlic cloves, crushed
2 carrots, coarsely grated
2 stalks celery, finely chopped
2/3 cup vegetable stock
4 ounces red or green lentils
14 ounce can chopped tomatoes
2 tablespoons tomato purée
1/2 teaspoon ground ginger
1 teaspoon fresh thyme
1 teaspoon chopped fresh rosemary
1 1/2 ounces low-fat margarine
1 1/2 ounces flour
2 1/2 cups skim milk
1 bay leaf
large pinch grated nutmeg
16–18 cannelloni tubes
1 ounce reduced-fat Cheddar
  cheese, grated
1 ounce grated Parmesan cheese
1 ounce fresh white bread crumbs
salt and ground black pepper
flat-leaf parsley, to garnish

1 To make the filling, put the onion, garlic, carrots and celery into a large saucepan. Add half the stock, cover and cook for 5 minutes or until tender.

2 Add the lentils, chopped tomatoes, tomato purée, ginger, thyme, rosemary and seasoning. Bring to a boil, cover and cook for 20 minutes. Remove the lid and cook for about 10 minutes until thick and soft. Let cool.

3 To make the sauce, put the margarine, flour, skim milk and bay leaf into a pan and whisk over the heat until thick and smooth. Season with salt, pepper and nutmeg. Discard the bay leaf.

flour

low-fat margarine

reduced-fat Cheddar cheese

onion *garlic* *celery*
rosemary

white bread crumbs

bay leaf *thyme*

skim milk

carrots

red lentils *Parmesan cheese*

nutmeg

cannelloni tubes

chopped tomatoes *vegetable stock* *tomato purée*

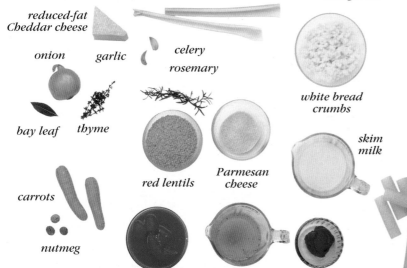

4 Fill the uncooked cannelloni by piping the filling into each tube. (It is easiest to hold them upright with one end flat on a cutting board, while piping into the other end.)

5 Preheat the oven to 350°F. Spoon half the sauce into the bottom of an 8-inch square ovenproof dish. Lay two rows of filled cannelloni on top and spoon over the remaining sauce.

6 Top with the cheeses and bread crumbs. Bake in the preheated oven for 30–40 minutes. Place under broiler to brown the top, if necessary. Garnish with flat-leaf parsley.

Spicy Ratatouille with Penne

Serves 6

INGREDIENTS
1 small eggplant
2 zucchini, thickly sliced
7 ounces firm tofu, cubed
3 tablespoons dark soy sauce
1 garlic clove, crushed
2 teaspoons sesame seeds
1 small red bell pepper, seeded
    and sliced
1 onion, finely chopped
1–2 garlic cloves, crushed
2/3 cup vegetable stock
3 firm ripe tomatoes, peeled, seeded
    and quartered
1 tablespoon chopped mixed herbs
8 ounces penne
salt and ground black pepper
crusty bread, to serve

tomatoes   *zucchini*

eggplant   *red bell pepper*   *tofu*

garlic

onion   *penne*   *sesame seeds*

vegetable stock   *soy sauce*

1 Wash and cut the eggplant into 1-inch cubes. Put into a colander with the zucchini, sprinkle with salt and leave to drain for 30 minutes.

2 Mix the tofu with the soy sauce, garlic and sesame seeds. Cover and marinate for 30 minutes.

3 Put the pepper, onion and garlic into a saucepan with the stock. Bring to a boil, cover and cook for 5 minutes until tender. Remove the lid and boil until all the stock has evaporated. Add the tomatoes and herbs and cook for 3 minutes more. Season to taste.

4 Meanwhile cook the pasta in a large pan of boiling, salted water until *al dente*. Drain thoroughly. Toss the pasta with the vegetables and tofu. Transfer to a shallow 10-inch square ovenproof dish and grill until lightly browned. Transfer to a serving dish and serve with fresh crusty bread.

Sun-dried Tomato and Parmesan Carbonara

Ingredients for this recipe can easily be doubled to serve four. Why not try it with plenty of garlic bread and a big green salad?

Serves 2

INGREDIENTS

6 ounces tagliatelle
2 ounces sun-dried tomatoes in olive oil, drained
2 eggs, beaten
⅔ cup heavy cream
1 tablespoon whole-grain mustard
⅔ cup Parmesan cheese, freshly grated
12 fresh basil leaves, shredded
salt and pepper
fresh basil leaves, to garnish
crusty bread, to serve

fresh basil

sun-dried tomatoes

Parmesan cheese

tagliatelle

whole-grain mustard

heavy cream

eggs

1 Cook the pasta in boiling, salted water until it is just tender but still retains a little bite (*al dente*).

2 Meanwhile, cut the sun-dried tomatoes into small pieces.

3 Combine the eggs, cream and mustard with plenty of seasoning.

4 Drain the pasta and immediately return to the hot saucepan with the cream mixture, sun-dried tomatoes, Parmesan cheese and shredded fresh basil. Return to very low heat for 1 minute, stirring gently, until the mixture thickens slightly. Adjust the seasoning and serve immediately, garnished with basil leaves. Serve with plenty of crusty bread.

Pasta with Roasted Bell Pepper and Tomato Sauce

Add other vegetables such as French beans or zucchini or even chick peas (garbanzos) to make this sauce more substantial.

Serves 4

INGREDIENTS
2 medium red bell peppers
2 medium yellow bell peppers
3 tbsp olive oil
1 medium onion, sliced
2 garlic cloves, crushed
½ tsp mild chili powder
14 oz canned chopped plum tomatoes
salt and pepper
4 cups dried pasta shells or spirals
freshly grated Parmesan cheese, to
    serve

bell peppers

pasta shells

onion

garlic

1 Preheat the oven to 400°F. Place the bell peppers on a baking sheet or in a roasting pan and bake for about 20 minutes or until beginning to char. Alternatively broil the peppers, turning frequently.

2 Rub the skins off the peppers under cold water. Halve, remove the seeds, and roughly chop the flesh.

3 Heat the oil in a medium saucepan and add the onion and garlic. Cook gently for 5 minutes until soft and golden.

4 Stir in the chili powder, cook for 2 minutes, then add the tomatoes and peppers. Bring to a boil and simmer for 10–15 minutes until slightly thickened and reduced. Season to taste.

5 Cook the pasta in plenty of boiling salted water according to the manufacturer's instructions. Drain well and toss with the sauce. Serve piping hot with lots of Parmesan cheese.

Tagliatelle with Gorgonzola Sauce

Gorgonzola is a creamy Italian blue cheese. As an alternative you could use Danish Blue.

Serves 4

INGREDIENTS
2 tbsp butter, plus extra for tossing
   the pasta
½ lb Gorgonzola cheese
⅔ cup heavy or whipping cream
2 tbsp dry vermouth
1 tsp cornstarch
1 tbsp chopped fresh sage
salt and pepper
1 lb tagliatelle

tagliatelle

Gorgonzola cheese

sage

I Melt 2 tbsp butter in a heavy saucepan (it needs to be thick-based to prevent the cheese from burning). Stir in 6 oz crumbled Gorgonzola cheese and stir over a very gentle heat for 2–3 minutes until the cheese is melted.

2 Pour in the cream, vermouth, and cornstarch, whisking well to amalgamate. Stir in the chopped sage, then taste and season. Cook, whisking all the time, until the sauce boils and thickens. Set aside.

3 Boil the pasta in plenty of salted water according to the manufacturer's instructions. Drain well and toss with a little butter.

4 Reheat the sauce gently, whisking well. Divide the pasta between 4 serving bowls, top with the sauce, and sprinkle over the remaining cheese. Serve immediately.

Pasta with Tomato and Cream Sauce

Here pasta is served with a deliciously rich version of ordinary tomato sauce.

Serves 4–6

INGREDIENTS
2 tbsp olive oil
2 garlic cloves, crushed
14 oz canned chopped tomatoes
⅔ cup heavy or whipping cream
2 tbsp chopped fresh herbs such as basil, oregano, or parsley
salt and pepper
4 cups pasta, any variety

olive oil

chopped tomatoes

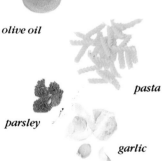

parsley

pasta

garlic

1 Heat the oil in a medium saucepan, add the garlic, and cook for 2 minutes until golden.

2 Stir in the tomatoes, bring to a boil and simmer uncovered for 20 minutes, stirring occasionally to prevent sticking. The sauce is ready when you can see the oil separating on top.

3 Add the cream, bring slowly to a boil again, and simmer until slightly thickened. Stir in the herbs, taste, and season well.

4 Cook the pasta in plenty of boiling salted water according to the manufacturer's instructions. Drain well and toss with the sauce. Serve piping hot, sprinkled with extra herbs if liked.

COOK'S TIP

If you are really in a hurry, buy a good ready-made tomato sauce and simply stir in the cream and simmer until thickened.

Tagliatelle with Pea Sauce, Asparagus and Broad Beans

A creamy pea sauce makes a wonderful combination with the crunchy young vegetables.

Serves 4

INGREDIENTS

1 tbsp olive oil
1 garlic clove, crushed
6 scallions, sliced
1 cup fresh or frozen baby peas, defrosted
12 oz fresh young asparagus
2 tbsp chopped fresh sage, plus extra leaves, to garnish
finely grated rind of 2 lemons
1¾ cups fresh vegetable stock or water
8 oz fresh or frozen broad beans, defrosted
1 lb tagliatelle
4 tbsp low-fat yogurt

lemon

garlic

asparagus

broad beans

peas

yogurt

tagliatelle

sage

scallions

1 Heat the oil in a pan. Add the garlic and scallions and cook gently for 2–3 minutes until softened.

2 Add the peas and ⅓ of the asparagus, together with the sage, lemon rind and stock or water. Bring to a boil, reduce the heat and simmer for 10 minutes until tender. Purée in a blender until smooth.

3 Meanwhile remove the outer skins from the broad beans and discard.

4 Cut the remaining asparagus into 2 in lengths trimming off any tough fibrous stems, and blanch in boiling water for 2 minutes.

5 Cook the tagliatelle following the instructions on the side of the package until *al dente*. Drain well.

COOK'S TIP

Frozen peas and beans have been suggested here to cut down the preparation time, but the dish tastes even better if you use fresh young vegetables when in season.

6 Add the cooked asparagus and shelled beans to the sauce and reheat. Stir in the yogurt and toss into the tagliatelle. Garnish with a few extra sage leaves and serve.

Tortellini with Cream, Butter and Cheese

This is an indulgent but quick alternative to macaroni and cheese. Meat-eaters could stir in some ham or pepperoni, though it's delicious as it is!

Serves 4–6

INGREDIENTS
4 cups fresh tortellini
salt and pepper
4 tbsp butter
1¼ cups heavy cream
¼ lb piece fresh Parmesan cheese
freshly grated nutmeg

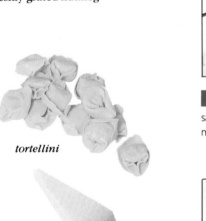

tortellini

Parmesan cheese

nutmeg

COOK'S TIP

Other hard grating cheeses can be used here, but don't try to use light cream or it will curdle.

1 Cook the pasta in plenty of boiling salted water according to the manufacturer's instructions.

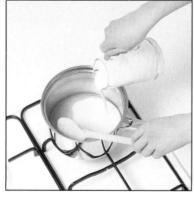

2 Meanwhile melt the butter in a medium saucepan and stir in the cream. Bring to a boil and cook for 2–3 minutes until slightly thickened.

3 Grate the Parmesan cheese and stir ¾ cup into the sauce until melted. Season to taste with salt, pepper, and nutmeg. Preheat the broiler.

4 Drain the pasta well and spoon into a buttered heatproof serving dish. Pour over the sauce, sprinkle over the remaining cheese, and place under the broiler until brown and bubbling. Serve immediately.

Baked Tortellini with Three Cheeses

Serve this straight out of the oven while the cheese is still runny. If smoked mozzarella cheese is not available, try using a smoked German cheese or even grated smoked Cheddar.

Serves 4–6

INGREDIENTS
1 lb fresh tortellini
salt and pepper
2 eggs
1½ cups ricotta or cottage cheese
2 tbsp butter
1 oz fresh basil leaves
¼ lb smoked cheese, sliced
4 tbsp freshly grated Parmesan cheese

tortellini

smoked cheese

basil

eggs

1 Preheat the oven to 375°F. Cook the tortellini in plenty of boiling salted water according to the manufacturer's instructions. Drain well.

2 Beat the eggs with the ricotta cheese and season well with salt and pepper. Use the butter to grease an ovenproof dish. Spoon in half the tortellini, pour over half the ricotta mixture, and cover with half the basil leaves.

3 Cover with the smoked cheese and remaining basil. Top with the rest of the tortellini and spread over the remaining ricotta.

4 Sprinkle evenly with the Parmesan cheese. Bake in the oven for 35–45 minutes or until golden brown and bubbling. Serve immediately.

Pasta Shells with Tomatoes and Arugula

This pretty-colored pasta dish relies for its success on a salad green called arugula. Available in large supermarkets, it is a leaf easily grown in the garden or a window box and tastes slightly peppery.

Serves 4

INGREDIENTS
1 lb shell pasta
salt and pepper
1 lb very ripe cherry tomatoes
3 tbsp olive oil
3 oz fresh arugula
Parmesan cheese

olive oil

pasta shells

cherry tomatoes

arugula

Parmesan cheese

1 Cook the pasta in plenty of boiling salted water according to the manufacturer's instructions. Drain well.

2 Halve the tomatoes. Trim, wash, and dry the arugula.

3 Heat the oil in a large saucepan, add the tomatoes, and cook for barely 1 minute. The tomatoes should only just heat through and not disintegrate.

4 Shave the Parmesan cheese using a rotary vegetable peeler.

5 Add the pasta, then the arugula. Carefully stir to mix and heat through. Season well with salt and freshly ground black pepper. Serve immediately with plenty of shaved Parmesan cheese.

Pasta Tossed with Broiled Vegetables

A hearty dish to be eaten with crusty bread and washed down with a robust red wine. Try barbecuing the vegetables for a really smoky flavor.

Serves 4

INGREDIENTS
1 medium eggplant
2 medium zucchini
1 medium red bell pepper
8 garlic cloves, unpeeled
about ⅔ cup good olive oil
salt and pepper
1 lb ribbon pasta (pappardelle)
few sprigs fresh thyme, to garnish

olive oil

zucchini

eggplant

ribbon pasta

thyme

garlic

pepper

1 Preheat the broiler. Slice the eggplant and zucchini lengthwise.

2 Halve the bell pepper, cut out the stalk and white pith, and scrape out the seeds. Slice lengthwise into 8 pieces.

3 Line a broiler pan with foil and arrange the vegetables and unpeeled garlic in a single layer on top. Brush liberally with oil and season well with salt and pepper.

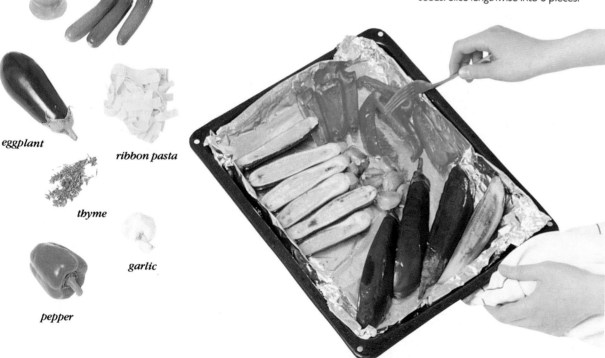

4 Grill until slightly charred, turning once. If necessary, cook the vegetables in 2 batches.

5 Cool the garlic, remove the charred skins, and halve. Toss the vegetables with olive oil and keep warm.

6 Meanwhile, cook the pasta in plenty of boiling salted water according to the manufacturer's instructions. Drain well and toss with the vegetables. Serve immediately, garnished with sprigs of thyme and accompanied by plenty of country bread.

Green Pasta with Avocado Sauce

This is an unusual sauce with a pale green color, studded with red tomato. It has a luxurious velvety texture. The sauce is rich, so you don't need much for a filling meal.

Serves 6

INGREDIENTS

3 ripe tomatoes
2 large ripe avocados
2 tbsp butter, plus extra for tossing
   the pasta
1 garlic clove, crushed
1½ cups heavy cream
salt and pepper
dash of Tabasco sauce
1 lb green tagliatelle
freshly grated Parmesan cheese
4 tbsp sour cream

tagliatelle

tomatoes

avocado

garlic

1 Halve the tomatoes and remove the cores. Squeeze out the seeds and cut the tomatoes into dice. Set aside.

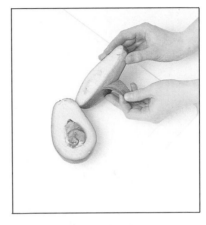

2 Halve the avocados, take out the pits, and peel. Roughly chop the flesh.

3 Melt the butter in a saucepan and add the garlic. Cook for 1 minute, then add the cream and chopped avocados. Raise the heat, stirring constantly to break up the avocados.

4 Add the diced tomatoes and season to taste with salt, pepper, and a little Tabasco sauce. Keep warm.

5 Cook the pasta in plenty of boiling salted water according to the manufacturer's instructions. Drain well and toss with a knob of butter.

6 Divide the pasta between 4 warmed bowls and spoon over the sauce. Sprinkle with grated Parmesan and top with a spoonful of sour cream.

Fettuccine all'Alfredo

A classic dish from Rome, Fettuccine all'Alfredo is simply pasta tossed with heavy cream, butter, and freshly grated Parmesan cheese. Popular less classic additions are peas and strips of ham.

Serves 4

INGREDIENTS
2 tbsp butter
⅔ cup heavy cream, plus 4 tbsp extra
1 lb fettuccine
freshly grated nutmeg
½ cup freshly grated Parmesan
  cheese, plus extra to serve
salt and pepper

fettuccine

nutmeg

Parmesan cheese

1 Place the butter and ⅔ cup cream in a heavy saucepan, bring to a boil, and simmer for 1 minute until slightly thickened.

2 Cook the fettuccine in plenty of boiling salted water according to the manufacturer's instructions, but for 2 minutes less time. The pasta should still be a little firm.

3 Drain very well and transfer to the pan with the cream sauce.

4 Place on the heat and toss the pasta in the sauce to coat.

5 Add the extra 4 tbsp cream, the cheese, salt and pepper to taste, and a little grated nutmeg. Toss until well coated and heated through. Serve immediately with extra grated Parmesan cheese.

Pasta with Pesto Sauce

Don't skimp on the fresh basil – this is the most wonderful sauce in the world! This pesto can also be used as a basting sauce for broiled chicken or fish, or rubbed over a leg of lamb before baking.

Serves 4

INGREDIENTS
2 garlic cloves
salt and pepper
½ cup pine nuts
1 cup fresh basil leaves
⅔ cup olive oil (not extra-virgin as it
  is too strong)
4 tbsp unsalted butter, softened
4 tbsp freshly grated Parmesan cheese
1 lb spaghetti

olive oil

spaghetti

pine nuts

Parmesan cheese

basil

1 Peel the garlic and process in a food processor with a little salt and the pine nuts until broken up. Add the basil leaves and continue mixing to a paste.

2 Gradually add the olive oil, little by little, until the mixture is creamy and thick.

3 Mix in the butter and season with pepper. Mix in the cheese. (Alternatively, you can make the pesto by hand using a pestle and mortar.)

4 Store the pesto in a jar (with a layer of olive oil on top to exclude the air) in the fridge until needed.

5 Cook the pasta in plenty of boiling salted water according to the manufacturer's instructions. Drain well.

COOK'S TIP

A good pesto can be made using parsley instead of basil and walnuts instead of pine nuts. To make it go further, add a spoonful or two of fromage frais. 'Red' pesto includes sun-dried tomato paste and pounded roasted red peppers.

6 Toss the pasta with half the pesto and serve in warm bowls with the remaining pesto spooned on top.

Margherita

(Tomato, Basil and Mozzarella)
This classic pizza is simple to prepare. The sweet flavor of sun-ripened tomatoes works wonderfully with the basil and mozzarella.

Serves 2–3

INGREDIENTS
1 pizza base, about 10–12 in
 diameter
2 tbsp olive oil
1 quantity Tomato Sauce
5 oz mozzarella
2 ripe tomatoes, thinly sliced
6–8 fresh basil leaves
2 tbsp freshly grated Parmesan
black pepper

basil

mozzarella

Parmesan

olive oil

tomatoes

Tomato Sauce

1 Preheat the oven to 425°F. Brush the pizza base with 1 tbsp of the oil and then spread over the Tomato Sauce.

2 Cut the mozzarella into thin slices.

3 Arrange the sliced mozzarella and tomatoes on top of the pizza base.

4 Roughly tear the basil leaves, add and sprinkle with the Parmesan. Drizzle over the remaining oil and season with black pepper. Bake for 15–20 minutes until crisp and golden. Serve immediately.

Marinara

(Tomato and Garlic)

The combination of garlic, good quality olive oil and oregano give this pizza an unmistakably Italian flavor.

Serves 2–3

INGREDIENTS
4 tbsp olive oil
1½ lb plum tomatoes, peeled, seeded and chopped
1 pizza base, about 10–12 in diameter
4 garlic cloves, cut into slivers
1 tbsp chopped fresh oregano
salt and black pepper

olive oil

oregano

plum tomatoes

garlic

I Preheat the oven to 425°F. Heat 2 tbsp of the oil in a pan. Add the tomatoes and cook, stirring frequently for about 5 minutes until soft.

2 Place the tomatoes in a strainer and leave to drain for about 5 minutes.

3 Transfer the tomatoes to a food processor or blender and purée until smooth.

4 Brush the pizza base with half the remaining oil. Spoon over the tomatoes and sprinkle with garlic and oregano. Drizzle over the remaining oil and season. Bake for 15–20 minutes until crisp and golden. Serve immediately.

Napoletana

(Tomato, Mozzarella and Anchovies)
This pizza is a speciality of Naples. It is both one of the simplest to prepare and the most tasty.

Serves 2–3

INGREDIENTS
1 pizza base, about 10–12 in
   diameter
2 tbsp olive oil
6 plum tomatoes
2 garlic cloves, chopped
4 oz mozzarella, grated
2 oz can anchovy fillets, drained and
   chopped
1 tbsp chopped fresh oregano
2 tbsp freshly grated Parmesan
black pepper

Parmesan

mozzarella

anchovy fillets

olive oil

plum tomatoes

garlic

oregano

1 Preheat the oven to 425°F. Brush the pizza base with 1 tbsp of the oil. Put the tomatoes in a bowl and pour over boiling water. Leave for 30 seconds, then plunge into cold water.

2 Peel, seed and coarsely chop the tomatoes. Spoon the tomatoes over the pizza base and sprinkle over the garlic.

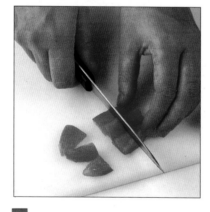

3 Mix the mozzarella with the anchovies and sprinkle over.

4 Sprinkle over the oregano and Parmesan. Drizzle over the remaining oil and season with black pepper. Bake for 15–20 minutes until crisp and golden. Serve immediately.

Quattro Formaggi

(Four Cheeses)

Rich and tasty, these individual pizzas are quick to assemble, and the aroma of melting cheese is irresistible.

Serves 4

INGREDIENTS
1 quantity Basic or Superquick Pizza
 Dough
1 tbsp Garlic Oil
½ small red onion, very thinly sliced
2 oz Saga Blue
2 oz mozzarella
2 oz Gruyère, grated
2 tbsp freshly grated Parmesan
1 tbsp chopped fresh thyme
black pepper

mozzarella

red onion

Parmesan

Garlic Oil

Saga Blue

Gruyère

thyme

1 Preheat the oven to 425°F. Divide the dough into four pieces and roll out each one on a lightly floured surface into a 5 in circle. Place well apart on two greased baking sheets, then pinch up the dough edges to make a thin rim. Brush with Garlic Oil and top with the red onion.

2 Cut the Saga Blue and mozzarella into cubes and scatter over the bases.

3 Mix together the Gruyère, Parmesan and thyme and sprinkle over.

4 Grind over plenty of black pepper. Bake for 15–20 minutes until crisp and golden and the cheese is bubbling. Serve immediately.

Fiorentina

Spinach is the star ingredient of this pizza. A grating of nutmeg to heighten its flavor gives this pizza its unique character.

Serves 2–3

INGREDIENTS
6 oz fresh spinach
3 tbsp olive oil
1 small red onion, thinly sliced
1 pizza base, about 10–12 in
   diameter
1 quantity Tomato Sauce
freshly grated nutmeg
5 oz mozzarella
1 large egg
1 oz Gruyere, grated

mozzarella

Gruyère

Tomato Sauce

spinach

red onion

nutmeg

egg

1 Preheat the oven to 425°F. Remove the stems from the spinach and wash the leaves in plenty of cold water. Drain well and pat dry with paper towels.

2 Heat 1 tbsp of the oil and fry the onion until soft. Add the spinach and continue to fry until just wilted. Drain off any excess liquid.

3 Brush the pizza base with half the remaining oil. Spread over the Tomato Sauce, then top with the spinach mixture. Grate some nutmeg over.

4 Thinly slice the mozzarella and arrange over the spinach. Drizzle the remaining oil over. Bake for 10 minutes, then remove from the oven.

5 Make a small well in the center and drop the egg into the hole.

6 Sprinkle over the Gruyère and return to the oven for a further 5–10 minutes until crisp and golden. Serve immediately.

Hot Pepperoni

This popular pizza is spiced with **green chilies** and **pepperoni**.

Serves 2–3

INGREDIENTS
1 pizza base, about 10–12 in
    diameter
1 tbsp olive oil
4 oz can peeled and chopped green
    chilies in brine, drained
1 quantity Tomato Sauce
3 oz sliced pepperoni
6 pitted black olives
1 tbsp chopped fresh oregano
4 oz mozzarella, grated
oregano leaves, to garnish

mozzarella

oregano

Tomato Sauce

pepperoni

olive oil

green chillies

black olives

1 Preheat the oven to 425°F. Brush the pizza base with the oil.

2 Stir the chilies into the sauce, and spread over the base.

3 Sprinkle the pepperoni over.

4 Halve the olives lengthwise and sprinkle over, with the oregano.

5 Sprinkle the grated mozzarella over and bake for 15–20 minutes until the pizza is crisp and golden.

VARIATION

You can make this pizza as hot as you like. For a really fiery version use fresh red or green chilies, cut into thin slices, in place of the chilies in brine.

6 Garnish with oregano leaves and serve immediately.

Prosciutto, Mushroom and Artichoke

Here is a pizza full of rich and varied flavors. For a delicious variation use mixed cultivated mushrooms.

Serves 2–3

INGREDIENTS
1 bunch scallions
4 tbsp olive oil
8 oz mushrooms, sliced
2 garlic cloves, chopped
1 pizza base, about 10–12 in
 diameter
8 slices prosciutto
4 bottled artichoke hearts in oil,
 drained and sliced
4 tbsp freshly grated Parmesan
salt and black pepper
thyme sprigs, to garnish

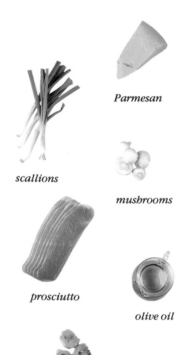

Parmesan

scallions

mushrooms

prosciutto

olive oil

artichoke hearts

1 Preheat the oven to 425°F. Trim the scallions, then chop all the white and some of the green stems.

2 Heat 2 tbsp of the oil in a frying pan. Add the scallions, mushrooms and garlic and fry over a moderate heat until all the juices have evaporated. Season and let cool.

3 Brush the pizza base with half the remaining oil. Arrange the prosciutto, mushrooms and artichoke hearts on top.

4 Sprinkle the Parmesan over, then drizzle the remaining oil over and season. Bake for 15–20 minutes. Garnish with thyme sprigs and serve immediately.

Sausage and Parsley

The combination of spicy chorizo and sweet, tender corn works well in this hearty and colorful pizza. For a simple variation you could use chopped fresh basil instead of Italian parsley.

Serves 2–3

INGREDIENTS
1 pizza base, about 10–12 in
   diameter
1 tbsp garlic oil
1 quantity Tomato Sauce
6 oz chorizo sausages
6 oz (drained weight) canned corn
   kernels
2 tbsp chopped fresh Italian
   parsley
2 oz mozzarella, grated
2 tbsp freshly grated Parmesan

Tomato Sauce

mozzarella

Italian parsley

Garlic Oil

chorizo sausages

Parmesan

sweetcorn

1 Preheat the oven to 425°F. Brush the pizza base with Garlic Oil and spread over the Tomato Sauce.

2 Skin and cut the chorizo sausages into chunks and scatter over the Tomato Sauce. Bake for 10 minutes then remove from the oven.

3 Sprinkle over the corn and Italian parsley.

4 Mix together the mozzarella and Parmesan and sprinkle over. Bake for a further 5–10 minutes until crisp and golden. Serve immediately.

Chicken, Shiitake Mushroom and Cilantro

The addition of shiitake mushrooms adds an earthy flavor to this colorful pizza, while fresh red chili provides a hint of spiciness.

Serves 3–4

INGREDIENTS

3 tbsp olive oil
12 oz chicken breast fillets, skinned and cut into thin strips
1 bunch scallions, sliced
1 fresh red chili, seeded and chopped
1 red bell pepper, seeded and cut into thin strips
3 oz fresh shiitake mushrooms, wiped and sliced
3–4 tbsp chopped fresh cilantro
1 pizza base, about 10–12 in diameter
1 tbsp chili oil
5 oz mozzarella
salt and black pepper

chicken breast fillets

scallions

red chili

cilantro

red bell pepper

olive oil

Chili Oil

shiitake mushrooms

1 Preheat the oven to 425°F. Heat 2 tbsp of the olive oil in a wok or large frying pan. Add the chicken, scallions, chili, pepper and mushrooms and stir-fry over a high heat for 2–3 minutes until the chicken is firm but still slightly pink within. Season to taste.

2 Pour off any excess oil, then set aside the chicken mixture to cool.

3 Stir the fresh cilantro into the chicken mixture.

4 Brush the pizza base with the chili oil.

5 Spoon the chicken mixture over and drizzle the remaining olive oil over.

6 Grate the mozzarella and sprinkle over. Bake for 15–20 minutes until crisp and golden. Serve immediately.

Pancetta, Leek and Smoked Mozzarella

Smoked mozzarella with its brownish smoky-flavored skin, pancetta and leeks make this an extremely tasty and easy-to-prepare pizza, ideal for a light lunch.

Serves 4

INGREDIENTS
2 tbsp freshly grated Parmesan
1 quantity Basic or Superquick Pizza
 Dough
2 tbsp olive oil
2 medium leeks
8–12 slices pancetta
5 oz smoked mozzarella
black pepper

pancetta

leeks

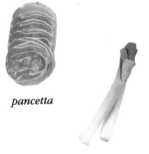
smoked mozzarella

olive oil

Parmesan

1 Preheat the oven to 425°F. Dust the work surface with the Parmesan, then knead into the dough. Divide the dough into four pieces and roll out each one to a 5 in circle. Place well apart on two greased baking sheets, then pinch up the edges to make a thin rim. Brush with 1 tbsp of the oil.

2 Trim and thinly slice the leeks.

3 Arrange the pancetta and leeks on the pizza bases.

4 Grate the smoked mozzarella and sprinkle over. Drizzle the remaining oil over and season with black pepper. Bake for 15–20 minutes until crisp and golden. Serve immediately.

Ham and Mozzarella Calzone

A calzone is a kind of "inside-out" pizza – the dough is on the outside and the filling on the inside. For a vegetarian version replace the ham with sautéed mushrooms or chopped cooked spinach.

Serves 2

INGREDIENTS
1 quantity Basic or Superquick Pizza
   Dough
4 oz ricotta
2 tbsp freshly grated Parmesan
1 egg yolk
2 tbsp chopped fresh basil
3 oz cooked ham, finely chopped
3 oz mozzarella, cut into small cubes
olive oil for brushing
salt and black pepper

basil

ricotta

egg

mozzarella

Parmesan

cooked ham

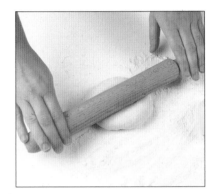

1 Preheat the oven to 425°F. Divide the dough in to two pieces and roll out each piece on a lightly floured surface to a 7 in circle.

2 In a bowl mix together the ricotta, Parmesan, egg yolk, basil and seasoning.

3 Spread the mixture over half of each circle, leaving a 1 in border, then scatter the ham and mozzarella on top. Dampen the edges with water, then fold over the other half of dough to enclose the filling.

4 Press the edges firmly together to seal. Place on two greased baking sheets. Brush with oil and make a small hole in the top of each to allow the steam to escape. Bake for 15–20 minutes until golden. Serve immediately.

Smoked Chicken, Yellow Pepper and Sun-dried Tomato Pizzettes

These ingredients complement each other perfectly and make a really delicious topping.

Serves 4

INGREDIENTS
1 quantity Basic or Superquick Pizza
   Dough
3 tbsp olive oil
4 tbsp sun-dried tomato paste
2 yellow bell peppers, seeded and cut
   into thin strips
6 oz sliced smoked chicken or turkey,
   chopped
5 oz mozzarella, cubed
2 tbsp chopped fresh basil
salt and black pepper

basil

mozzarella

yellow bell peppers

olive oil

smoked chicken

sun-dried tomato paste

1 Preheat the oven to 425°F. Divide the dough into four pieces and roll out each one on a lightly floured surface to a 5 in circle. Place well apart on two greased baking sheets, then pinch up the dough edges to make a thin rim. Brush with 1 tbsp of the oil.

2 Brush the pizza bases generously with the sun-dried tomato paste.

3 Stir-fry the peppers in half the remaining oil for 3–4 minutes.

4 Arrange the chicken and peppers on top of the sun-dried tomato paste.

5 Scatter the mozzarella and basil over. Season with salt and black pepper.

VARIATION

For a vegetarian pizza with a similar smoky taste, omit the chicken, roast the yellow peppers and remove the skins before using, and replace the mozzarella with Gouda smoked cheese.

6 Drizzle over the remaining oil and bake for 15–20 minutes until crisp and golden. Serve immediately.

Caramelized Onion, Salami and Black Olive

The flavor of the sweet caramelized onion is enhanced by the salty black olives and the mixed herbs in the pizza base and the sprinkling of Parmesan to finish.

Serves 4

INGREDIENTS
1½ lb red onions
4 tbsp olive oil
12 pitted black olives
1 quantity Basic or Superquick Pizza Dough
1 teaspoon dried mixed herbs
6–8 slices Italian salami, quartered
2–3 tbsp freshly grated Parmesan
black pepper

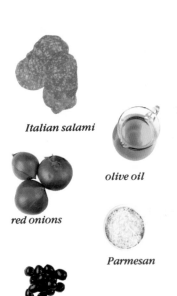

Italian salami

olive oil

red onions

Parmesan

black olives

mixed herbs

1 Preheat the oven to 425°F. Thinly slice the onions.

2 Heat 2 tbsp of the oil in a pan and add the onions. Cover and cook gently for 15–20 minutes, stirring occasionally until the onions are soft and very lightly colored. Leave to cool.

3 Finely chop the black olives.

4 Knead the dough on a lightly floured surface, adding the black olives and the herbs. Roll out the dough and use to line a 12 x 7 inch Swiss-roll pan. Push up the dough edges to make a thin rim and brush with half the remaining oil.

5 Spoon half the onions over the base, top with the salami and the remaining onions.

6 Grind over plenty of black pepper and drizzle over the remaining oil. Bake for 15–20 minutes until crisp and golden. Remove from the oven and sprinkle the Parmesan over to serve.

Zucchini, Corn and Plum Tomato Whole-wheat Pizza

This tasty whole-wheat pizza can be served hot or cold with a mixed bean salad and fresh crusty bread or baked potatoes. It is also ideal as a snack for the road.

Serves 6

INGREDIENTS
2 cups whole-wheat flour
pinch of salt
2 teaspoons baking powder
¼ cup polyunsaturated margarine
⅔ cup skim milk
2 tablespoons tomato paste
2 teaspoons dried *herbes de Provence*
2 teaspoons olive oil
1 onion, sliced
1 garlic clove, crushed
2 small zucchini, sliced
1½ cups mushrooms, sliced
⅔ cup frozen corn kernels
2 plum tomatoes, sliced
½ cup reduced-fat Cheddar cheese, finely grated
½ cup mozzarella cheese, finely grated
salt and ground black pepper
basil sprigs, to garnish

whole-wheat flour

salt

baking powder

dried herbes de Provence

olive oil

onion

zucchini

mushrooms

plum tomatoes

corn

reduced-fat Cheddar cheese

mozzarella cheese

garlic

polyunsaturated margarine

skim milk

tomato paste

1 Preheat the oven to 425°F. Line a baking sheet with nonstick baking paper. Put the flour, salt and baking powder in a bowl and rub the margarine lightly into the flour until the mixture resembles bread crumbs.

2 Add enough milk to form a soft dough and knead lightly. On a lightly floured surface, roll the dough out to a circle about 10 inches in diameter.

3 Place the dough on the prepared baking sheet and pinch the edges until they are slightly thicker than the center. Spread the tomato paste over the base and sprinkle the herbs on top.

4 Heat the oil in a frying pan, add the onion, garlic, zucchini and mushrooms and cook gently, stirring occasionally, for 10 minutes.

5 Spread the vegetable mixture over the pizza crust and sprinkle with the corn and seasoning. Arrange the tomato slices on top.

6 Mix together the cheeses and sprinkle over the pizza. Bake for 25–30 minutes, until the pizza is cooked and golden brown. Serve hot or cold in slices, garnished with basil sprigs.

COOK'S TIP
This pizza is ideal for freezing in portions or slices. Freeze for up to three months.

Pan-baked Pepperoni Pizza

This pizza is made using a scone base which happily does not require proving! The topping can be varied to include whatever you like best – tunafish, shrimp, ham or salami are all good alternatives to the pepperoni.

Serves 2–3

INGREDIENTS
1 tbsp chopped fresh mixed herbs
1 quantity Scone Pizza Dough
2 tbsp tomato paste
14 oz can crushed tomatoes, drained well
2 oz mushrooms, thinly sliced
3 oz sliced pepperoni
6 pitted black olives, chopped
2 oz Edam, grated
2 oz sharp Cheddar, grated
1 tbsp chopped fresh basil, to garnish

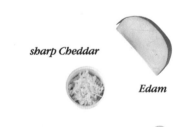
sharp Cheddar

Edam

chopped tomatoes

mushrooms

black olives
basil
fresh mixed herbs

pepperoni
tomato paste

1 Add the herbs to the scone mix before mixing to a soft dough.

2 Turn the dough on to a lightly floured surface and knead lightly until smooth. Roll out to fit a well-greased frying pan, about 8½ in diameter.

3 Cook the dough in the pan over a low heat for about 5 minutes until the base is golden. Lift carefully with a spatula to check.

4 Turn the base on to a baking sheet, then slide it back into the pan, with the cooked side uppermost.

5 Mix together the tomato paste and drained tomatoes and spread over the pizza base. Scatter over the mushrooms, pepperoni, olives and cheeses. Continue to cook for about 5 minutes until the underside is golden.

6 When it is ready, transfer the pan to a preheated moderate broiler for 4–5 minutes to melt the cheese. Scatter the basil over and serve immediately.

Mixed Seafood

Here is a pizza that gives you the full flavor of the Mediterranean, ideal for a summer evening supper!

Serves 3–4

INGREDIENTS

1 pizza base, 10–12 in diameter
2 tbsp olive oil
1 quantity Tomato Sauce
14 oz mixed cooked seafood
  (including mussels, shrimp and squid)
3 garlic cloves
2 tbsp chopped fresh parsley
2 tbsp freshly grated Parmesan, to garnish

mixed seafood

olive oil

garlic

parsley

Tomato Sauce

Parmesan

1 Preheat the oven to 425°F. Brush the pizza base with 1 tbsp of the oil.

2 Spread the Tomato Sauce over. Bake in the oven for 10 minutes. Remove from the oven.

3 Pat the seafood dry using paper towels, then arrange on top.

4 Chop the garlic and sprinkle over.

5 Sprinkle the parsley over, then drizzle the remaining oil over.

VARIATION

If you prefer, this pizza can be made with mussels or shrimp on their own, or any combination of your favorite seafood.

6 Bake for a further 5–10 minutes until the seafood is warmed through and the base is crisp and golden. Sprinkle with Parmesan and serve immediately.

Salmon and Avocado

Smoked and fresh salmon make a delicious pizza topping when mixed with avocado. Smoked salmon trimmings are cheaper than smoked salmon slices and could be used instead.

Serves 3–4

INGREDIENTS
5 oz salmon fillet
½ cup dry white wine
1 pizza base, 10–12 in diameter
1 tbsp olive oil
14 oz can chopped tomatoes, drained well
4 oz mozzarella, grated
1 small avocado
2 tsp lemon juice
2 tbsp crème fraîche
3 oz smoked salmon, cut into strips
1 tbsp capers
2 tbsp chopped fresh chives, to garnish
black pepper

lemon

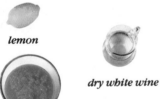

dry white wine

chopped tomatoes

mozzarella

avocado

smoked salmon

salmon fillet

crème fraîche

1 Preheat the oven to 425°F. Place the salmon fillet in a frying pan, pour the wine over and season with black pepper. Bring slowly to a boil, remove from the heat, cover and cool. (The fish will continue to cook in the cooling liquid.) Skin and flake the salmon into small pieces, removing any bones.

2 Brush the pizza base with the oil and spread over the drained tomatoes. Sprinkle 2 oz of the mozzarella over. Bake for 10 minutes, then remove from the oven.

3 Meanwhile, halve, pit and peel the avocado. Cut the flesh into small cubes and toss carefully in the lemon juice.

4 Dot teaspoonsful of the crème fraîche over the pizza base.

5 Arrange the fresh and smoked salmon, avocado, capers and remaining mozzarella on top. Season with black pepper. Bake for a further 5–10 minutes until crisp and golden.

6 Sprinkle the chives over and serve immediately.

Shrimp, Sun-dried Tomato and Basil Pizzettes

Sun-dried tomatoes with their concentrated caramelized tomato flavor make an excellent topping for pizzas. Serve these pretty pizzettes as an appetizer or snack.

Serves 4

INGREDIENTS

1 quantity Basic or Superquick Pizza
   Dough
2 tbsp chili oil
3 oz mozzarella, grated
1 garlic clove, chopped
½ small red onion, thinly sliced
4–6 pieces sun-dried tomatoes, thinly
   sliced
4 oz cooked shrimp, peeled
2 tbsp chopped fresh basil
salt and black pepper
shredded basil leaves, to garnish

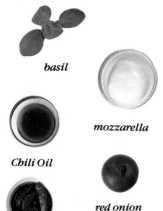

basil

mozzarella

Chili Oil

red onion

sun-dried tomatoes

garlic

1 Preheat the oven to 425°F. Divide the dough into eight pieces.

2 Roll out each one on a lightly floured surface to a small oval about ¼ in thick. Place well apart on two greased baking sheets. Prick all over with a fork.

3 Brush the pizza bases with 1 tbsp of the chili oil and top with the mozzarella, leaving a ½ in border.

4 Divide the garlic, onion, sun-dried tomatoes, shrimp and basil between the pizza bases. Season and drizzle the remaining chili oil over. Bake for 8–10 minutes until crisp and golden. Garnish with basil leaves and serve immediately.

Crab and Parmesan Calzonelli

These miniature calzone owe their popularity to their impressive presentation. If preferred, you can use shrimp instead of crab.

Makes 10–12

INGREDIENTS
1 quantity Basic or Superquick Pizza
   Dough
4 oz mixed prepared crabmeat,
   defrosted if frozen
1 tbsp heavy cream
2 tbsp freshly grated Parmesan
2 tbsp chopped fresh parsley
1 garlic clove, crushed
salt and black pepper
parsley sprigs, to garnish

Parmesan

heavy cream

crabmeat

parsley

garlic

1 Preheat the oven to 400°F. Roll out the dough on a lightly floured surface to ⅛ in thick. Using a 3 in plain round cutter stamp out 10–12 circles.

2 In a bowl mix together the crabmeat, cream, Parmesan, parsley, garlic and seasoning.

3 Spoon a little of the filling on to one half of each circle. Dampen the edges with water and fold over to enclose filling.

4 Seal the edges by pressing with a fork. Place well apart on two greased baking sheets. Bake for 10–15 minutes until golden. Garnish with parsley sprigs.

Mussel and Leek Pizzettes

Serve these tasty seafood pizzettes with a crisp green salad for a light lunch.

Serves 4

INGREDIENTS
1 lb live mussels
½ cup dry white wine
1 quantity Basic or Superquick Pizza
    Dough
1 tbsp olive oil
2 oz Gruyère
2 oz mozzarella
2 small leeks
salt and black pepper

olive oil

dry white wine

mozzarella

mussels

Gruyère

leeks

1 Preheat the oven to 425°F. Place the mussels in a bowl of cold water to soak, and scrub well. Remove the beards and discard any mussels that are open.

2 Place the mussels in a pan. Pour over the wine, cover and cook over a high heat, shaking the pan occasionally, for 5–10 minutes until the mussels have opened.

3 Drain off the cooking liquid. Remove the mussels from their shells, discarding any that remain closed. Leave to cool.

4 Divide the dough into four pieces and roll out each one on a lightly floured surface to a 5 in circle. Place well apart on two greased baking sheets, then pinch up the dough edges to form a thin rim. Brush the pizza bases with the oil. Grate the cheeses and sprinkle half evenly over the bases.

5 Thinly slice the leeks, then scatter over the cheese. Bake for 10 minutes, then remove from the oven.

VARIATION

Frozen or canned mussels can also be used, but will not have the same flavor and texture. Make sure you defrost the mussels properly.

6 Arrange the mussels on top. Season and sprinkle the remaining cheese over. Bake for a further 5–10 minutes until crisp and golden. Serve immediately.

Anchovy, Pepper and Tomato

This pretty, summery pizza is utterly simple, yet quite delicious. It's well worth broiling the peppers as they take on a subtle smoky flavor.

Serves 2–3

INGREDIENTS
6 plum tomatoes
3 tbsp olive oil
1 tsp salt
1 large red bell pepper
1 large yellow bell pepper
1 pizza base, 10–12 in diameter
2 garlic cloves, chopped
2 oz can anchovy fillets, drained
    and chopped
black pepper
basil leaves, to garnish

olive oil

*red and yellow
bell peppers*

plum tomatoes

garlic

anchovy fillets

1 Halve the tomatoes lengthwise and scoop out the seeds.

2 Coarsely chop the flesh and place in a bowl with 1 tbsp of the oil and the salt. Mix well, then leave to marinate for 30 minutes.

3 Meanwhile, preheat the oven to 425°F. Slice the peppers in half lengthwise and remove the seeds. Place the pepper halves, skin-side up, on a baking sheet and broil until the skins of the peppers are evenly charred.

4 Place the peppers in a covered bowl for 10 minutes, then peel off the skins. Cut the flesh into thin strips.

5 Brush the pizza base with half the remaining oil. Drain the tomatoes, then scatter over the base with the peppers and garlic.

6 Sprinkle on the anchovy fillets and season with black pepper. Drizzle over the remaining oil and bake for 15–20 minutes until crisp and golden. Garnish with basil leaves and serve immediately.

Tuna, Anchovy and Caper

This pizza makes a substantial supper dish which will provide two to three generous portions accompanied by a simple salad.

Serves 2–3

INGREDIENTS

1 quantity Scone Pizza Dough
2 tbsp olive oil
1 quantity Tomato Sauce
1 small red onion
7 oz can tuna, drained
1 tbsp capers
12 pitted black olives
3 tbsp freshly grated Parmesan
2 oz can anchovy fillets, drained and halved lengthways
black pepper

Tomato Sauce

olive oil

Parmesan

black olives

tuna

red onion

capers

1 Preheat the oven to 425°F. Roll out the dough on a lightly floured surface to a 10 in circle. Place on a greased baking sheet and brush with 1 tbsp of the oil. Spread the Tomato Sauce evenly over the dough.

2 Cut the onion into thin wedges and arrange on top.

3 Coarsely flake the tuna with a fork and scatter the onion over.

4 Sprinkle the capers, black olives and Parmesan over.

5 Lattice the anchovy fillets over the top of the pizza.

6 Drizzle the remaining oil over, then grind over plenty of black pepper. Bake for 15–20 minutes until crisp and golden. Serve immediately.

Roasted Vegetable and Goat Cheese

Here is a pizza which incorporates the smoky flavors of oven-roasted vegetables with the distinctive taste of goat cheese.

Serves 3

INGREDIENTS
1 eggplant, cut into thick chunks
2 small zucchini, sliced lengthwise
1 red bell pepper, quartered and seeded
1 yellow bell pepper, quartered and seeded
1 small red onion, cut into wedges
6 tbsp Garlic Oil
1 pizza base, 10–12 in diameter
1 × 14 oz can chopped tomatoes, drained well
1 × 4 oz goat cheese (with rind)
1 tbsp chopped fresh thyme
black pepper
green olive tapenade, to serve

zucchini

eggplant

goat cheese

Garlic Oil

tapenade

crushed tomatoes

red and yellow bell peppers

1 Preheat the oven to 425°F. Place the eggplant, zucchini, peppers and onion in a large roasting pan. Brush with 4 tbsp of the Garlic Oil. Roast for about 30 minutes until lightly charred, turning the peppers halfway through cooking. Remove from the oven and set aside.

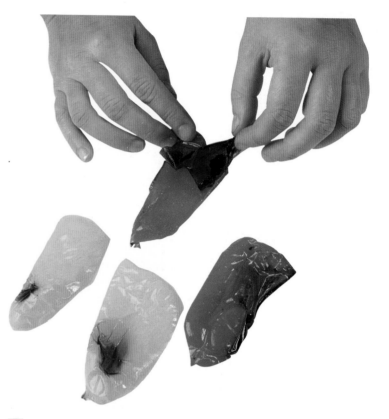

2 When the peppers are cool enough to handle, peel off the skins and cut the flesh into thick strips.

3 Brush the pizza base with half the remaining Garlic Oil and spread over the drained tomatoes.

4 Arrange the roasted vegetables on top of the pizza.

5 Cube the goat cheese and arrange on top. Scatter the thyme over.

COOK'S TIP
If you place the roasted peppers in a paper bag while they cool, peeling off the skins becomes easier.

6 Drizzle the remaining Garlic Oil over and season with black pepper. Bake for 15–20 minutes until crisp and golden. Spoon the tapenade over to serve.

New Potato, Rosemary and Garlic

New potatoes, smoked mozzarella, rosemary and garlic make the flavor of this pizza unique. For a delicious variation, use sage instead of rosemary.

Serves 2–3

INGREDIENTS
12 oz new potatoes
3 tbsp olive oil
2 garlic cloves, crushed
1 pizza base, 10–12 in diameter
1 red onion, thinly sliced
5 oz smoked mozzarella, grated
2 tsp chopped fresh rosemary
salt and black pepper
2 tbsp freshly grated Parmesan, to garnish

olive oil

Parmesan

new potatoes

smoked mozzarella

rosemary

red onion

garlic

I Preheat the oven to 425°F. Cook the potatoes in boiling salted water for 5 minutes. Drain well. When cool, peel and slice thinly.

2 Heat 2 tbsp of the oil in a frying pan. Add the sliced potatoes and garlic and fry for 5–8 minutes until tender.

3 Brush the pizza base with the remaining oil. Scatter the onion over, then arrange the potatoes on top.

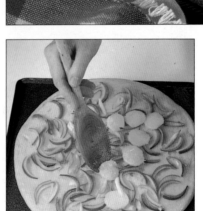

4 Sprinkle over the mozzarella and rosemary. Grind over plenty of black pepper and bake for 15–20 minutes until crisp and golden. Remove from the oven and sprinkle the Parmesan over to serve.

Wild Mushroom Pizzettes

Serve these extravagant pizzas as a side dish. Fresh wild mushrooms add a distinctive flavor to the topping but a mixture of cultivated mushrooms such as shiitake, oyster and chestnut mushrooms would do just as well.

Serves 4

INGREDIENTS

3 tbsp olive oil
12 oz fresh wild mushrooms, washed
   and sliced
2 shallots, chopped
2 garlic cloves, finely chopped
2 tbsp chopped fresh mixed thyme
   and Italian parsley
1 quantity Basic or Superquick Pizza
   Dough
1½ oz Gruyère, grated
2 tbsp freshly grated Parmesan
salt and black pepper

Gruyère

Italian parsley

olive oil

thyme

Parmesan

garlic   *shallots*

wild mushrooms

I Preheat the oven to 425°F. Heat 2 tbsp of the oil in a frying pan. Add the mushrooms, shallots and garlic and fry over a moderate heat until all the juices have evaporated.

2 Stir in half the herbs and seasoning, then set aside to cool.

3 Divide the dough into four pieces and roll out each one on a lightly floured surface to a 5 in circle. Place well apart on two greased baking sheets, then pinch up the dough edges to form a thin rim. Brush the pizza bases with the remaining oil and top with the wild mushroom mixture.

4 Mix together the Gruyère and Parmesan, then sprinkle over. Bake for 15–20 minutes until crisp and golden. Remove from the oven and sprinkle the remaining herbs over to serve.

Tomato, Pesto and Black Olive

These individual pizzas take very little time to put together. Marinating the tomatoes gives them extra flavor.

Serves 4

INGREDIENTS
2 plum tomatoes
1 garlic clove, crushed
4 tbsp olive oil
1 quantity Basic or Superquick Pizza
  Dough
2 tbsp red pesto
5 oz mozzarella, thinly sliced
4 pitted black olives, chopped
1 tbsp chopped fresh oregano
salt and black pepper
oregano leaves, to garnish

red pesto

mozzarella

oregano

plum tomatoes

black olives

1 Slice the tomatoes thinly crosswise, then cut each slice in half. Place the tomatoes in a shallow dish with the garlic. Drizzle 2 tbsp of the oil over and season. Let marinate for 15 minutes.

2 Meanwhile, preheat the oven to 425°F. Divide the dough into four pieces and roll out each one on a lightly floured surface to a 5 in circle. Place well apart on two greased baking sheets, then pinch up the dough edges to make a rim. Brush the pizza bases with half the remaining oil and spread over the pesto.

3 Drain the tomatoes, then arrange a fan of alternate slices of tomatoes and mozzarella on each base.

4 Sprinkle over the olives and oregano. Drizzle over the remaining oil on top and bake for 15–20 minutes until crisp and golden. Garnish with the oregano leaves and serve immediately.

Fresh Herb

Cut this pizza into thin wedges and serve as part of a mixed antipasti.

Serves 8

INGREDIENTS

4 oz mixed fresh herbs, such as
   parsley, basil and oregano
3 garlic cloves, crushed
½ cup heavy cream
1 pizza base, 10–12 in diameter
1 tbsp garlic oil
4 oz Pecorino, grated
salt and black pepper

1 Preheat the oven to 425°F. Chop the herbs in a food processor if you have one.

heavy cream

Garlic Oil

Pecorino

basil

parsley

garlic

2 In a bowl mix together the herbs, garlic, cream and seasoning.

3 Brush the pizza base with the Garlic Oil, then spread the herb mixture over.

4 Sprinkle the Pecorino over. Bake for 15–20 minutes until crisp and golden and the topping is still moist. Cut into thin wedges and serve immediately.

Eggplant, Shallot and Sun-dried Tomato Calzone

Eggplant, shallots and sun-dried tomatoes make an unusual filling for calzone. Add more or less red chili flakes, depending on personal taste.

Serves 2

INGREDIENTS

3 tbsp olive oil
3 shallots, chopped
4 baby eggplants
1 garlic clove, chopped
2 oz (drained weight) sun-dried
    tomatoes in oil, chopped
¼ tsp dried red chilli flakes
2 tsp chopped fresh thyme
1 quantity Basic or Superquick Pizza
    Dough
3 oz mozzarella, cubed
salt and black pepper
1–2 tbsp freshly grated Parmesan, to
    serve

Parmesan

mozzarella

thyme

olive oil

baby eggplants

shallots

red chili flakes

1 Preheat the oven to 425°F. Heat 2 tbsp of the oil in a frying pan. Add the shallots and cook until soft. Trim the eggplants, then cut into small cubes.

2 Add the eggplants to the shallots with the garlic, sun-dried tomatoes, red chili flakes, thyme and seasoning. Cook for 4–5 minutes, stirring frequently, until the eggplant is beginning to soften. Remove from the heat and let cool.

3 Divide the dough in half and roll out each piece on a lightly floured surface to a 7 in circle.

4 Spread the eggplant mixture over half of each circle, leaving a 1 in border, then scatter the mozzarella over.

5 Dampen the edges with water, then fold over the other half of dough to enclose the filling. Press the edges firmly together to seal. Place on two greased baking sheets.

6 Brush with half the remaining oil and make a small hole in the top of each to allow the steam to escape. Bake for 15–20 minutes until golden. Remove from the oven and brush with the remaining oil. Sprinkle the Parmesan over and serve immediately.

Tomato, Fennel and Parmesan

This pizza relies on the winning combination of tomatoes, fennel and Parmesan. The fennel adds both a crisp texture and a distinctive flavor.

Serves 2–3

INGREDIENTS
1 fennel bulb
3 tbsp garlic oil
1 pizza base, 10–12 in diameter
1 quantity Tomato Sauce
2 tbsp chopped fresh Italian parsley
2 oz mozzarella, grated
2 oz Parmesan, grated
salt and black pepper

Italian parsley

mozzarella

Parmesan

Tomato Sauce

fennel bulb

Garlic Oil

1 Preheat the oven to 425°F. Trim and quarter the fennel lengthwise. Remove the core and slice each quarter of fennel thinly.

2 Heat 2 tbsp of the Garlic Oil in a frying pan and sauté the fennel for 4–5 minutes until just tender. Season.

3 Brush the pizza base with the remaining Garlic Oil and spread over the Tomato Sauce. Spoon the fennel on top and scatter the Italian parsley over.

4 Mix together the mozzarella and Parmesan and sprinkle over. Bake for 15–20 minutes until crisp and golden. Serve immediately.

Red Onion, Gorgonzola and Sage

This topping combines the richness of Gorgonzola with the earthy flavors of sage and sweet red onions.

Serves 4

INGREDIENTS
1 quantity Basic or Superquick Pizza
  Dough
2 tbsp garlic oil
2 small red onions
5 oz Gorgonzola
2 garlic cloves
2 tsp chopped fresh sage
black pepper

sage

Gorgonzola

garlic

Garlic Oil

red onions

1 Preheat the oven to 425°F. Divide the dough into eight pieces and roll out each one on a lightly floured surface to a small oval about ¼ in thick. Place well apart on two greased baking sheets and prick with a fork. Brush the bases of each oval well with 1 tbsp of the Garlic Oil.

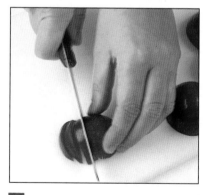

2 Halve, then slice the onions into thin wedges. Scatter over the pizza bases.

3 Remove the rind from the Gorgonzola. Cut the cheese into small cubes, then scatter it over the onions.

4 Cut the garlic lengthwise into thin strips and sprinkle over, along with the sage. Drizzle the remaining oil on top and grind over plenty of black pepper. Bake for 10–15 minutes until crisp and golden. Serve immediately.

Onion and Three Cheese

You can use any combination of cheese you like. Edam and Cheddar both have good flavors and melting properties.

Serves 3–4

INGREDIENTS
3 tbsp olive oil
3 medium onions, sliced
1 pizza base, 10–12 in diameter
4 small tomatoes, peeled, seeded and
    cut into thin wedges
2 tbsp chopped fresh basil
4 oz Saga Blue
5 oz mozzarella
4 oz Red Leicester
black pepper
fresh basil leaves, to garnish

tomatoes

basil

mozzarella

Red Leicester

Saga Blue

olive oil

onions

1 Preheat the oven to 425°F. Heat 2 tbsp of the oil in a frying pan, add the onions and gently fry for about 10 minutes, stirring occasionally. Remove from the heat and let cool.

2 Brush the pizza base with the remaining oil. Spoon the onions and tomatoes over, then scatter the basil leaves over.

3 Thinly slice the cheeses and arrange over the tomatoes and onions.

4 Grind over plenty of black pepper and bake for 15–20 minutes until crisp and golden. Garnish with basil leaves and serve immediately.

Roasted Garlic and Oregano

This is a pizza for garlic lovers! Mash down the cloves as you eat – they should be soft and will have lost their pungency.

Serves 4

INGREDIENTS
1 medium garlic head, unpeeled
3 tbsp olive oil
1 medium red bell pepper, quartered
   and seeded
1 medium yellow bell pepper,
   quartered and seeded
2 plum tomatoes
1 quantity Basic or Superquick Pizza
   Dough
6 oz feta, crumbled
black pepper
1–2 tbsp chopped fresh oregano, to
   garnish

oregano

feta

plum tomatoes

olive oil

*red and yellow
bell peppers*

garlic head

1 Preheat the oven to 425°F. Break the head of garlic into cloves, discarding the outer papery layers. Toss in 1 tbsp of the oil.

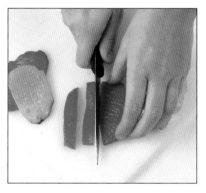

2 Place the peppers skin-side up on a baking sheet and broil until the skins are evenly charred. Place in a covered bowl for 10 minutes, then peel off the skins. Cut the flesh into strips.

3 Put the tomatoes in a bowl and pour boiling water over. Leave for 30 seconds, then plunge into cold water. Peel, seed and coarsely chop the flesh. Divide the dough into four pieces and roll out each one on a lightly floured surface to a 5 in circle.

4 Place the dough circles well apart on two greased baking sheets, then pinch up the dough edges to form a thin rim. Brush with half the remaining oil and scatter the chopped tomatoes over. Top with the peppers, crumbled feta and garlic cloves. Drizzle over the remaining oil and season with black pepper. Bake for 15–20 minutes until crisp and golden. Garnish with chopped oregano and serve immediately.

Spring Vegetable and Pine Nuts

This colorful pizza is well worth the time it takes to prepare. You can vary the ingredients according to availability.

Serves 2–3

INGREDIENTS
1 pizza base, 10–12 in diameter
3 tbsp Garlic Oil
1 quantity Tomato Sauce
4 scallions
2 zucchini
1 leek
4 oz asparagus tips
1 tbsp chopped fresh oregano
2 tbsp pine nuts
2 oz mozzarella, grated
2 tbsp freshly grated Parmesan
black pepper

Parmesan

mozzarella

Tomato Sauce

scallions

leek

zucchini

asparagus

pine nuts

1 Preheat the oven to 425°F. Brush the pizza base with 1 tbsp of the Garlic Oil, then spread the Tomato Sauce over.

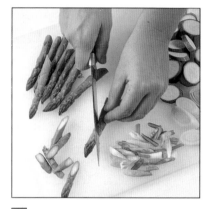

2 Slice the scallions, zucchini, leek and asparagus.

3 Heat half the remaining Garlic Oil in a frying pan and stir-fry the vegetables for 3–5 minutes.

4 Arrange the vegetables over the Tomato Sauce.

5 Sprinkle the oregano and pine nuts over the pizza.

6 Mix together the mozzarella and Parmesan and sprinkle over. Drizzle the remaining Garlic Oil over and season with black pepper. Bake for 15–20 minutes until crisp and golden. Serve immediately.

Spinach and Ricotta Panzerotti

These make great party food to serve with drinks or as tasty appetizers for a crowd.

Makes 20–24

INGREDIENTS
4 oz frozen chopped spinach,
    defrosted and squeezed dry
2 oz ricotta
2 oz freshly grated Parmesan
generous pinch freshly grated nutmeg
2 quantities Basic or Superquick Pizza
    Dough
1 egg white, lightly beaten
vegetable oil for deep-frying
salt and black pepper

nutmeg

ricotta

vegetable oil

egg

frozen spinach

Parmesan

1 Place the spinach, ricotta, Parmesan, nutmeg and seasoning in a bowl and beat until smooth.

2 Roll out the dough on a lightly floured surface to about ⅛ in thick. Using a 3 in plain round cutter stamp out 20–24 circles.

3 Spread a teaspoon of spinach mixture over one half of each circle.

4 Brush the edges of the dough with a little egg white.

5 Fold the dough over the filling and press the edges firmly together to seal.

COOK'S TIP
Do serve these as soon as possible after frying, they will become much less appetizing if left to cool.

6 Heat the oil in a large heavy-based pan or deep-fat fryer to 350°F. Deep-fry the panzerotti a few at a time for 2–3 minutes until golden. Drain on paper towels and serve immediately.

Feta, Pimiento and Pine Nut

Delight your guests with these tempting pizzas. Substitute goat cheese for the feta if you prefer.

Makes 24

INGREDIENTS
2 quantities Basic or Superquick Pizza
   Dough
4 tbsp olive oil
2 tbsp black olive tapenade
6 oz feta
1 large canned pimiento, drained
2 tbsp chopped fresh thyme
2 tbsp pine nuts
black pepper
thyme sprigs, to garnish

pimiento

thyme

feta cheese

tapenade

pine nuts

1 Preheat the oven to 425°F. Divide the dough into 24 pieces and roll out each one on a lightly floured surface to a small oval, about ⅛ in thick. Place the ovals, well apart, on greased baking sheets and prick all over with a fork. Brush each one with 2 tbsp of the oil.

2 Spread a thin layer of the black olive tapenade on each oval and crumble the feta over.

3 Cut the pimiento into thin strips and pile on top.

4 Sprinkle each one with thyme and pine nuts. Drizzle the remaining oil over and grind over plenty of black pepper. Bake for 10–15 minutes until crisp and golden. Garnish with thyme sprigs and serve immediately.

Sun-dried Tomatoes, Basil and Olive Pizza Bites

This quick and easy recipe uses scone pizza dough with the addition of chopped fresh basil.

Makes 24

INGREDIENTS
18–20 fresh basil leaves
1 quantity Scone Pizza Dough
2 tbsp tomato oil (from jar of sun-dried tomatoes)
1 quantity Tomato Sauce
4 oz (drained weight) sun-dried tomatoes in oil, chopped
10 pitted black olives, chopped
2 oz mozzarella, grated
2 tbsp freshly grated Parmesan
shredded basil leaves, to garnish

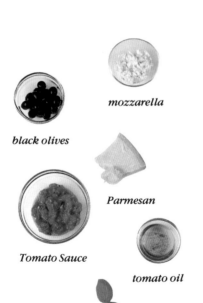

mozzarella

black olives

Parmesan

Tomato Sauce

tomato oil

basil

sun-dried tomatoes

1 Preheat the oven to 425°F. Tear the basil leaves into small pieces. Add half to the scone mix before mixing to a soft dough. Set aside the remainder.

2 Knead the dough gently on a lightly floured surface until smooth. Roll out and use to line a 12 × 7 in jelly roll pan. Pinch up the edges to make a thin rim.

3 Brush the base with 1 tbsp of the tomato oil, then spread the Tomato Sauce over. Scatter the sun-dried tomatoes, olives and remaining basil over.

4 Mix together the mozzarella and Parmesan and sprinkle over. Drizzle the remaining tomato oil over. Bake for about 20 minutes. Cut lengthwise and across into 24 bite-size pieces. Garnish with extra shredded basil leaves and serve immediately.

Farmhouse Pizza

This is the ultimate party pizza. Served cut into fingers, it is ideal for a crowd.

Serves 8

INGREDIENTS
6 tbsp olive oil
8 oz mushrooms, sliced
2 quantities Basic or Superquick Pizza
   Dough
1 quantity Tomato Sauce
10 oz mozzarella, thinly sliced
4 oz paper-thin smoked ham slices
6 bottled artichoke hearts in oil,
   drained and sliced
2 oz can anchovy fillets, drained and
   halved lengthwise
10 pitted black olives, halved
2 tbsp chopped fresh oregano
3 tbsp freshly grated Parmesan
black pepper

anchovy fillets

mozzarella

artichoke hearts

smoked ham

olive oil

Tomato Sauce

black olives

mushrooms

1 Preheat the oven to 425°F. Heat 2 tbsp of the oil in a large frying pan, add the mushrooms and fry for about 5 minutes until all the juices have evaporated. Leave to cool.

2 Roll out the dough on a lightly floured surface to a 12 × 10 in rectangle. Transfer to a greased baking sheet, then pinch up the dough edges to make a thin rim. Brush the dough with 2 tbsp of the oil.

3 Spread the Tomato Sauce over.

4 Arrange the sliced mozzarella over the sauce.

5 Scrunch up the ham and arrange on top with the artichoke hearts, mushrooms and anchovies.

6 Dot with the olives, then sprinkle the oregano and Parmesan over. Drizzle over the remaining oil and season with black pepper. Bake for about 25 minutes until crisp and golden. Serve immediately.

Quick Seafood Pizza

Make four mini pizzas or one large one with the same quantities of ingredients. The larger one will take about 40 minutes to cook. If you are really running out of time, use a pizza-base mix instead of making the dough.

Serves 4

INGREDIENTS
For the pizza base
1 tsp quick-blend yeast
1 tbsp sugar
1¼ cups lukewarm
  water
2 tbsp extra virgin olive oil
1 tsp sea salt
4 cups plain unbleached
  flour

For the fish topping
1 tbsp olive oil
1 onion, finely chopped
1¾ lb canned or fresh plum tomatoes,
  chopped
salt and freshly ground black pepper
1 tbsp fresh chopped thyme
12 fresh anchovies or 1 can anchovies,
  drained
fresh, peeled shrimp
4 oz cherry tomatoes, halved
a few sprigs of fresh thyme, to garnish

anchovies

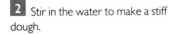

plum tomatoes

shrimp

cherry tomatoes

1 Stir the yeast into the flour and mix well. Add the sugar, salt and olive oil.

2 Stir in the water to make a stiff dough.

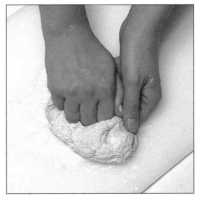

3 Knead the dough for about 10 minutes. Cover and leave in a warm place to double in size.

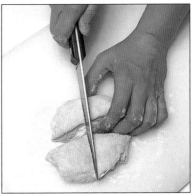

4 Punch down the dough and knead for 5 minutes, then cut the dough into four. Shape into four 5 in circles. Pre-heat the oven to 400°F.

5 Fry the onions until soft. Add the canned tomatoes, seasoning and thyme and simmer for 15 minutes.

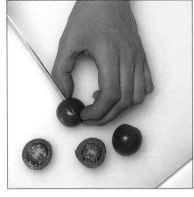

6 Meanwhile cut the cherry tomatoes in half. Assemble the pizza with a spoonful of the sauce, a couple of anchovies and shrimp and the cherry tomatoes. Bake for 20 minutes until golden and crispy. Scatter a few fresh sprigs of thyme on top to serve.

VARIATION
Add your favorite seafood such as fresh or canned mussels to the topping.

Barbecued Goat Cheese

Pizzas cooked on the barbecue have a beautifully crisp and golden base.

Serves 4

5 oz package pizza dough mix
olive oil for brushing
²/₃ cup crushed tomatoes
2 tbsp red pesto sauce
1 small red onion, thinly sliced
8 cherry tomatoes, halved
4 oz firm goat's cheese, thinly
  sliced
handful chopped fresh basil
  leaves
salt and freshly ground black
  pepper

crushed tomatoes

pizza dough mix

goat's cheese

red pesto sauce

red onion

basil

cherry tomatoes

COOK'S TIP

If the pizza starts to brown too much underneath, raise the grill rack away from the fire, or slip a piece of foil under the pizza, to slow down the cooking.

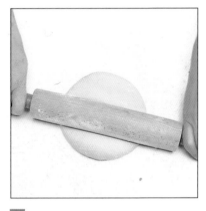

1 Make up the pizza dough, according to package directions. Roll out to a round of about a 10-in diameter.

2 Brush the dough with oil and place, oiled-side down, on a medium-hot barbecue. Cook for about 6–8 minutes, until firm and golden underneath.

3 Brush the top of the dough with oil and turn the dough over, to cook the other side.

4 Mix together the crushed tomatoes and pesto sauce and quickly spread over the cooked side of the pizza, to within about ¹/₂ in of the edge.

5 Arrange the onion, tomatoes and cheese slices on top and sprinkle with salt and pepper.

6 Cook the pizza for 8–10 minutes more, or until the dough is golden brown and crisp. Sprinkle with chopped basil and serve.

VEGETARIAN MEALS AND SIDE DISHES

Vegetables have always played a big part in Italian cooking, particularly in the south of the country where meat used to be considered a luxury. The true flavor of the Mediterranean is captured in dishes such as Frittata with Sun-dried Tomatoes and Grilled Mediterranean Vegetables with Marbled Yogurt Pesto.

Potato Gnocchi with Hazelnut Sauce

These delicate potato dumplings are dressed with a creamy hazelnut sauce.

Serves 4

INGREDIENTS
1½ lb large potatoes
1 cup plain flour

FOR THE HAZELNUT SAUCE
½ cup skinned, roasted hazelnuts
1 garlic clove, roughly chopped
½ tsp grated lemon rind
½ tsp lemon juice
2 tbsp sunflower oil
scant ¾ cup low-fat ricotta cheese
salt and freshly ground black pepper

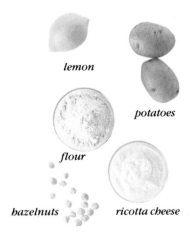

lemon

potatoes

flour

hazelnuts *ricotta cheese*

garlic

1 Place ⅓ cup of the hazelnuts in a blender with the garlic, grated lemon rind and juice. Blend until coarsely chopped. Gradually add the oil and blend until smooth. Spoon into a bowl and mix in the ricotta cheese. Season to taste.

2 Place the potatoes in a pan of cold water. Bring to the boil and cook for 20–25 minutes. Drain well in a colander.

When cool, peel and purée the potatoes while still warm by passing them through a food mill into a bowl.

3 Add the flour a little at a time (you may not need all the flour as potatoes vary in texture). Stop adding flour when the mixture is smooth and slightly sticky. Add salt to taste.

4 Roll out the mixture onto a floured board, into a long sausage about ½ in in diameter. Cut into ¾ in lengths.

5 Take 1 piece at a time and press it on to a floured fork. Roll each piece slightly while pressing it along the prongs and off the fork. Flip onto a floured plate or tray. Continue with the rest of the mixture.

COOK'S TIP

A light touch is the key to making soft gnocchi, so handle the dough as little as possible to prevent the mixture from becoming tough.

6 Bring a large pan of water to a boil and drop in 20–25 pieces at a time. They will rise to the surface very quickly. Let them cook for 10–15 seconds more, then lift them out with a slotted spoon. Drop into a dish and keep warm. Continue with the rest of the gnocchi. To heat the sauce, place in a heatproof bowl over a pot of simmering water and heat gently, being careful not to let the sauce curdle. Pour the sauce over the gnocchi. Roughly chop the remaining hazelnuts and scatter over the sauce.

Zucchini and Asparagus en Papillote

An impressive dinner party accompaniment, these puffed paper parcels should be broken open at the table by each guest, so that the wonderful aroma can be fully appreciated.

Serves 4

INGREDIENTS

2 medium zucchini
1 medium leek
8 oz young asparagus, trimmed
4 tarragon sprigs
4 whole garlic cloves, unpeeled
salt and freshly ground black pepper
1 egg, beaten

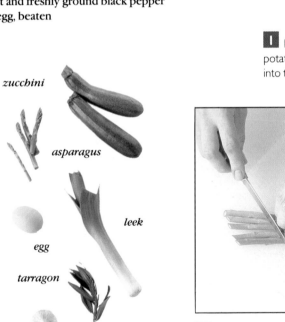

zucchini

asparagus

leek

egg

tarragon

garlic

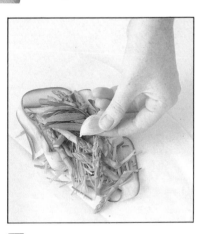

1 Preheat the oven to 400°F. Using a potato peeler slice the zucchini lengthwise into thin strips.

2 Cut the leek into very fine julienne strips and cut the asparagus evenly into 2 in lengths.

3 Cut out 4 sheets of parchment paper 12 × 15 in in size and fold each in half. Draw a large curve to make a heart shape when unfolded. Cut along the inside of the line and open out.

4 Divide the zucchini, asparagus and leek evenly between each paper heart, positioning the filling on one side of the fold line, and topping each with a sprig of tarragon and an unpeeled garlic clove. Season to taste.

COOK'S TIP

Experiment with other vegetables and
herbs such as sugar-snap peas and
mint or baby carrots and rosemary.
The possibilities are endless.

5 Brush the edges lightly with the
beaten egg and fold over.

6 Pleat the edges together so that each
parcel is completely sealed. Lay the
parcels on a cookie sheet and cook for 10
minutes. Serve immediately.

Pumpkin and Pistachio Risotto

This elegant combination of creamy golden rice and orange pumpkin can be as pale or bright as you like by adding different quantities of saffron.

Serves 4

INGREDIENTS

5 cups fresh vegetable stock or water
generous pinch of saffron threads
2 tbsp olive oil
1 medium onion, chopped
2 garlic cloves, crushed
1 lb arborio rice
2 lb pumpkin, peeled, seeded and cut
   into ¾ in cubes
¾ cup dry white wine
½ oz Parmesan cheese, finely grated
½ cup pistachios
3 tbsp chopped fresh marjoram or
   oregano, plus extra leaves, to
   garnish
salt, freshly grated nutmeg and ground
   black pepper

1 Bring the stock or water to a boil and reduce to a low simmer. Ladle a little stock into a small bowl. Add the saffron threads and leave to infuse.

2 Heat the oil in a large saucepan. Add the onion and garlic and cook gently for about 5 minutes until softened. Add the rice and pumpkin and cook for a few more minutes until the rice looks transparent.

3 Pour in the wine and allow it to boil hard. When it is absorbed add ¼ of the stock and the infused saffron and liquid. Stir constantly until all the liquid is absorbed.

4 Gradually add the stock or water, a ladleful at a time, allowing the rice to absorb the liquid before adding more and stirring all the time. After 20–30 minutes the rice should be golden yellow and creamy, and *al dente* when tested.

saffron

pumpkin

white wine

onion

garlic

marjoram

Parmesan

arborio rice

pistachios

5 Stir in the Parmesan cheese, cover the pan and leave to stand for 5 minutes.

6 To finish, stir in the pistachios and marjoram or oregano. Season to taste with a little salt, nutmeg and pepper, and scatter over a few extra marjoram or oregano leaves.

COOK'S TIP
Italian arborio rice must be used to make an authentic risotto. Choose unpolished white arborio as it contains more starch.

Caponata

Caponata is a quintessential part of Sicilian antipasti and is a rich, spicy mixture of eggplants, tomatoes, capers and celery.

Serves 4

INGREDIENTS
4 tbsp olive oil
1 large onion, sliced
2 celery stalks, sliced
1 lb eggplant, diced
5 ripe tomatoes, chopped
1 garlic clove, crushed
3 tbsp red wine vinegar
1 tbsp sugar
2 tbsp capers
12 olives
pinch of salt
4 tbsp chopped fresh parsley,
    to garnish
warm crusty bread, to serve
olives, to serve

celery

eggplants

onion

tomatoes

olives

capers

1 Heat half the oil in a large heavy saucepan. Add the onion and celery and cook over a gentle heat for about 3–4 minutes to soften.

2 Add the remainder of the oil with the eggplants and stir to absorb the oil. Cook until the eggplants begin to color, then add the chopped tomatoes, garlic, vinegar and sugar.

3 Cover the surface of the vegetables with a circle of waxed paper and simmer for 8–10 minutes.

4 Add the capers and olives, then season to taste with salt. Turn the caponata out into a bowl, garnish with parsley and serve at room temperature with warm crusty bread and olives.

Cannellini Bean Purée with Grilled Radicchio

The slightly bitter flavors of the radicchio and chicory make a wonderful marriage with the creamy citrus flavored bean purée.

Serves 4

INGREDIENTS
14 oz can cannellini beans
3 tbsp low-fat ricotta cheese
finely grated rind and juice of 1
   large orange
1 tbsp finely chopped fresh rosemary
4 heads of chicory
2 medium radicchio
1 tbsp walnut oil

chicory

ricotta cheese

cannellini beans

rosemary

radicchio

orange

1 Drain the beans, rinse, and drain again. Purée the beans in a blender or food processor with the ricotta cheese, orange juice and rosemary. Set aside.

2 Cut the chicory in half lengthwise.

3 Cut each radicchio into 8 wedges.

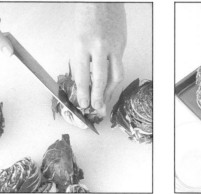

4 Lay out the chicory and radicchio on a baking tray and brush with walnut oil. Grill for 2–3 minutes. Serve with the sauce and scatter over the orange rind.

COOK'S TIP
Other suitable beans to use are navy, mung or broad beans.

Creamy Cannellini Beans with Asparagus

Cannellini beans in a creamy sauce contrast with tender asparagus in this tasty toast topper.

Serves 2

INGREDIENTS
2 tsp butter
1 small onion, finely chopped
1 small carrot, grated
1 tsp fresh thyme leaves
14 oz can cannellini beans, drained
$2/3$ cup light cream
4 oz young asparagus spears, trimmed
2 slices of fresh sliced whole wheat bread
salt and freshly ground black pepper

whole wheat bread *carrot* *thyme*

butter

asparagus spears

light cream

onion

cannellini beans

parsley

1 Melt the butter in a pan. Add the onion and carrot, and fry over a moderate heat for 4 minutes until soft. Add the thyme leaves.

2 Rinse the cannellini beans under cold running water. Drain thoroughly. Then add to the onion and carrot. Mix lightly.

3 Pour in the cream, and heat slowly to just below boiling point, stirring occasionally. Remove the pan from the heat, and add salt and pepper to taste. Preheat the broiler.

4 Place the asparagus spears in a saucepan. Pour over just enough boiling water to cover. Poach for 3–4 minutes until the spears are just tender.

5 Meanwhile, toast the bread under the broiler until both sides are golden.

6 Place the toast on individual plates. Drain the asparagus, and divide the spears between the slices of toast. Spoon the bean mixture over each portion, and serve.

COOK'S TIP
Use your favorite variety of canned beans such as borlotti, haricot or flageolets.

Potato, Spinach and Pine Nut Gratin

Pine nuts add a satisfying crunch to this gratin of wafer-thin potato slices and spinach in a creamy cheese sauce.

Serves 2

INGREDIENTS
1 lb potatoes
1 garlic clove, crushed
3 scallions, thinly sliced
²/₃ cup light cream
1 cup milk
8 oz frozen chopped spinach, thawed
4 oz Cheddar cheese, grated
¹/₄ cup pine nuts
salt and freshly ground black pepper

spinach

potatoes

garlic clove

pine nuts

Cheddar cheese

scallions

light cream

1 Peel the potatoes, and cut them carefully into wafer-thin slices. Spread them out in a large, heavy-bottomed, nonstick frying pan.

2 Sprinkle the crushed garlic and sliced scallions evenly over the potatoes.

3 Pour the cream and milk over the potatoes. Place the pan over a gentle heat. Cover, and cook for 8 minutes or until the potatoes are tender.

4 Using both hands, squeeze the spinach dry. Add the spinach to the potatoes, mixing lightly. Cover the pan, and cook for 2 minutes more.

5 Add salt and pepper to taste, then spoon the mixture into a shallow casserole. Preheat the broiler.

6 Sprinkle the grated cheese and pine nuts over the spinach mixture. Heat under the broiler for 2–3 minutes until the topping is golden. A simple lettuce and tomato salad makes an excellent accompaniment to this dish.

Eggplant, Tomato and Basil Rolls

Grilled eggplants wrapped around tangy feta cheese, flavored with basil and sun-dried tomatoes, make a wonderful combination of sunshine flavors.

Serves 4

2 large eggplants
olive oil
10–12 sun-dried tomatoes in
 oil, drained
handful of large, fresh basil
 leaves
5 oz feta cheese
salt and freshly ground black
 pepper

olive oil

eggplants

feta cheese

basil

sun-dried tomatoes in oil

COOK'S TIP

Vegetarians or vegans could use tofu in place of the feta cheese. For extra flavor, sprinkle the tofu with a little soy sauce before wrapping.

1 Slice the eggplants lengthwise into ¼-in thick slices. Sprinkle with salt and layer in a colander. Allow to drain for about 30 minutes.

2 Rinse the eggplants in cold water and dry well. Brush with oil on both sides and grill on a hot barbecue for 2–3 minutes, turning once, until golden brown and softened.

3 Arrange the sun-dried tomatoes over one end of each eggplant slice and top with the basil leaves. Cut the feta into short sticks and place on top. Season with salt and pepper.

4 Roll the eggplant slices around to enclose the filling. Cook on the barbecue for 2–3 minutes more, until hot. Serve with a thick French loaf.

Tuscan Baked Beans

Beans, both dried and fresh, are particularly popular in Tuscany, where they are cooked in many different ways. In this vegetarian dish, the beans are flavored with fresh sage leaves.

Serves 6–8

INGREDIENTS
1 pound, 6 ounces dried beans,
    such as Great Northern
¼ cup olive oil
2 garlic cloves, crushed
3 fresh sage leaves
1 leek, finely sliced
1 can (14 ounces) plum tomatoes,
    chopped, with their juice
salt and ground black pepper

Great Northern beans

olive oil

garlic

canned tomatoes

leek

sage

COOK'S TIP
If fresh sage is unavailable, use ¼ cup chopped fresh parsley instead.

1 Carefully pick over the beans, discarding any stones or other particles. Place the beans in a large bowl and cover with water. Let soak for at least 6 hours or overnight. Drain.

2 Preheat the oven to 350°F. In a small saucepan, heat the oil and sauté the garlic cloves and sage leaves for 3–4 minutes. Remove from the heat and set aside.

3 In a large, deep baking dish, combine the beans with the leek and tomatoes. Stir in the oil with the garlic and sage. Add enough fresh water to cover the beans by 1 inch. Mix well. Cover the dish with a lid or foil and place in the center of the oven. Bake for 1¾ hours.

4 Remove the dish from the oven, stir the beans and season with salt and pepper. Return the beans to the oven, uncovered, and cook for another 15 minutes, or until the beans are tender. Remove from the oven and let stand for 7–8 minutes before serving. Alternatively, let cool and serve at room temperature.

Malfatti with Red Sauce

If you ever felt dumplings were a little heavy, try these light spinach and ricotta malfatti instead. Serve with a tomato and red bell pepper sauce.

Serves 4–6

INGREDIENTS
1 pound fresh leaf spinach, stems trimmed
1 small onion, chopped
1 garlic clove, finely chopped
1 tablespoon olive oil
14 ounces (1¾ cups) ricotta cheese
3 eggs, beaten
2 tablespoons butter, melted
1 cup dried bread crumbs
½ cup all-purpose flour
1 teaspoon salt
½ cup freshly grated Parmesan cheese, plus shavings to garnish
grated nutmeg, to taste
salt and ground black pepper

FOR THE SAUCE
1 large red bell pepper, seeded and chopped
1 small red onion, chopped
2 tablespoons olive oil
1 can (14 ounces) chopped tomatoes
⅔ cup water
generous pinch of dried oregano
2 tablespoons light cream

spinach
onion
ricotta cheese
garlic
olive oil
flour
bread crumbs
eggs
nutmeg
Parmesan cheese
light cream
canned tomatoes
red bell pepper
butter
dried oregano
red onion

1 Blanch the spinach in the tiniest amount of water until it is limp. Drain well, pressing it in a sieve with the back of a ladle or spoon. Chop finely.

2 Lightly fry the onion and garlic in the oil in a large frying pan for 5 minutes. Allow to cool, then mix in the spinach, ricotta, eggs, melted butter, bread crumbs, flour, 1 teaspoon salt, grated Parmesan and grated nutmeg to taste.

3 Mold the spinach mixture into 12 small quenelles (see Cook's Tip).

4 Meanwhile, make the sauce. Lightly sauté the red pepper and onion in the oil in a saucepan for 5 minutes. Add the canned tomatoes, water, oregano and seasoning. Bring to a boil, then simmer gently for 5 minutes.

5 Remove the sauce from the heat and blend to a purée in a food processor. Return to the pan, then stir in the cream. Adjust the seasoning if necessary.

COOK'S TIP

Quenelles are oval-shaped dumplings. To shape the malfatti into quenelles you need two dessertspoons. Scoop up the mixture with one spoon, making sure that it is mounded up, then, using the other spoon, scoop the mixture off the first spoon, twisting the top spoon into the bowl of the second. Repeat this action two or three times until the quenelle is nice and smooth, and then gently knock it off on to a plate ready to cook. Repeat the process with the rest of the mixture.

6 Bring a shallow pan of salted water to a gentle boil, drop the malfatti into it a few at a time and poach them for about 5 minutes. Drain them well and keep them warm in a low oven.

7 Arrange the malfatti on warm plates and drizzle over the sauce. Serve topped with slivers of Parmesan.

Polenta with Mushrooms

This dish is delicious made with a mixture of wild and regular button mushrooms.

Serves 6

INGREDIENTS

2 tablespoons dried porcini
    mushrooms (omit if using
    wild mushrooms)
¼ cup olive oil
1 small onion, finely chopped
1½ pounds mushrooms, wild
    or button, or a combination
    of both
2 garlic cloves, finely chopped
3 tablespoons chopped fresh parsley
3 medium tomatoes, peeled
    and diced
1 tablespoon tomato paste
¾ cup warm water
¼ teaspoon fresh thyme leaves,
    or 1 large pinch dried thyme
1 bay leaf
2½ cups polenta or yellow cornmeal
salt and ground black pepper
fresh parsley sprigs, to garnish

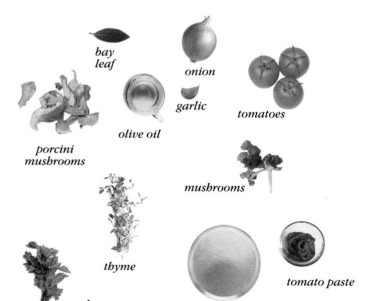

bay leaf
onion
garlic
tomatoes
olive oil
porcini mushrooms
mushrooms
thyme
parsley
polenta
tomato paste

1 Soak the dried mushrooms, if using, in a small bowl of warm water for about 20 minutes. Remove the mushrooms with a slotted spoon. Filter the soaking water through a layer of paper towels placed in a sieve and reserve. Rinse the mushrooms well in several changes of cold water.

2 In a large frying pan, heat the oil and sauté the onion over low heat until soft and golden.

3 Clean the fresh mushrooms by wiping them with a damp cloth. Cut into slices. When the onion is soft, add the mushrooms to the pan. Stir over medium to high heat until they release their liquid. Add the garlic, parsley and diced tomatoes. Cook for 4–5 minutes.

4 Soften the tomato paste in the warm water (use only ½ cup water if using dried mushrooms). Add the paste mixture to the pan with the herbs. Add the dried mushrooms and soaking liquid, if using, and season. Reduce the heat to low and cook for 15–20 minutes. Set aside.

5 Bring 6¼ cups water to a boil in a large, heavy saucepan. Add 1 tablespoon salt. Reduce the heat to a simmer and begin to add the polenta in a fine stream. Stir constantly with a whisk until the polenta has all been incorporated.

COOK'S TIP
Just a few dried porcini mushrooms will help give button mushrooms a more complex and interesting flavor.

6 Switch to a long-handled wooden spoon and continue to stir the polenta over low to medium heat until it is a thick mass and pulls away from the sides of the pan. This may take 25–50 minutes, depending on the type of polenta used. For best results, never stop stirring the polenta until you remove it from the heat. When the polenta has almost finished cooking, gently reheat the mushroom sauce.

7 To serve, spoon the polenta onto a warmed serving platter. Make a well in the center. Spoon some of the mushroom sauce into the well, and garnish with parsley sprigs. Serve immediately, passing the remaining sauce in a separate bowl.

Frittata with Sun-Dried Tomatoes

Adding just a few sun-dried tomatoes gives this frittata a distinctly Mediterranean flavor.

Serves 3–4

INGREDIENTS

6 sun-dried tomatoes, dry or in oil and drained
¼ cup olive oil
1 small onion, finely chopped
pinch of fresh thyme leaves
6 eggs
½ cup (2 ounces) freshly grated Parmesan cheese
salt and ground black pepper

sun-dried tomatoes

Parmesan cheese

eggs

thyme

onion

olive oil

1 Place the dry tomatoes in a small bowl and pour in enough hot water to just cover them. Soak for about 15 minutes. Lift the tomatoes out of the water, and slice them into thin strips. Reserve the soaking water.

2 Heat the oil in a large nonstick or heavy frying pan. Stir in the onion, and cook for 5–6 minutes, or until soft and golden. Add the tomatoes and thyme. Stir over medium heat for 2–3 minutes. Season with salt and pepper.

3 Break the eggs into a bowl and beat lightly. Stir in 3–4 tablespoons of the tomato soaking water and the grated Parmesan. Raise the heat under the pan.

VARIATION
Replace the sun-dried tomatoes with ⅓ cup diced ham or prosciutto and 1 cup chopped cooked spinach. When frying the onion, add a finely chopped garlic clove if desired.

4 When the oil is sizzling, pour in the eggs. Mix them quickly into the other ingredients, and stop stirring. Lower the heat to medium and cook for 4–5 minutes on the first side, or until the frittata is puffed and golden brown.

5 Take a large plate, place it upside down over the pan and, holding it firmly with oven mitts, turn the pan and the frittata over onto it. Slide the frittata back into the pan, and continue cooking until golden on the second side, 3–4 more minutes. Serve immediately.

Herb Polenta with Grilled Tomatoes

Golden polenta with fresh summer herbs and sweet grilled tomatoes.

COOK'S TIP

Any mixture of fresh herbs can be used, or try using just basil or chives alone, for a really distinctive flavor.

Serves 4

3²/₃ cups stock or water
1 tsp salt
1 cup polenta
2 tbsp butter
5 tbsp mixed chopped fresh parsley, chives and basil, plus extra, to garnish
olive oil for brushing
4 large plum or beef tomatoes, halved
salt and freshly ground black pepper

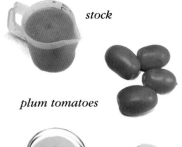
stock

plum tomatoes

polenta   *butter*
thyme   *chives*
parsley   *basil*

1 Prepare the polenta in advance: place the water or stock in a pan, with the salt, and bring to a boil. Reduce the heat and stir in the polenta.

2 Stir constantly over moderate heat for 5 minutes, until the polenta begins to thicken and come away from the sides of the pan.

3 Remove from the heat and stir in the butter, herbs and black pepper.

4 Pour the mixture into a wide, greased pan or dish and spread it evenly. Leave until completely cool and set.

5 Turn out the polenta and cut it into squares or stamp out rounds with a large cookie cutter. Brush with oil.

6 Brush the tomatoes with oil and sprinkle with salt and pepper. Cook the tomatoes and polenta on a medium hot barbecue for 5 minutes, turning once. Serve garnished with fresh herbs.

Baked Onions with Sun-Dried Tomatoes

This wonderfully simple vegetable dish of baked onions brings together the flavors of a hot Italian summer—tomatoes, fresh herbs and olive oil.

Serves 4

INGREDIENTS

1 pound small onions, peeled
2 teaspoons chopped fresh rosemary
    or 1 teaspoon dried rosemary
2 garlic cloves, chopped
1 tablespoon chopped fresh parsley
½ cup sun-dried tomatoes in oil,
    drained and chopped
6 tablespoons olive oil
1 tablespoon white wine vinegar
salt and ground black pepper

olive oil

garlic

rosemary

small onions

sun-dried tomatoes

white wine vinegar

parsley

1 Preheat the oven to 300°F. Grease a shallow baking dish. Drop the onions into a saucepan of boiling water and cook for 5 minutes. Drain in a colander.

2 Spread the onions in the bottom of the prepared baking dish.

VARIATIONS

Other herbs can be used instead of the rosemary and parsley in this dish. Try using shredded fresh basil, which will enhance the flavor of the sun-dried tomatoes, or fresh thyme, which complements the flavor of baked onions perfectly. If you can find small red onions, these would make a nice change, or even mix the two colors.

3 Combine the rosemary, garlic, parsley, salt and pepper in a small mixing bowl and sprinkle the mixture evenly over the onions in the dish.

4 Sprinkle the chopped sun-dried tomatoes over the onions. Drizzle the olive oil and vinegar on top.

5 Cover the dish with a sheet of foil and bake for 45 minutes, basting occasionally. Remove the foil and bake for about 15 minutes more, until the onions are golden brown all over. Serve immediately from the dish.

Broiled Eggplant Bundles

These are delicious little bundles of tomatoes, mozzarella cheese and fragrant fresh basil, wrapped in slices of eggplant.

Serves 4

INGREDIENTS
2 large, long eggplants
8 ounces mozzarella cheese
2 plum tomatoes
16 large basil leaves
2 tablespoons olive oil
salt and ground black pepper

FOR THE DRESSING
¼ cup olive oil
1 teaspoon balsamic vinegar
1 tablespoon sun-dried tomato
    paste
1 tablespoon lemon juice

FOR THE GARNISH
2 tablespoons pine nuts, toasted
torn basil leaves

mozzarella
cheese

eggplant

basil

lemon

balsamic vinegar

sun-dried
tomato paste

plum
tomatoes

olive oil

pine nuts

1 To make the dressing, whisk together the olive oil, vinegar, sun-dried tomato paste and lemon juice. Season to taste and set aside.

2 Remove the stalks from the eggplants and cut the eggplants lengthwise into thin slices—the aim is to get 16 slices total (each about ¼ inch thick), disregarding the first and last slices. (If you have a mandoline, it will cut perfect, even slices for you; otherwise use a sharp, long-bladed knife.)

3 Bring a large pan of salted water to a boil and cook the eggplant slices for about 2 minutes, or until just softened. Drain the sliced eggplant, then dry on paper towels. Set aside.

4 Cut the cheese into thin slices. Cut each tomato into eight slices, not counting the first and last slices.

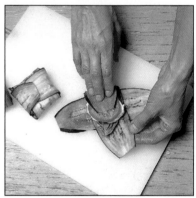

5 Take two eggplant slices and place on a baking sheet or in a large flameproof dish, forming a cross. Place a slice of tomato in the center of the cross, season with salt and pepper, then add a basil leaf, followed by a slice of cheese, another basil leaf, a slice of tomato and more seasoning.

6 Fold the ends of the eggplant slices around the cheese and tomato filling to make a neat bundle. Repeat with the rest of the assembled ingredients to make eight bundles. Chill the bundles for about 20 minutes.

7 Preheat the broiler. Brush the bundles with olive oil and cook for about 5 minutes on each side, or until golden. Serve hot, with the dressing, and sprinkled with pine nuts and basil.

Zucchini with Onion and Garlic

Use a good-quality olive oil and sunflower oil. The olive oil gives the dish a delicious fragrance without overpowering the zucchini.

Serves 4

INGREDIENTS
1 tablespoon olive oil
1 tablespoon sunflower oil
1 large onion, chopped
1 garlic clove, finely chopped
6–7 small zucchini, cut into
    ½-inch slices
⅔ cup chicken or vegetable broth
½ teaspoon chopped fresh oregano
salt and ground black pepper
chopped fresh parsley, to garnish

garlic

zucchini

olive oil

chicken broth

sunflower oil

oregano

onion

parsley

1 Heat the olive and sunflower oils together in a large frying pan and add the chopped onion and garlic. Fry over medium heat for 5–6 minutes, until the onion has softened and is beginning to brown.

2 Add the zucchini slices and fry for about 4 minutes, until they just begin to be flecked with brown, stirring frequently.

3 Stir in the broth, oregano and seasoning and simmer gently for 8–10 minutes, or until the liquid has almost evaporated.

4 Spoon the zucchini into a warmed serving dish, sprinkle with chopped parsley and serve.

COOK'S TIP
Zucchini are very popular in Italy, grown in many kitchen gardens. They make a lovely summer dish, and take very little time to prepare. If you can find them, choose small zucchini, which tend to be much sweeter than the larger ones.

Sun-dried Tomato Bread

This savory bread tastes delicious on its own, but it also makes exceptional sandwiches.

Makes 1 loaf

INGREDIENTS
3¼ cups bread flour
1 tsp salt
2 tsp rapid-rise dried yeast
2 oz (drained weight) sun-dried
   tomatoes in oil, chopped
¾ cup lukewarm water
5 tbsp lukewarm olive oil, plus extra
   for brushing
plain flour for dusting

water

flour

olive oil

rapid-rise yeast

sun-dried tomatoes

salt

1 Sift the flour and salt into a large mixing bowl.

2 Stir in the yeast and sun-dried tomatoes.

3 Make a well in the center of the dry ingredients. Pour in the water and oil, and mix until the ingredients come together and form a soft dough.

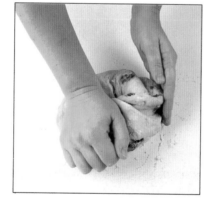

4 Turn the dough on to a lightly floured surface and knead for about 10 minutes.

5 Shape into an oblong loaf, without making the top too smooth, and place on a greased baking sheet. Brush the top with oil, cover with plastic wrap, then let rise in a warm place for about 1 hour.

6 Meanwhile, preheat the oven to 425°F. Remove the plastic wrap, then sprinkle the top of the loaf lightly with flour. Bake for 30–40 minutes until the loaf sounds hollow when tapped on the bottom. Serve warm.

Rosemary and Sea Salt Focaccia

Focaccia is an Italian flat bread made with olive oil. Here it is given added flavor with rosemary and coarse sea salt.

Makes 1 loaf

INGREDIENTS
3 cups unbleached all-purpose
    flour
½ tsp salt
2 tsp rapid-rise dried yeast
1 cup lukewarm water
3 tbsp olive oil
1 small red onion
leaves from 1 large rosemary sprig
1 tsp coarse sea salt

coarse sea salt

water

olive oil

flour

rapid-rise yeast

red onion

rosemary

1 Sift the flour and salt into a large mixing bowl. Stir in the yeast, then make a well in the center of the dry ingredients. Pour in the water and 2 tbsp of the oil. Mix well, adding a little more water if the mixture seems dry.

2 Turn the dough on to a lightly floured surface and knead for about 10 minutes until smooth and elastic.

3 Place the dough in a greased bowl, cover and let rise in a warm place for about 1 hour until doubled in size. Punch down and knead the dough for 2–3 minutes.

4 Meanwhile, preheat the oven to 425°F. Roll out the dough to a large circle, about ½ in thick, and transfer to a greased baking sheet. Brush with the remaining oil.

5 Halve the onion and slice into thin wedges. Sprinkle over the dough with the rosemary and sea salt, pressing in lightly.

6 Using a finger make deep indentations in the dough. Cover the surface with greased plastic wrap, then let rise in a warm place for 30 minutes. Remove the plastic wrap and bake for 25–30 minutes until golden. Serve warm.

Saffron Focaccia

A dazzling yellow bread that is light in texture and distinctive in flavor.

Makes 1 loaf

INGREDIENTS
pinch of saffron threads
⅔ cup boiling water
2 cups flour
½ tsp salt
1 tsp easy-blend dry yeast
1 tbsp olive oil

FOR THE TOPPING
2 garlic cloves, sliced
1 red onion, cut into thin wedges
rosemary sprigs
12 black olives, pitted and coarsely
    chopped
1 tbsp olive oil

flour

garlic

rosemary

red onion

olives

saffron

yeast

1 Place the saffron in a heatproof cup and pour on the boiling water. Leave to stand and infuse until lukewarm.

2 Place the flour, salt, yeast and olive oil in a food processor. Turn on and gradually add the saffron and its liquid. Process until the dough forms into a ball.

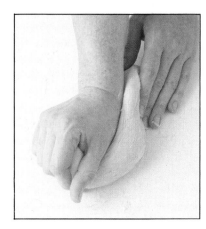

3 Turn onto a floured board and knead for 10–15 minutes. Place in a bowl, cover and leave to rise for 30–40 minutes until doubled in size.

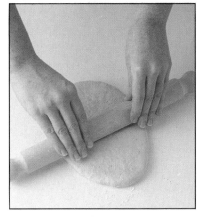

4 Punch down the risen dough on a lightly floured surface and roll out into an oval shape, ½ in thick. Place on a lightly greased cookie sheet and leave to rise for 20–30 minutes.

5 Preheat the oven to 400°F. Press small indentations all over the surface of the focaccia with your fingers.

6 Cover with the topping ingredients, brush lightly with olive oil, and bake for 25 minutes or until the loaf sounds hollow when tapped on the bottom. Leave to cool on a wire rack.

Mini Focaccia with Pine Nuts

Pine nuts add little bites of nutty texture to these mini focaccias.

Makes 4 mini loaves

INGREDIENTS

3 cups unbleached all-purpose
  flour
½ tsp salt
2 tsp rapid-rise dried yeast
1 cup lukewarm water
3 tbsp olive oil
3–4 tbsp pine nuts
2 tsp coarse sea salt

water

sea salt

olive oil

flour

rapid-rise yeast

pine nuts

1 Sift the flour and salt into a large mixing bowl. Stir in the yeast, then make a well in the center of the dry ingredients. Pour in the water and 2 tbsp of the oil. Mix well, adding more water if the mixture seems dry. Turn on to a lightly floured surface and knead for about 10 minutes until smooth and elastic. Place the dough in a greased bowl, cover and let rise in a warm place for about 1 hour until doubled in size. Punch down and knead the dough for 2–3 minutes.

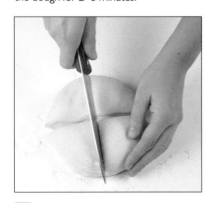

2 Divide the dough into four pieces.

3 Using your hands pat out each piece on greased baking sheets to a 4 × 3 in oblong, rounded at the ends.

4 Scatter the pine nuts over and gently press them into the surface. Sprinkle with salt and brush with the remaining oil. Cover with greased plastic wrap and let rise for about 30 minutes. Meanwhile, preheat the oven to 425°F. Remove the plastic wrap and bake the focaccias for 15–20 minutes until golden. Serve warm.

Walnut Bread

The nutty flavor of this wonderfully textured bread is excellent. Try it toasted and topped with melting goat cheese for a mouthwatering snack.

Makes 2 loaves

INGREDIENTS
4 cups bread flour
2 tsp salt
2 tsp rapid-rise dried yeast
1¼ cups chopped walnuts
4 tbsp chopped fresh parsley
1⅔ cups lukewarm water
4 tbsp olive oil

flour

oliu

rapid-rise yeast

parsley

walnuts

salt

1 Sift the flour and salt into a large mixing bowl. Stir in the yeast, walnuts and parsley.

2 Make a well in the center of the dry ingredients. Pour in the water and oil and mix to a soft dough. Turn the dough on to a lightly floured surface and knead for about 10 minutes until smooth and elastic. Place in a greased bowl, cover and let rise in a warm place for about 1 hour until doubled in size.

3 Punch down and knead the dough for 2–3 minutes. Divide in half and shape each piece into a thick roll about 7–8 in long. Place on greased baking sheets, cover with plastic wrap and let rise for about 30 minutes.

4 Meanwhile, preheat the oven to 425°F. Remove the plastic wrap, then lightly slash the top of each loaf. Bake for 10 minutes, then reduce the oven temperature to 350°F. and bake for a further 25–30 minutes until the loaves sound hollow when tapped. Serve warm.

Olive Bread

Green olives are added to heighten the flavor of this moist bread. Use a combination of green and black olives if you prefer.

Makes 2 loaves

INGREDIENTS
6 cups bread flour
1 tsp salt
sachet of rapid-rise dried yeast
1 tbsp chopped fresh oregano
1½ cups lukewarm water
7 tbsp olive oil
about 30 stoned green olives

green olives

flour

oregano

rapid-rise yeast

olive oil

salt

1 Sift the flour and salt into a large mixing bowl. Stir in the yeast and oregano.

2 Measure the water into a bowl, then stir in 6 tbsp of the oil. Make a well in the center of the dry ingredients, pour in the liquid and mix to a soft dough.

3 Turn the dough on to a lightly floured surface and knead for about 10 minutes until smooth and elastic. Place in a greased bowl, cover with plastic wrap and let rise in a warm place for about 1 hour until doubled in size.

4 Punch down and knead the dough for 2–3 minutes. Divide in half, then press the dough on greased baking sheets into two ovals, about ½ in thick.

5 Using a clean finger make about 15 deep indentations over the surface of each loaf. Press an olive into each indentation.

6 Brush the loaves with the remaining oil, cover with plastic wrap and let rise for 30 minutes. Meanwhile, preheat the oven to 425°F. Remove the plastic wrap and bake for 20–25 minutes until the loaves sound hollow when tapped. Serve warm.

Saffron and Basil Breadsticks

Saffron lends its delicate aroma and flavor, as well as rich yellow color, to these tasty breadsticks.

Makes 32

INGREDIENTS
generous pinch saffron strands
4 cups bread flour
1 tsp salt
2 tsp rapid-rise dried yeast
1¼ cups lukewarm water
3 tbsp olive oil
3 tbsp chopped fresh basil

flour

water

olive oil

basil

rapid-rise yeast

saffron strands

salt

1 Infuse the saffron strands in 2 tbsp hot water for 10 minutes.

2 Sift the flour and salt into a large mixing bowl. Stir in the yeast, then make a well in the center of the dry ingredients. Pour in the water and saffron liquid and start to mix a little.

3 Add the oil and basil and continue to mix to a soft dough.

4 Turn out and knead the dough on a lightly floured surface for about 10 minutes until smooth and elastic. Place in a greased bowl, cover with plastic wrap and let rise for about 1 hour until it has doubled in size.

5 Punch down and knead the dough on a lightly floured surface for 2–3 minutes.

6 Preheat the oven to 425°F. Divide the dough into 32 pieces and shape into long sticks. Place well apart on greased baking sheets, then let rise for a further 15–30 minutes until they become puffy. Bake for about 15 minutes until crisp and golden. Serve warm.

Olive and Oregano Bread

This is an excellent accompaniment to all salads, and it is particularly good served warm.

Serves 8–10

INGREDIENTS

1¼ cups warm water
1 tsp dried yeast
pinch of sugar
1 tbsp olive oil
1 onion, chopped
4 cups white bread flour
1 tsp salt
¼ tsp freshly ground black pepper
⅓ cup pitted black olives, coarsely chopped
1 tbsp black olive paste
1 tbsp chopped fresh oregano
1 tbsp chopped fresh parsley

fresh oregano *fresh parsley* *black olives*

white bread flour

black pepper

olive oil *black olive paste*

water

dried yeast *salt* *onion*

1 Put half the warm water in a small pitcher. Sprinkle the yeast over the top. Add the sugar, mix well, and let stand for 10 minutes.

2 Heat the olive oil in a frying pan, and fry the onion until golden brown.

3 Sift the flour into a mixing bowl with the salt and pepper. Make a well in the center. Add the yeast mixture, the fried onion (with the oil), the olives, olive paste, herbs and remaining water. Gradually incorporate the flour, and mix to make a soft dough, adding a little more water, if necessary.

4 Turn the dough onto a floured surface, and knead for 5 minutes until smooth and elastic. Place in a clean bowl, cover with a damp dish towel, and let rise in a warm place for about 2 hours, or until doubled in bulk. Lightly grease a baking sheet.

5 Turn the dough onto a floured surface, and knead again for a few minutes. Shape into an 8 in round, and place on the prepared baking sheet. Using a sharp knife, make crisscross cuts over the top, cover, and let stand in a warm place for 30 minutes until well risen. Preheat the oven to 425°F.

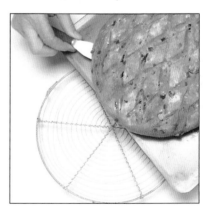

6 Dust the loaf with a little flour, and bake for 10 minutes. Lower the oven temperature to 400°F. Bake the loaf for 20 minutes more, or until it sounds hollow when it is tapped on the bottom. Transfer to a wire rack to cool slightly before serving.

Prosciutto and Parmesan Bread

This nourishing bread is almost a meal in itself.

Serves 8

INGREDIENTS

2 cups self-rising whole-wheat
2 cups self-rising white flour
1 tsp baking powder
1 tsp salt
1 tsp freshly ground black pepper
3 oz prosciutto, chopped
2 tbsp freshly grated Parmesan cheese
2 tbsp chopped fresh parsley
3 tbsp French mustard
1½ cups buttermilk
skim milk, for glazing

parsley

salt

Parmesan cheese

black pepper

self-rising whole-wheat flour

self-rising white flour

French mustard

buttermilk

prosciutto

baking powder

1 Preheat the oven to 400°F. Flour a baking sheet. Place the whole-wheat flour in a bowl, and sift in the white flour, baking powder and salt. Add the pepper and the prosciutto. Reserve about 1 tbsp of the grated Parmesan, and stir the rest into the flour mixture. Stir in the parsley. Make a well in the center.

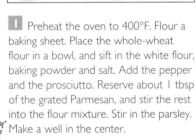

2 Mix the mustard and buttermilk in a pitcher, add to the flour mixture, and quickly mix to make a soft dough.

3 Turn the dough onto a floured surface, and knead briefly. Shape into an oval loaf, brush with milk, and sprinkle with the remaining cheese. Place the loaf on the prepared baking sheet.

4 Bake the loaf for 25–30 minutes, or until golden brown. Transfer to a wire rack to cool.

Ham and Tomato Biscuits

These make an ideal accompaniment for soup. Choose a strongly flavored ham, and chop it fairly finely, so that a little goes a long way.

Makes 12

INGREDIENTS
2 cups self-rising flour
1 tsp dry mustard
1 tsp paprika, plus extra for
   sprinkling
½ tsp salt
2 tbsp margarine
1 tbsp snipped fresh basil
⅓ cup drained, oil packed sun-dried
   tomatoes, chopped
2 ounces chopped, cooked ham
½–⅔ cup skim milk, plus extra
   for brushing

margarine

paprika

salt

skim milk

self-rising flour

fresh basil

dry mustard

sun-dried tomatoes

ham

1 Preheat the oven to 400°F. Flour a large baking sheet. Sift together the flour, mustard, paprika and salt into a bowl. Work in the margarine until the mixture resembles bread crumbs.

2 Stir in the basil, sun-dried tomatoes and ham, and mix lightly. Add enough milk to make a soft dough.

3 Turn the dough onto a lightly floured surface, knead lightly, and roll out to an 8 x 6 in rectangle. Cut into 2 in squares, and arrange on the baking sheet.

4 Brush lightly with milk, sprinkle with paprika, and bake for 12–15 minutes. Transfer to a wire rack to cool.

Focaccia with Hot Artichokes and Olives

Focaccia makes an excellent base for different broiled toppings. Artichoke hearts bottled in oil are best for this.

Makes 3

INGREDIENTS
4 tbsp olive paste
3 Mini Focaccia
1 small red bell pepper, halved and
 seeded
10 oz bottled or canned artichoke
 hearts, drained
3 oz pepperoni, sliced
1 tsp dried oregano

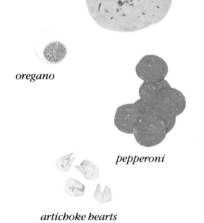

red bell pepper

mini focaccia

oregano

pepperoni

artichoke hearts

1 Preheat the oven to 425°F. Spread the olive paste over the focaccia. Broil the red bell pepper until blackened, put in a plastic bag, seal, and allow to cool for 10 minutes. Skin the pepper and cut into strips.

2 Cut the artichoke hearts in quarters and arrange over the olive paste with the pepperoni.

3 Sprinkle over the red pepper strips and the oregano. Place in the oven for 5–10 minutes until heated through.

OLIVE FOCACCIA

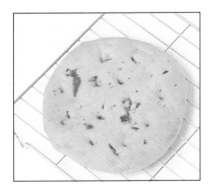

Focaccia is an Italian flat bread made with olive oil and often with olives as well. The amount of water needed varies with the type of flour used, so you may need a little less – or a little more – than the quantity given.

Makes 2 loaves

4 cups bread flour
1 tsp salt
1 tsp dried yeast
pinch of sugar
1¼ cups warm water
4 tbsp olive oil
1 cup black olives, pitted and roughly
 chopped
½ tsp dried oregano

Mix the flour and salt together in a mixing bowl. Put the yeast in a small bowl and mix with half the water and a pinch of sugar to help activate the yeast. Leave for about 10 minutes until dissolved. Add the yeast mixture to the flour along with the oil, olives, and remaining water, and mix to a soft dough, adding a little more water if necessary.

Transfer the dough out to a floured surface and knead for 5 minutes until it is smooth and elastic. Place in a mixing bowl, cover with a damp dish towel and leave in a warm place to rise for about 2 hours or until doubled in size.

Preheat the oven to 425°F. Transfer the dough out to a floured surface and knead again for a few minutes. Divide into 2 portions, then roll out each to a thickness of ½ in in either a round or oblong shape. Place on an oiled baking sheet, using a floured rolling pin to lift the dough. Make indentations all over the surface with your fingertips and sprinkle with the oregano. Bake in the oven for about 15–20 minutes.

FOCACCIA WITH SUN-DRIED TOMATOES AND MOZZARELLA

Spread the focaccia with 3 tbsp chopped sun-dried tomatoes. Slice ½ lb mozzarella cheese and arrange over the top. Sprinkle with 8 pitted and quartered black olives, and heat through in the oven as for the main recipe.

MINI FOCACCIA

Divide the dough into 6 balls. On a floured surface, roll these out to 6 in circles. Finish as for Olive Focaccia, baking for 12–15 minutes.

Pan Bagna

This literally means 'bathed bread' and is basically a Salade Niçoise stuffed into a baguette or roll. The olive oil dressing soaks into the bread when it is left for an hour or so with a weight on top of it.

Makes 4

INGREDIENTS
1 large baguette
⅔ cup French Dressing
1 small onion, thinly sliced
3 tomatoes, sliced
1 small green or red bell pepper, seeded and sliced
2 oz can anchovy fillets, drained
3½ oz can tuna fish, drained
2 oz black olives, halved and pitted

baguette

French Dressing

bell peppers

tomatoes

tuna fish

onion

anchovy fillets

olives

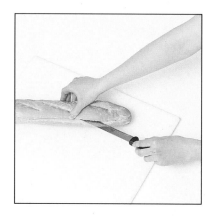

1 Split the baguette horizontally along one side without cutting all the way through the crust.

2 Open the bread out so that it lies flat and sprinkle the French Dressing evenly over the top.

3 Arrange the onion, tomatoes, green or red pepper, anchovies, tuna, and olives on one side of the bread. Close the 2 halves, pressing firmly together.

4 Wrap in plastic wrap, lay a board on top, put a weight on it, and leave for about 1 hour: as well as allowing the dressing to soak into the bread, this makes it easier to eat.

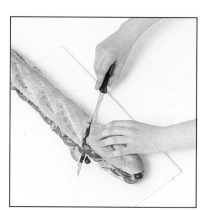

5 Cut the loaf diagonally into 4 equal portions.

FRENCH DRESSING

Olive oil is a must for this dressing; it imparts a rich, fruity flavor, especially if you use that lovely green, virgin olive oil. Make a large quantity at a time and store it in a wine bottle, ready for instant use.

Makes about scant 2 cups

1½ cups extra-virgin olive oil
6 tbsp red-wine vinegar
1 tbsp Moutarde de Meaux
1 garlic clove, crushed
1 tsp clear honey
salt and pepper

Pour the olive oil into a measuring jug and make up to a scant 2 cups with the vinegar. Add the remaining ingredients, then, using a funnel pour into a wine bottle. Put in the cork firmly, give the mixture a thorough shake, and store.

Ciabatta Sandwich

If you can find a ciabatta flavored with sun-dried tomatoes, it improves the flavor of the sandwich. The proscuitto should be sliced very thinly and then cut into strips to make it easier to eat.

Makes 3

INGREDIENTS
4 tbsp mayonnaise
2 tbsp pesto sauce
1 ciabatta loaf
¼ lb provolone or mozzarella cheese, sliced
3 oz prosciutto, cut into strips
4 plum tomatoes, sliced
sprigs fresh basil, torn into pieces

ciabatta loaf

provolone cheese

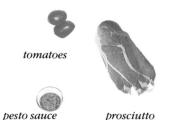
tomatoes

pesto sauce   prosciutto

basil

1 Thoroughly mix together the mayonnaise and pesto sauce.

2 Cut the ciabatta in half horizontally and spread the cut side of both halves with the pesto mayonnaise. Lay the cheese over one half of the ciabatta.

3 Cut the prosciutto into strips and arrange over the top. Cover with the sliced tomatoes and torn basil leaves. Sandwich together with the other half and cut into 3 pieces.

Crostini with Tomato and Anchovy

Crostini are little rounds of bread cut from a crusty loaf and toasted or fried, then covered with a savory topping such as melted cheese, olive paste, anchovy, tomato or chicken liver.

Makes 8

INGREDIENTS
1 small crusty loaf (large enough to cut into 8 slices)
2 tbsp olive oil
2 garlic cloves, chopped
4 tomatoes, peeled and chopped
1 tbsp chopped fresh basil
1 tbsp tomato paste
salt and pepper
8 canned anchovy fillets
12 black olives, halved and pitted
1 sprig fresh basil, to garnish

olive oil

crusty loaf

garlic

black olives

basil

anchovy fillets

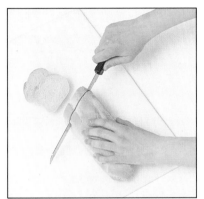

1 Cut the bread diagonally into 8 slices about ½ in thick and toast until golden on both sides.

CROSTINI WITH ONION AND OLIVE

Fry 2 cups sliced onions in 2 tbsp olive oil until golden brown. Stir in 8 roughly chopped anchovy fillets, 12 halved, pitted black olives, some seasoning, and 1 tsp dried thyme. Spread the toasted bread with 1 tbsp black olive paste and spread a spoonful of the onion mixture over each one.

2 Heat the oil and fry the garlic and tomatoes for 4 minutes. Stir in the basil, tomato paste, and seasoning.

3 Spoon a little tomato mixture on each slice of bread. Place an anchovy fillet on each one and sprinkle with olives. Serve garnished with a sprig of basil.

Ham and Asparagus Slice

Be creative in your arrangement of the ingredients here. You could make ham cornets, or wrap the asparagus in the ham, or use different meats such as salami or mortadella.

Makes 4

INGREDIENTS
12 asparagus spears
½ cups (about ¼ lb) cream cheese
4 slices rye bread
4 slices ham
few leaves frisée lettuce
2 tbsp mayonnaise
4 radish roses, to garnish

rye bread

frisée lettuce

ham

asparagus

1 Cook the asparagus until tender, drain, pat dry with paper towels, and cool.

2 Spread cream cheese over the rye bread and arrange the ham in folds over the top.

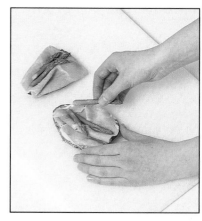

3 Lay 3 asparagus spears on each sandwich.

4 Arrange the lettuce on top of the spears and spoon over some mayonnaise.

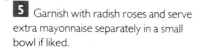

5 Garnish with radish roses and serve extra mayonnaise separately in a small bowl if liked.

SALAMI AND COTTAGE CHEESE ON RYE

Omit the asparagus. Arrange 3 salami slices on top with a spoonful of cottage cheese and chopped fresh chives. Garnish with watercress, chives, and chive flowers.

Artichoke and Pepper Pizzettes

Crunchy bread makes an ideal base for these quick pizzas.

Serves 4

INGREDIENTS
1 tbsp sunflower oil
1 onion, chopped
1 green bell pepper, seeded and
  chopped
7 oz can chopped tomatoes
1 tbsp tomato paste
½ crusty loaf
14 oz can artichoke hearts, drained
4 oz mozzarella cheese, sliced
1 tbsp poppy seeds
salt and freshly ground black pepper

mozzarella cheese

crusty loaf

tomato paste

chopped tomatoes

green bell pepper

poppy seeds

onion

artichoke hearts

1 Heat the oil in a frying pan. Add the chopped onion and bell pepper, and cook for 4 minutes until just softened.

2 Stir in the chopped tomatoes and tomato paste. Cook for 4 minutes. Remove from the heat, and add salt and pepper to taste.

3 Cut the piece of crusty loaf in half lengthwise. Cut each half in fourths to make eight pieces in all.

4 Spoon a little of the pepper and tomato mixture over each piece of bread. Preheat the broiler.

5 Slice the artichoke hearts. Arrange them on top of the pepper and tomato mixture. Cover with the mozzarella slices, and sprinkle with the poppy seeds.

6 Arrange the crusty bread pizzas on a rack over a broiler pan and broil for 6–8 minutes until the cheese melts and is beginning to brown. Serve immediately.

Crusty Rolls with Zucchini and Saffron

Split, crusty rolls are filled with zucchini in a creamy tomato sauce flavored with saffron. Use a mixture of green zucchini and yellow summer squash, if possible.

Serves 4

INGREDIENTS

1½ lb small zucchini
1 tbsp olive oil
2 shallots, finely chopped
4 crusty rolls
7 oz can chopped tomatoes
pinch of sugar
a few saffron threads
¼ cup light cream
salt and freshly ground black pepper

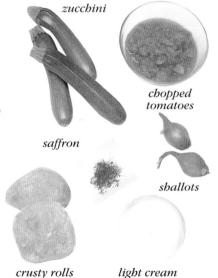

zucchini

chopped tomatoes

saffron

shallots

crusty rolls   *light cream*

1 Preheat the oven to 350°F. Remove the ends from the zucchini, then, using a sharp knife, cut the zucchini into 1½ in lengths. Cut each piece into quarters lengthwise.

COOK'S TIP

To avoid heating your oven, heat the rolls in a microwave. Put them on a plate, cover with paper towels, and heat on **HIGH** for 30–45 seconds.

2 Heat the oil in a large frying pan. Add the shallots, and fry over moderate heat for 1–2 minutes. Put the rolls into the oven to warm through.

3 Add the zucchini to the shallots. Mix well, and cook for 6 minutes, stirring frequently, until just beginning to soften.

4 Stir in the tomatoes and sugar. Steep the saffron threads in a little hot water for a few minutes, then add to the pan with the cream. Cook for 4 minutes, stirring occasionally. Season to taste. Split open the rolls, and fill with the zucchini and sauce.

Fried Mozzarella Sandwich

This sandwich is very popular in southern Italy, where it is known as *Mozzarella in Carrozza*. Be sure to use mozzarella packed in brine for the best flavor. This is also excellent made with Cheddar or Swiss cheese.

Makes 2

INGREDIENTS
¼ lb mozzarella cheese, thickly sliced
4 thick slices white bread, crusts
   removed
salt and pepper
1 egg
2 tbsp milk
oil for shallow-frying

1 Lay the mozzarella slices on 2 slices of bread, sprinkle with salt and pepper, then top with the remaining bread slices to make 2 cheese sandwiches.

2 Mix the egg and milk together, season, and place in a large shallow dish.

3 Lay the sandwiches in the egg mixture, turn over so that they are saturated and leave there for a few minutes. Pour enough oil into a skillet to give ½ in depth. Heat the oil and fry the sandwich for 3–4 minutes, turning once, until golden brown and crisp. Drain well on paper towels.

mozzarella cheese

white bread

egg

VARIATION
Add 2 chopped sun-dried tomatoes or some black olive paste to the sandwich before soaking in egg.

CAKES AND DESSERTS

Anyone with a sweet tooth will not be able to resist Italy's most tempting cakes and desserts. As well as the ever-popular Tiramisu and Chocolate Amaretti, sample some more adventurous sweet pasta delights such as Strawberry Conchiglie Salad with Kirsch and Raspberry Sauce, or Dark Chocolate Ravioli with White Chocolate and Cream Cheese Filling.

Choux Pastries with Two Custards

Italian pastry shops are filled with displays of sweetly scented pastries such as these.

Makes about 48

INGREDIENTS
scant 1 cup water
8 tablespoons (1 stick) butter
1-inch piece vanilla bean, split
     lengthways
1¼ cups all-purpose flour
5 eggs
pinch of salt

FOR THE CUSTARD FILLINGS
2 ounces semisweet chocolate
1¼ cups milk
4 egg yolks
scant ⅓ cup granulated sugar
generous ⅓ cup all-purpose flour
1 teaspoon pure vanilla extract
1¼ cups whipping cream
unsweetened cocoa powder and
     confectioners' sugar, for dusting

butter   eggs

granulated
sugar

unsweetened   confectioners'
chocolate   sugar

water   cocoa
                powder

        milk

vanilla
extract

flour   whipping
                cream

1 Preheat the oven to 375°F. Heat the water with the butter, vanilla bean and salt. When the butter has just melted, whisk in the flour.

2 Cook over low heat, stirring constantly, for about 8 minutes. Remove from the heat. Beat in the eggs one at a time. Remove the vanilla bean.

3 Butter a baking sheet. Spoon the mixture into a pastry bag fitted with a plain tip. Squeeze the mixture out onto the sheet into about 48 balls the size of small walnuts, leaving space between the rows to allow for spreading. Bake for 20–25 minutes, or until the pastries are golden brown. Remove from the oven and let cool thoroughly before filling.

4 Meanwhile, prepare the custard fillings. Melt the chocolate in the top half of a double boiler, or in a bowl set over a pan of simmering water. Heat the milk in a small saucepan over low to medium heat, taking care not to let it boil.

5 Beat the egg yolks with a wire whisk or electric beater. Gradually add the sugar and continue beating until the mixture is pale yellow. Beat in the flour. Add the hot milk very gradually, pouring it in through a sieve. When all the milk has been added, pour the mixture into a heavy saucepan and bring to a boil. Simmer for 5–6 minutes, stirring.

COOK'S TIP

Although the choux pastries can be made in advance, do not add the filling until the very last minute before serving, as it will make the pastry soggy and unappetizing.

6 Remove from the heat and divide the custard between two bowls. Add the melted chocolate to one and stir the vanilla extract into the other. Let cool completely.

7 Whip the cream. Fold half of it carefully into each of the custards. Fill two pastry bags fitted with plain tips with the custards. Fill half of the choux pastries with the chocolate custard, and the rest with the vanilla custard, making a little hole and piping the filling in through the side of each pastry. Dust the tops of the chocolate-filled pastries with cocoa powder, and the rest with confectioners' sugar. Serve immediately.

Fresh Orange Granita

A granita is like an Italian ice, but coarser and quite grainy in texture, hence its name. It makes a refreshing dessert after a rich main course, or a cooling treat on a hot summer's day.

Serves 6

INGREDIENTS
4 large oranges
1 large lemon
¾ cup granulated sugar
2 cups water
amaretti cookies, to serve

oranges   *sugar*

amaretti cookies

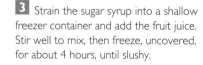

lemon

COOK'S TIP
To make the decoration, slice the orange and lemon zest into thin strips. Blanch for 2 minutes, refresh under cold water and dry before using.

1 Thinly pare the zest from the oranges and lemon, trying to avoid the bitter white pith, and set a few pieces aside for decoration. Halve the fruit and squeeze the juice into a pitcher. Set aside.

2 Heat the sugar and water in a heavy saucepan, stirring over low heat, until the sugar dissolves. Bring to a boil, then boil without stirring for about 10 minutes, until a syrup forms. Remove the syrup from the heat, add the orange and lemon zest and shake the pan. Cover and let cool.

3 Strain the sugar syrup into a shallow freezer container and add the fruit juice. Stir well to mix, then freeze, uncovered, for about 4 hours, until slushy.

4 Take the half-frozen mixture from the freezer and mix with a fork. Freeze for 4 more hours, or until hard. To serve, let sit at room temperature for about 10 minutes, then break up with a fork and pile into long-stemmed glasses. Decorate with strips of zest (see Cook's Tip) and serve with amaretti cookies.

Tiramisu

The name of this popular dessert translates as "pick me up," which is said to derive from the fact that it is so good that it literally makes you swoon when you eat it. There are many, many versions, and the recipe can be adapted to suit your own taste—you can vary the amounts of the ingredients, or make it in individual serving dishes, if desired.

Serves 6–8

INGREDIENTS

3 eggs, separated
2 cups mascarpone cheese, at room
   temperature
1 teaspoon vanilla sugar
¾ cup cold, very strong black coffee
½ cup Kahlua or other coffee-
   flavored liqueur
18 savoiardi (Italian sponge fingers)
sifted unsweetened cocoa powder
   and grated bittersweet chocolate,
   to finish

vanilla sugar

eggs

cocoa powder

bittersweet chocolate

mascarpone cheese

coffee-flavored liqueur

savoiardi

coffee powder

1 Put the egg whites in a grease-free bowl and beat with an electric mixer until stiff and in peaks.

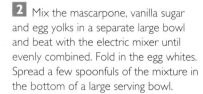

2 Mix the mascarpone, vanilla sugar and egg yolks in a separate large bowl and beat with the electric mixer until evenly combined. Fold in the egg whites. Spread a few spoonfuls of the mixture in the bottom of a large serving bowl.

3 Combine the coffee and liqueur in a shallow dish. Dip a sponge finger in the mixture, turn it quickly so that it becomes saturated but does not disintegrate, and place it on top of the mascarpone mixture in the bowl. Add five more dipped sponge fingers, placing them side by side.

4 Spoon in about one-third of the remaining mascarpone mixture and spread it out. Make more layers in the same way, ending with mascarpone. Level the surface, then sift cocoa powder over it. Cover and chill overnight. Before serving, sprinkle with more cocoa and the grated chocolate.

Zabaglione

A much-loved, simple Italian pudding traditionally made with Marsala, an Italian fortified wine. Madeira is a good alternative.

Serves 4

INGREDIENTS
4 egg yolks
¼ cup granulated sugar
¼ cup Marsala or Madeira wine
amaretti cookies, to serve

eggs *sugar*

Marsala

amaretti cookies

1 Place the egg yolks and sugar in a large, clean heatproof bowl and beat with an electric mixer until the mixture is pale and thick and forms fluffy peaks when the beaters are lifted out of the egg mixture.

2 Gradually add the Marsala, beating well after each addition (at this stage the mixture will be quite runny).

3 Now place over a pan of gently simmering water and continue to beat for 5–7 minutes, until the mixture becomes thick and mousse-like; when the beaters are lifted, they should leave a thick trail on the surface of the mixture.

4 Pour into four warmed stemmed glasses and serve immediately, with the amaretti cookies for dipping.

COOK'S TIP
Make sure the zabaglione is thick and mousse-like; if you don't beat the mixture for long enough, the zabaglione will be too runny and will probably separate.

VARIATION
If you don't have any Marsala or Madeira, you could use a medium-sweet sherry or a dessert wine.

Stuffed Peaches with Mascarpone Cream

Mascarpone is a thick, velvety Italian cream cheese, made from cow's milk. It is often used in desserts, or eaten with fresh fruit.

Serves 4

INGREDIENTS
4 large peaches, halved and pitted
¾ cup amaretti cookie crumbs
2 tablespoons ground almonds
3 tablespoons granulated sugar
1 tablespoon unsweetened
   cocoa powder
⅔ cup sweet wine
2 tablespoons butter

FOR THE MASCARPONE CREAM
2 tablespoons superfine sugar
3 egg yolks
1 tablespoon sweet wine
1 cup mascarpone cheese
⅔ cup heavy cream

1 Preheat the oven to 400°F. Using a teaspoon, scoop some of the flesh from the cavities in the peaches to make a reasonable space for stuffing. Chop the scooped-out flesh.

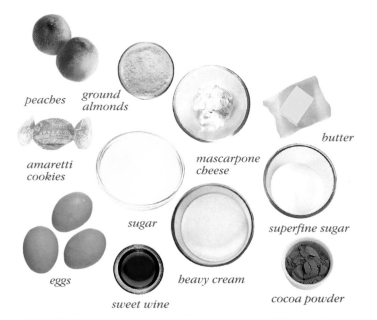

peaches   ground almonds   butter   mascarpone cheese   amaretti cookies   sugar   superfine sugar   eggs   heavy cream   sweet wine   cocoa powder

2 Combine the amaretti cookies, ground almonds, sugar, cocoa and peach flesh in a bowl. Add enough wine to make the mixture into a thick paste. Place the peaches in a buttered ovenproof dish and fill them with the amaretti and almond stuffing. Dot with butter, then pour the remaining wine into the dish. Bake for 35 minutes.

3 To make the mascarpone cream, beat the sugar and egg yolks until thick and pale. Stir in the wine, then fold in the mascarpone. Whip the cream until it forms soft peaks and fold into the mixture. Remove the peaches from the oven and let cool. Serve the peaches at room temperature, with the mascarpone cream.

Dark Chocolate Ravioli with White Chocolate and Cream Cheese Filling

This is a spectacular, chocolatey pasta, with cocoa powder added to the flour. The pasta packets contain a rich creamy-white filling.

Serves 4

INGREDIENTS
1½ cups all-purpose flour
¼ cup cocoa powder
2 tbsp confectioners' sugar
2 large eggs
salt
light cream and grated chocolate, to serve

FILLING
6 oz white chocolate
3 cups cream cheese
1 egg, plus 1 beaten egg to seal

eggs

cream cheese

cocoa powder

white chocolate

1 Make the pasta following the instructions for Basic Pasta Dough, but sifting the flour with the cocoa and confectioners' sugar before adding the eggs. Cover and rest for 30 minutes.

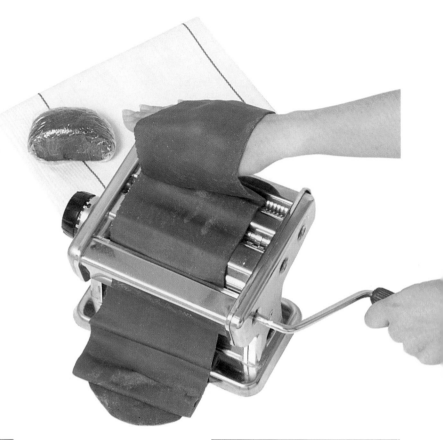

2 For the filling, break up the white chocolate and melt it in a bowl standing in a pan of barely simmering water. Cool slightly, then beat into the cream cheese with the egg. Spoon into a pastry bag fitted with a plain tip.

3 Cut the dough in half and wrap one portion in clear film (plastic wrap). Roll the pasta out thinly to a rectangle on a lightly floured surface, or use a pasta machine. Cover with a clean damp tea (dish) towel and repeat with the remaining pasta.

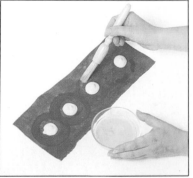

4 Pipe small mounds (about 1 tsp) of filling in even rows, spacing them at 1½ in intervals, across one piece of the dough. Using a pastry brush, brush the spaces of dough between the mounds with some beaten egg.

5 Using a rolling pin, lift the remaining sheet of pasta over the dough with the filling. Press down firmly between the pockets of filling, pushing out any trapped air. Cut into rounds with a serrated ravioli cutter or sharp knife. Transfer to a floured dish towel. Rest for 1 hour.

6 Bring a large pan of salted water to a boil and add the ravioli a few at a time, stirring to prevent them sticking together. Simmer gently for 3–5 minutes, remove with a perforated spoon. Serve with a generous splash of light cream and some grated chocolate.

Cinnamon Tagliatelle with Creamy Custard Sauce

The secret of this pudding is to roll the pasta out very thinly, giving delicious ribbons coated in a delicate vanilla sauce.

Serves 4

INGREDIENTS
1½ cups all-purpose flour
pinch of salt
2 tbsp confectioners' sugar
2 tsp ground cinnamon, plus extra for
   dusting the pasta
2 large eggs
melted butter, for tossing the pasta

CUSTARD
1 vanilla bean
2½ cups milk
6 egg yolks
¼–⅓ cup superfine sugar

1 Make the pasta following the instructions for Basic Pasta Dough, but sifting the flour with the confectioners' sugar and cinnamon before adding the eggs. Roll out thinly and cut into tagliatelle. Spread out on a clean, lightly floured dish towel to dry.

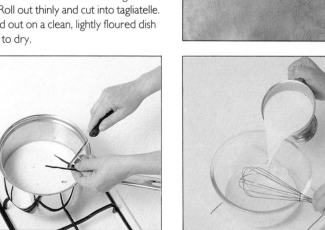

butter

eggs

cinnamon

vanilla bean

2 For the custard, split the vanilla bean and scrape out the seeds into a saucepan. Add the pod itself to the pan with the milk and slowly bring to a boil. Take the pan off the heat and allow to infuse for 10 minutes, then strain to remove the vanilla bean and seeds.

3 Whisk the egg yolks and sugar together in a medium bowl until pale and creamy. Slowly stir in the strained milk, return the pan to a low heat, and cook, stirring, until slightly thickened. Do not boil or the custard will curdle. Strain and keep warm.

4 Drop the tagliatelle into plenty of boiling salted water and cook until the water returns to the boil or until *al dente*. The pasta should have no hard core, and should be very pliable. Strain and toss with a little butter. Serve in warm bowls with the custard poured over. Dust with extra cinnamon if liked.

Tiramisu Surprise

The small pasta shapes incorporated into this dessert make a very pretty dish served in tall glasses.

Serves 4

INGREDIENTS
¼ lb small pasta shapes
salt
16 small ratafias, macaroons, or
   Amaretti cookies
6 tbsp very strong black coffee
2 tbsp brandy
4 tbsp dark rum
1¾ cups mascarpone or other cream
   cheese
½ cup confectioners' sugar, sifted
⅔ cup whipping cream
3 oz chocolate shavings, to decorate

dark rum

pasta shapes

brandy   *chocolate*

ratafias

1 Cook the pasta in plenty of boiling salted water according to the manufacturer's instructions. Drain well and cool.

2 Place the ratafias in 4 individual glasses and spoon over a layer of pasta. Mix together the coffee, brandy, and 2 tbsp of the rum, and pour this over the pasta layer.

3 Beat the mascarpone with the sugar and remaining rum until smooth. Stir in the cream and spoon the mixture equally between the glasses.

4 Sprinkle the chocolate shavings thickly on top of the cheese mixture to decorate and refrigerate for at least 1 hour before serving.

Pasta Timbales with Apricot Sauce

Orzo, or rice-shaped, pasta inspired this dessert made like a rice pudding, but with a difference! Other small soup pastas can be used if orzo cannot be found.

Serves 4

INGREDIENTS
¼ lb orzo or other soup pasta
⅓ cup superfine sugar
salt
2 tbsp butter
1 vanilla bean, split
3⅔ cups milk
1¼ cups ready-made vanilla pudding
3 tbsp kirsch
1 tbsp powdered gelatin
oil, for greasing
14 oz canned apricots in juice
lemon juice
fresh flowers, to decorate (optional)

custard

pasta

lemon

butter

apricots

1 Place the pasta, sugar, a pinch of salt, the butter, vanilla bean, and milk into a heavy saucepan and bring to a boil. Turn down the heat and simmer for 25 minutes until the pasta is tender and most of the liquid is absorbed. Stir frequently to prevent it from sticking.

2 Remove the vanilla bean and transfer the pasta to a bowl to cool. Stir in the custard and 2 tbsp of the kirsch.

3 Sprinkle the gelatin over 3 tbsp water in a small bowl set in a pan of barely simmering water. Allow to become spongy and heat gently to dissolve. Stir into the pasta.

4 Lightly oil 4 timbale molds and spoon in the pasta. Refrigerate for about 2 hours until set.

5 Meanwhile, liquidize the apricots, pass through a strainer, and add lemon juice and kirsch to taste. Dilute with a little water if too thick.

6 Loosen the pasta timbales from their molds and turn out onto individual plates. Spoon some apricot sauce around and serve, decorated with a few fresh flowers if liked.

Strawberry Conchiglie Salad with Kirsch and Raspberry Sauce

A divinely decadent dessert laced with liqueur and luscious raspberry sauce.

Serves 4

INGREDIENTS
6 oz pasta shells (conchiglie)
salt
½ lb fresh or frozen raspberries,
   thawed if frozen
1–2 tbsp superfine sugar
lemon juice
1 lb small fresh strawberries
flaked almonds
3 tbsp kirsch

pasta shells

raspberries

strawberries

almonds

1 Cook the pasta in plenty of boiling salted water according to the manufacturer's instructions. Drain well and cool.

2 Purée the raspberries in a food processor and pass through a strainer to remove the seeds.

3 Put the purée in a small saucepan with the sugar and simmer for 5–6 minutes, stirring occasionally. Add lemon juice to taste. Set aside to cool.

4 Hull the strawberries and halve if necessary. Toss with the pasta and transfer to a serving bowl.

5 Spread the almonds on a baking sheet and toast under the broiler until golden. Cool.

6 Stir the kirsch into the raspberry sauce and pour over the salad. Scatter with the toasted almonds and serve.

Nectarines with Marzipan and Mascarpone

A luscious dessert that no one can resist – dieters may like to use low-fat soft cheese or ricotta instead of mascarpone.

Serves 4

4 firm, ripe nectarines or
   peaches
3 oz marzipan
5 tbsp mascarpone cheese
3 macaroons crushed

mascarpone cheese

nectarines

marzipan

macaroons

1 Cut the nectarines or peaches in half, removing the pits.

2 Cut the marzipan into eight pieces and press one piece into the pit cavity of each nectarine half.

3 Spoon the mascarpone on top. Sprinkle the crushed macaroons over the mascarpone.

4 Place the half-fruits on a hot barbecue for 3–5 minutes, until they are hot and the mascarpone starts to melt.

COOK'S TIP
Either peaches or nectarines can be used for this recipe. If the pit does not pull out easily when you halve the fruit, use a small, sharp knife to cut around it.

Panettone

This famous Italian fruit cake is often served with a glass of red wine.

Makes 1 cake

INGREDIENTS
⅔ cup lukewarm milk
1 envelope (2¼ teaspoons) active dry yeast
3 cups all-purpose flour
6 tablespoons sugar
2 teaspoons salt
2 eggs, plus 5 egg yolks
12 tablespoons (1½ sticks) butter
⅔ cup raisins
grated rind of 1 lemon
½ cup chopped candied peel

milk

lemon rind

butter

salt

raisins

flour

egg yolks

sugar

candied peel

eggs

active dry yeast

1 Mix the milk and yeast in a large warmed bowl and let sit for 10 minutes, until frothy. Stir in 1 cup of the flour, cover loosely and leave in a warm place for 30 minutes. Sift in the remaining flour. Make a well in the center and add the sugar, salt, eggs and egg yolks.

2 Stir with a spoon, then with your hands to obtain a soft, sticky dough.

3 Soften the butter, then smear it on top of the dough and work it in. Cover and let rise in a warm place for 3–4 hours, until the dough has doubled in bulk.

4 Line the bottom of an 8¾-cup charlotte mold with baking parchment, then grease well. Punch down the dough and transfer to a floured surface. Knead in the raisins, lemon rind and candied peel. Shape the dough and fit it into the prepared mold.

5 Cover the mold with a plastic bag and let the dough rise for about 2 hours, until it is well above the top of the mold.

6 Preheat the oven to 400°F. Bake for 15 minutes, cover the top with foil and lower the heat to 350°F. Bake for 30 minutes more. Allow to cool in the mold for about 5 minutes, then transfer to a wire rack, remove the paper and cool completely.

COOK'S TIP
If you do not have a charlotte mold, you can use a perfectly clean 2-pound coffee or fruit can.

Fresh Fig, Apple and Date Dessert

Sweet Mediterranean figs and dates combine especially well with crisp dessert apples. A hint of almond serves to unite the flavors.

Serves 4

INGREDIENTS
6 large apples
juice of ½ lemon
6 oz fresh dates
1 oz white marzipan
1 tsp orange flower water
4 tbsp plain yogurt
4 green or purple figs
4 almonds, toasted

apples

figs   *almonds*

dates

1 Core the apples. Slice thinly, then cut into fine matchsticks. Toss with lemon juice to keep them white.

2 Remove the pits from the dates and cut the flesh into fine strips, then combine with the apple slices.

3 Soften the marzipan with orange flower water and combine with the yogurt. Mix well.

4 Pile the apples and dates in the center of 4 plates. Remove the stem from each of the figs and divide the fruit into quarters without cutting right through the base. Squeeze the base with the thumb and forefinger of each hand to open up the fruit.

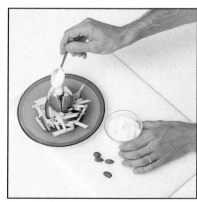

5 Place a fig in the center of the salad, spoon in the yogurt filling, and decorate with a toasted almond.

Chocolate Truffles

Truffles can be simply dusted with cocoa, confectioners' sugar, finely chopped nuts or coated in melted chocolate.

Makes 20 large or 30 medium truffles

INGREDIENTS
1 cup heavy cream
10 oz fine quality bittersweet or semi-sweet chocolate, chopped
3 tbsp unsalted butter, cut into small pieces
3 tbsp brandy, whisky or other liqueur

TO FINISH (OPTIONAL)
unsweetened cocoa for dusting
finely chopped pistachios
14 oz bittersweet chocolate

bittersweet chocolate

brandy

pistachios

cocoa

1 In a saucepan over medium heat, bring cream to a boil. Remove from heat and add chocolate all at once. Stir gently until melted. Stir in butter until melted, then stir in brandy or liqueur. Strain into a bowl and cool to room temperature. Cover and refrigerate for 4 hours or overnight.

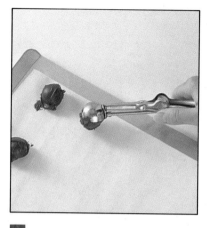

2 Using a small ice cream scoop, melon baller or tablespoon, scrape up mixture into 20 large balls or 30 medium balls and place on a wax paper-lined cookie sheet.

3 If dusting with cocoa, sift a thick layer of cocoa on to a dish or pie plate. Roll truffles in cocoa, rounding them between the palms of your hands. (Dust your hands with cocoa to prevent truffles sticking.) Do not worry if the truffles are not perfectly round as the irregular shape looks more authentic.

4 Alternatively, roll in very finely chopped pistachios. Refrigerate for up to 10 days or freeze for up to 2 months.

5 If coating with chocolate, do not roll in cocoa or nuts, but freeze for 1 hour. Temper the chocolate. Alternatively, truffles can be coated with chocolate melted by the direct heat method if refrigerated immediately. In a small bowl, melt chocolate by either method. Using a fork, dip truffles into melted chocolate, one at a time, tapping fork on edge of bowl to shake off excess. Place on a parchment paper or waxed paper-lined baking sheet. If chocolate begins to thicken, reheat gently until smooth. Refrigerate until set.

Chocolate Pine Nut Tart

Lemon zest could be used instead of orange and a
combination of white and plain chocolates substituted
for all plain.

Serves 8

INGREDIENTS
1½ cups flour
¼ cup superfine sugar
pinch of salt
grated zest of ½ orange
½ cup unsalted butter, cut into small
     pieces
3 egg yolks, lightly beaten
1–2 tbsp iced water

FILLING
2 eggs
3 tbsp superfine sugar
grated zest of 1 orange
1 tbsp orange-flavor liqueur
1 cup whipping cream
4 oz plain chocolate, chopped
¾ cup pine nuts, toasted

TO DECORATE
1 orange
¼ cup granulated sugar
½ cup water

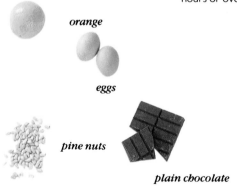

orange

eggs

pine nuts

plain chocolate

1 In a food processor with metal blade,
process flour, sugar, salt and zest to blend
Add butter and process for 20–30
seconds until mixture resembles coarse
crumbs. Add yolks and using pulse-action
process until dough begins to stick
together; do not allow dough to form a
ball or pastry will be tough. If dough
appears dry, add 1–2 tbsp iced water,
little by little, just until dough holds
together. Turn dough on to lightly floured
surface and knead gently until blended.
Shape into flat disc and wrap in waxed
paper or clear plastic. Refrigerate for 2–3
hours or overnight.

2 Lightly butter a 9 in tart pan with
removable bottom. Soften dough for
5–10 minutes at room temperature. On a
well-floured surface, roll out dough into
an 11 in round, about ⅛ in thick. Roll
dough loosely around rolling pin and
unroll over tart pan. Ease dough into pan.
With floured fingers, press overhang
down slightly towards center (making top
edge thicker).

3 Roll a rolling pin over edge to cut off
excess dough. Now press thicker top
edge against side of pan to form rim
slightly higher than pan. Prick bottom with
fork. Refrigerate for 1 hour. Preheat oven
to 400°F. Line tart pan with foil or waxed
paper; fill with dry beans or rice. Bake for
5 minutes, then lift out foil with beans and
bake 5 more minutes, until set. Remove
to wire rack to cool slightly. Lower
temperature to 350°F.

4 Prepare filling. In a medium bowl
beat the eggs, sugar, zest and liqueur.
Blend in the cream. Sprinkle the chocolate
evenly over bottom of tart shell, then
sprinkle over pine nuts. Place pan on
cookie sheet and gently pour egg and
cream mixture into tart shell. Bake tart
for 20–30 minutes, until pastry is golden
and custard is set. Remove to wire rack to
cool slightly.

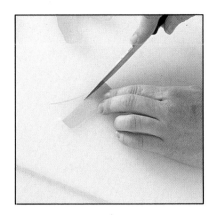

5 Prepare decoration. With vegetable peeler, remove thin strips of orange zest and cut into julienne strips. In a small saucepan over high heat, bring julienne strips, sugar and water to a boil. Boil for 5–8 minutes until syrup is thickened; then stir in 1 tbsp cold water to stop cooking.

6 With a pastry brush, carefully glaze tart with the orange-sugar syrup and arrange julienne orange strips over tart. Remove side of tart pan and slide tart on to plate. Serve warm.

COOK'S TIP
If you do not wish to prepare the garnish, simply heat 2 tbsp marmalade and 1 tsp water until dissolved. Brush over surface of warm tart.

Chocolate Tiramisu Tart

This version of the famous Italian dessert, tiramisu (or 'pick-me-up') does not contain coffee-soaked biscuits, as they would cause the crust to become soggy.

Serves 12–16

INGREDIENTS
8 tbsp unsalted butter
1 tbsp coffee-flavor liqueur or water
1½ cups flour
¼ cup unsweetened cocoa
¼ cup confectioners' sugar
pinch of salt
¼ tsp vanilla extract
unsweetened cocoa for dusting

CHOCOLATE LAYER
½ cup heavy cream
1 tbsp light corn syrup
4 oz bittersweet chocolate, chopped
2 tbsp unsalted butter, cut into pieces
2 tbsp coffee-flavor liqueur

FILLING
1 cup whipping cream
12 oz mascarpone or cream cheese, at
    room temperature
3 tbsp confectioners' sugar
3 tbsp cold espresso or strong coffee
3 tbsp coffee-flavor liqueur
3½ oz semi-sweet chocolate, grated

mascarpone cheese

bittersweet chocolate

1 Prepare pastry. Lightly grease a 9 in springform pan. In a saucepan, heat butter and liqueur or water over medium heat until hot. Into a bowl, sift together flour, cocoa, sugar and salt. Remove butter mixture from the heat, stir in vanilla extract and gradually stir into the flour mixture until a soft dough forms. Knead lightly until smooth. Press on to bottom and up side of pan to within ¾ in of top. Prick dough. Refrigerate for 40 minutes. Preheat oven to 375°F. Bake pastry for 8–10 minutes. If pastry puffs up, prick with fork and bake for 2–3 minutes more until set. Remove to rack to cool.

2 Prepare chocolate layer. In a saucepan over medium heat, bring cream and syrup to a boil. Remove from heat and add chocolate, stirring until melted. Beat in butter and liqueur and pour into the cooked pastry. Cool completely, then refrigerate.

3 Prepare filling. In a bowl with an electric mixer, whip cream until soft peaks form. In another bowl, beat cheese until soft, then beat in sugar until smooth and creamy. Gradually beat in cold coffee and liqueur; gently fold in whipped cream and chocolate. Spoon filling into the chocolate-lined pastry level with the crust. Refrigerate until ready to serve.

4 To serve, run a sharp knife around the side of the pan to loosen the crust. Unclip the pan side. Sift a layer of cocoa over the tart.

Chocolate Amaretti

As an alternative decoration, lightly press a few raw sugar crystals on top of each cookie before baking or dust with confectioners' sugar when cold.

Makes about 24

INGREDIENTS
1 cup blanched whole almonds
½ cup superfine sugar
1 tbsp unsweetened cocoa
2 tbsp confectioners' sugar
2 egg whites
pinch of cream of tartar
1 tsp almond extract
slivered almonds to decorate

eggs

cocoa

almonds

almond extract

1 Preheat oven to 350°F. Place almonds on a small cookie sheet and bake for 10–12 minutes, stirring occasionally, until almonds are golden brown. Remove from oven and cool to room temperature. Reduce oven temperature to 325°F.

Line a large cookie sheet with parchment paper or foil. In a food processor fitted with a metal blade, process the toasted almonds with ¼ cup sugar until almonds are finely ground but not oily. Transfer to a medium bowl and sift in the cocoa and confectioners' sugar; stir to blend. Set aside.

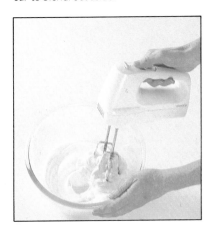

2 In a medium mixing bowl with electric mixer, beat the egg whites and cream of tartar until stiff peaks form. Sprinkle in remaining ¼ cup sugar a tablespoon at a time, beating well after each addition, and continue beating until whites are glossy and stiff. Beat in almond extract.

3 Sprinkle over almond-sugar mixture and gently fold into beaten egg whites until just blended. Spoon mixture into a large piping bag fitted with a plain ½ in tip. Pipe 1½ in rounds about 1 in apart on prepared cookie sheet. Press a slivered almond into the center of each.

4 Bake cookies for 12–15 minutes or until they appear crisp. Remove cookie sheets to wire rack to cool for 10 minutes. With metal spatula, remove cookies to wire rack to cool completely. When cool, dust with confectioners' sugar and store in an airtight container.

Mango and Amaretti Pastries

Fresh mango and crushed amaretti wrapped in wafer-thin filo pastry make a special treat that is just as delicious made with apricots or plums.

Serves 4

INGREDIENTS
1 large mango
grated rind of 1 lemon
2 amaretti cookies
3 tbsp raw sugar
4 tbsp whole-wheat bread crumbs
2 sheets filo pastry, each 19 x 11 in
4 tsp margarine, melted
1 tbsp chopped almonds
confectioner's sugar, for dusting

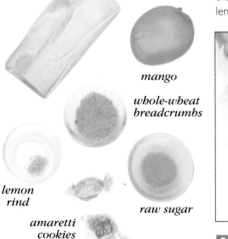

filo pastry

mango

whole-wheat breadcrumbs

lemon rind

raw sugar

amaretti cookies

chopped almonds

soft margarine

1 Preheat the oven to 375°F. Lightly grease a large baking sheet. Halve, pit and peel the mango. Cut into cubes, then place them in a bowl, and sprinkle with the grated lemon rind.

2 Crush the amaretti cookies, and mix them with the raw sugar and the whole-wheat bread crumbs.

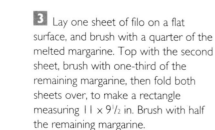

3 Lay one sheet of filo on a flat surface, and brush with a quarter of the melted margarine. Top with the second sheet, brush with one-third of the remaining margarine, then fold both sheets over, to make a rectangle measuring 11 x 9½ in. Brush with half the remaining margarine.

4 Sprinkle the filo with the amaretti mixture, leaving a 2 in border on each long side. Arrange the mango cubes over the top.

5 Roll up the filo from one of the long sides, jelly roll fashion. Lift the strudel onto the baking sheet with the join underneath. Brush with the remaining melted margarine, and sprinkle with the chopped almonds.

6 Bake for 20–25 minutes until golden brown, then transfer to a board. Dust with the icing sugar, slice diagonally and serve warm.

COOK'S TIP
The easiest way to prepare a mango is to cut horizontally through the fruit, keeping the knife blade close to the stone. Repeat on the other side of the stone and peel off the skin. Remove the remaining skin and flesh from around the stone.

Chocolate Amaretto Marquise

A 9 in springform cake pan is ideal for this recipe, but for special occasions it is worth taking extra time to line a heart-shaped pan carefully.

Serves 10–12

INGREDIENTS
1 tbsp flavorless vegetable oil, such as sunflower
7–8 amaretti biscuits, finely crushed
2 tbsp unblanched almonds, toasted and finely chopped
1 lb fine quality bittersweet or semi-sweet chocolate, broken into pieces or chopped
⅓ cup Amaretto liqueur
⅓ cup corn syrup
2 cups heavy cream
unsweetened cocoa for dusting

AMARETTO CREAM (OPTIONAL)
1½ cups whipping or heavy cream for serving
2–3 tbsp Amaretto liqueur

bittersweet chocolate

amaretti biscuits

Amaretto liqueur

almonds

1 Lightly oil a 9 in heart-shaped or springform cake pan. Line the bottom with parchment paper and oil the paper. In a small bowl, combine the crushed amaretti biscuits and the chopped almonds. Sprinkle evenly on to the bottom of the pan.

2 Place the chocolate, Amaretto liqueur and corn syrup in a medium saucepan over a very low heat. Stir frequently until chocolate is melted and mixture is smooth. Allow to cool until mixture feels just warm to the touch, about 6–8 minutes.

3 In a bowl with electric mixer, beat the cream until it just begins to hold its shape. Stir in a large spoonful to the chocolate mixture, then add quickly remaining cream and gently fold into the chocolate mixture. Pour into the prepared pan and tap pan gently on the work surface to release any large air bubbles. Cover the pan with plastic wrap and refrigerate overnight.

4 To unmold, run a thin-bladed sharp knife under hot water and dry carefully. Run the knife around the edge of the pan to loosen dessert. Place a serving plate over the pan, then invert to unmold the dessert. Carefully peel off the paper, replacing any crust that sticks to it, and dust with cocoa. To serve, whip the cream and Amaretto liqueur until soft peaks form and serve separately.

Chocolate Truffle Tart

Any flavor liqueur can be substituted for brandy – orange, raspberry, coffee and whisky all go very well with chocolate.

Serves 12

INGREDIENTS

1 cup flour
⅓ cup unsweetened cocoa
  (preferably Dutch-processed)
¼ cup superfine sugar
½ tsp salt
½ cup cold unsalted butter, cut into
  pieces
1 egg yolk
1–2 tbsp iced water
1 oz fine quality white or milk
  chocolate, melted
whipped cream for serving (optional)

TRUFFLE FILLING

1⅓ cups heavy cream
12 oz couverture or fine quality
  bittersweet chocolate, chopped
4 tbsp unsalted butter, cut into pieces
2 tbsp brandy or other liqueur

bittersweet chocolate

milk chocolate

eggs

brandy

cocoa

1 Prepare pastry. Into a small bowl, sift flour and cocoa. In a food processor fitted with metal blade, process flour mixture, sugar and salt to blend. Add butter and process for 15–20 seconds, until mixture resembles coarse crumbs.

2 In a bowl, lightly beat yolk with iced water. Add to flour mixture and using pulse action, process until dough begins to stick together. Turn out dough on to plastic wrap. Use to help shape dough into flat disc and wrap tightly. Refrigerate for 1–2 hours.

Lightly grease a 9 in tart pan with removable base. Soften dough for 5–10 minutes. Roll out dough between sheets of waxed paper or plastic wrap to a 22 in round, about ¼ in thick. Peel off top sheet and invert dough into pan. Remove bottom sheet. Ease dough on to base and side of pan. Prick base with fork. Refrigerate for 1 hour.

Preheat oven to 350°F. Line tart with foil or parchment paper; fill with dried beans. Bake for 5–7 minutes; lift out foil with beans and bake for 5–7 minutes more, until just set. (Pastry may look slightly underdone on bottom but it will dry out.) Remove to rack to cool.

3 Prepare filling. In a medium saucepan over medium heat, bring cream to a boil. Remove pan from heat and stir in chocolate until melted and smooth. Stir in butter and liqueur. Strain into prepared tart pan, tilting slightly to even surface, but do not touch surface.

4 Spoon melted chocolate into a paper cone and cut tip about ¼ in in diameter. Drop rounds of chocolate over surface of tart and with a skewer or toothpick gently draw point through chocolate to produce marbled effect. Refrigerate for 2–3 hours until set. To serve, allow tart to soften slightly at room temperature, about 30 minutes.

Cappuccino Coffee Cups

Coffee-lovers will love this one – and it tastes rich and creamy, even though it's very light.

Serves 4

INGREDIENTS
2 eggs
7.7 oz can low-fat milk
5 tsp instant coffee granules or
    powder
2 tbsp granulated artificial sweetener
2 tsp powdered gelatin
4 tbsp light crème fraîche
extra cocoa powder or ground
    cinnamon, to decorate

evaporated low-fat milk

powdered gelatin

granulated artificial sweetener

instant coffee   *eggs*

crème fraîche

cocoa powder

COOK'S TIP
It's important to insure that the gelatin is completely dissolved before spooning the mixture into the dishes, otherwise the texture will not be smooth.

1 Separate one egg and reserve the white. Beat the yolk with the whole of the remaining egg.

2 Put the evaporated milk, coffee granules, sweetener and beaten eggs in a pan; whisk until evenly combined.

3 Put the pan over a low heat and stir constantly until the mixture is hot, but not boiling. Cook, stirring constantly, without boiling, until the mixture is slightly thickened and smooth.

4 Remove the pan from the heat. Sprinkle the gelatin over the pan and whisk until the gelatin has completely dissolved.

5 Spoon the coffee custard into four individual dishes or glasses and chill them until set.

6 Whisk the reserved egg white until stiff. Whisk in the crème fraîche and then spoon the mixture over the desserts. Sprinkle with cocoa or cinnamon and serve.

VARIATION
Strained plain yogurt can be used instead of crème fraîche, if you prefer.

Black and White Ginger Florentines

These florentines can be refrigerated in an airtight container for one week.

Makes about 30

INGREDIENTS
½ cup heavy cream
¼ cup unsalted butter
½ cup granulated sugar
2 tbsp honey
1⅔ cups slivered almonds
⅓ cup flour
½ tsp ground ginger
⅓ cup diced candied orange peel
½ cup diced stem ginger
2 oz semi-sweet chocolate, chopped
5 oz bittersweet chocolate, chopped
5 oz fine quality white chocolate, chopped

bittersweet chocolate

honey

candied orange peel

white chocolate

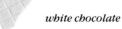

slivered almonds

1 Preheat oven to 350°F. Lightly grease 2 large cookie sheets. (Non-stick sheets are ideal for these caramel-like cookies.) In a medium saucepan over medium heat, stir cream, butter, sugar and honey until sugar dissolves. Bring mixture to the boil, stirring constantly. Remove from heat and stir in almonds, flour and ground ginger until well blended. Stir in orange peel, stem ginger and chopped semi-sweet chocolate.

2 Drop teaspoons of mixture on to prepared sheets at least 3 in apart. Spread each round as thinly as possible with the back of the spoon. (Dip spoon into water to prevent sticking.)

3 Bake for 8–10 minutes or until edges are golden brown and cookies are bubbling. Do not underbake or they will be sticky, but be careful not to over-bake as the high sugar and fat content allows them to burn easily. Continue baking in batches. If you wish, use a 3 in cookie cutter to neaten the edges of the florentines while on the cookie sheet.

4 Remove to wire rack to cool for 10 minutes until firm. Using a metal spatula, carefully remove cookies to wire rack to cool completely.

5 In a small saucepan over very low heat, heat the bittersweet chocolate, stirring frequently, until melted and smooth. Cool slightly. In the top of a double boiler over low heat, melt the white chocolate until smooth, stirring frequently. Remove top of double boiler from bottom and cool for about 5 minutes, stirring occasionally until slightly thickened.

6 Using a small metal spatula, spread half the florentines with the bittersweet chocolate on flat side of each cookie, swirling to create a decorative surface, and place on wire rack, chocolate side up. Spread remaining florentines with the melted white chocolate and place on rack, chocolate side up. Refrigerate for 10–15 minutes to set completely.

INDEX